Please return this book on or before the due date below

ʋ 2015

st copy.
of print

WITHDRAWN

NO

The Reformation of Emotions in the Age of Shakespeare

The Reformation of Emotions in the Age of Shakespeare

STEVEN MULLANEY

The University of Chicago Press ❊ *Chicago and London*

STEVEN MULLANEY
is associate professor of
English at the University
of Michigan. He is
the author of *The Place
of the Stage: License,
Play, and Power in
Renaissance England.*

The University of Chicago Press, Chicago 60637
The University of Chicago Press, Ltd., London
© 2015 by The University of Chicago
All rights reserved. Published 2015.
Printed in the United States of America
24 23 22 21 20 19 18 17 16 15   1 2 3 4 5
ISBN-13: 978-0-226-54763-3 (cloth)
ISBN-13: 978-0-226-11709-6 (e-book)
DOI: 10.7208/chicago/9780226117096.001.0001

Library of Congress Cataloging-in-Publication Data

Mullaney, Steven, author.
    The reformation of emotions in the age of Shakespeare /
Steven Mullaney.
        pages cm
    Includes bibliographical references and index.
    ISBN 978-0-226-54763-3 (cloth : alk. paper)
    ISBN 978-0-226-11709-6 (e-book)
    1. Shakespeare, William, 1564–1616—Criticism and
interpretation.   I. Title.
    PR2976.M77 2015
    822'.309—dc23

                                    2014044798

♾ This paper meets the requirements of ANSI/NISO
Z39.48-1992 (Permanence of Paper).

Contents

Acknowledgments vii

Prologue *1*

Introduction: Structures of Feeling and
the Reformation of Emotions *7*

1   Affective Irony in *The Spanish Tragedy, Titus Andronicus,*
and *The Merchant of Venice 51*

2   The Wreckage of History: Memory and Forgetting in
Shakespeare's First History Tetralogy *94*

3   What's Hamlet to Habermas? Theatrical Publication
and the Early Modern Stage *144*

Epilogue *175*

Notes 181   Index 225

Acknowledgments

A great many institutions, intellectual communities, colleagues, students, friends, and loved ones have contributed to the completion of this book. It is a great pleasure to thank them all and to recollect some of the particular debts in this space.

The University of Michigan has fostered me in many ways, not only through direct support but also, and most importantly, through its remarkable dedication to intellectual speculation and dialogue across disciplines, nations, peoples, and histories. The Department of English Language and Literature at Michigan has been a welcome home for many years and I want to thank the many faculty and staff whose labors have helped it endure and grow. I am indebted as well to the Institute for the Humanities at Michigan, a garden of intellectual delights, and to the Committee for the Study of Social Transformations (CSST), whose founding troika—William Sewall, Geoff Eley, and Terry McDonald—deserve special thanks for introducing me to so many brilliant colleagues and ideas beyond the humanities. Further afield, I am ever-grateful to the National Humanities Center and the Institute for Advanced Studies for the research time and community they provided so generously.

A number of audiences have generously allowed me to try out some of the ideas and approaches of this book, which is all the better for their kind insights. I want especially to thank the Sainsbury Institute for Art at the University of East Anglia and its Head, Bronwen Wilson; the Five Colleges Renaissance Seminar at the University of Massachusetts, Amherst, where I resided for rich and full week; the English Department at Pennsylvania State College; the Centre of Excellence for the History of Emotions in Perth, at the University of Western Australia, where I met and learned from theater practitioners as well as scholars; to the graduate students and faculty of Queen's University (Ontario); the German Shakespeare Association, where Andreas Hoefele made me feel heroic for simply arriving in Bochum, through clouds of Icelandic ash; and the Renaissance Society of America, the University of Sydney, University of Melbourne, Northwestern University, St. Andrews University, Oxford University, University of Stirling, the Shakespeare Institute in Stratford, UK, and the Shakespeare Seminar at the University of London. Special thanks to audiences at the Shakespeare Association of America (SAA), where colleagues attending a number of annual meetings have listened so patiently (or read in seminar) most of this work over the years, and to the SAA and its wonderful staff as well. The Folger Shakespeare Library has been a mainstay. I am indebted to the Social Sciences and Humanities Research Council (SSHRC) of Canada and to McGill University in Montreal, under whose auspices I have regularly enjoyed something rare for scholars in the humanities—collaborative, funded research and discussion with a large and dynamic group of scholars and graduate students from a number of disciplines and many countries and institutions. A grant from SSHRC supported five years (2005–2010) of a rich and productive group project, *Making Publics in Early Modern Europe*; a second grant from SSHRC has enabled another, ongoing interdisciplinary project, *Early Modern Conversions: Religions, Cultures, Cognitive Ecologies*, which began in 2013 and will conclude in 2018. I could never list the colleagues, graduate students, post-docs, and staff who made these lectures and projects so fruitful. They have reinforced my belief that the life of the mind works best when it takes place outside the skull and in social conversation and interactions.

Specific colleagues and friends have contributed to the ideas and concerns that have shaped *The Reformation of Emotions*, perhaps even more than they knew at the time. Among them, David Halperin has served the longest. I have known David for many years and have been his delighted colleague in a number of climes, from Palo Alto to Boston to Ann Arbor. He has been a loyal (and evidently persistent) friend and mentor who has helped see me through many self-doubts and taught me, or tried to teach me, when to trust my own instincts and ideas. Thank you, David. It has been my immense delight to work with and learn from Paul Yachnin over the past fifteen years on so many projects, large and small. I am deeply grateful to him for his friendship, the intellectual worlds he has shared with me, and the example he has provided. Special mention should also go to Jean Howard. She has directly and indirectly encouraged and nurtured my thinking, most recently with her sagacious, astute, and invaluable reading of this book in its earlier forms. I am grateful for her generosity and friendship; I understand why her students regard her as one of the wonders of the world.

For the intellectual friendship as well as the feedback and advice they have provided, I want to thank (in alphabetical order) Sara Blair, Nick Dirks, Peter Donaldson, Lincoln Faller, Jonathan Friedman, Lucy Hart, John Knott, Christina Lupton, Stephen Orgel, Michael Schoenfeldt, David Thorburn, Valerie Traub, Douglas Trevor, Angela Vanhaelan, Martha Vicinus, William West, Bronwen Wilson, and James Winn. Jeffrey Doty and Musa Gurnis read the entire manuscript, in a much longer and messier form, and gave me brilliant and generous comments— gifts of time and attention that were extraordinarily helpful as well as touching. Both Stephen Spiess and Sheila Coursey have read the manuscript, not only proofing, fact-checking, and offering suggestions for bibliography, but also sharing their own insights and occasionally challenging my own thinking so aptly, productively, and generously. Among the many other graduate students I would like to thank are Amanda Bailey, Stephen Whitworth, Amy Rogers, Katherine Wills, Katherine Brokaw, Sarah Linwick, and Andrew Bozio.

I am deeply grateful to Alan Thomas, my editor at the University of Chicago Press, for his patience, support, and friendship over the years.

My family has borne the most over the years, in times thick and thin, and have never wavered in their encouragement, tolerance, or charity. Emma and Megan grew up with this book but have matured more efficiently and completely: I thank them for putting up with so many irritable avatars of Dad, and doing so with such love and grace.

As ever, I am in awe of Linda Gregerson. She sustains me; I can never thank her enough.

>>><<<

An early version of chapter 3 appeared in *Making Space Public in Early Modern Europe: Performance, Geography, Privacy*, ed. Angela Vanhaelen and Joseph P. Ward (Routledge, 2013), 17–40; it appears here with the kind permission of Routledge, Taylor and Francis Group. Scattered throughout the book are fragments of an essay that appeared in *Environment and Embodiment in Early Modern England*, ed. Mary Floyd-Wilson and Garrett Sullivan (Palgrave Macmillan 2007), 71–89. My thanks to Palgrave Macmillan for permission to reuse portions of that material.

Prologue

During the night of April 10, 1549, a procession of carts rumbled through the streets of London on a course that began at the Pardon Churchyard of St. Paul's and ended at a nondescript marsh outside of Moorgate, in the vicinity of Finsbury Field. Without ceremony, one cart after another emptied its contents into the marsh and then returned for another load, in a cycle repeated many times over—"more than one thousand cartloads," according to John Stow—before the carters could be paid and sent home. Afterwards, the area was covered over with "soylage of the citie."[1] It was as though what lay there had to be defiled as well as banished from the city and hidden out of sight, as though it could only be consigned to oblivion if it—or they, depending on one's point of view—were also made to suffer such degrading rites of humiliation.

It, or they? The choice of pronouns goes to the heart of the matter, for the carts were filled with human remains: the bones of countless men, women, and children who had lived and died in the neighborhood and environs of St. Paul's during the previous 400 years. Up until this night in April, they had been lodged in the great ossuary of the cathedral, founded during the reign of King Stephen in the twelfth century and located under the Chapel of the Blessed Virgin.[2] A charnel house, in other words, sometimes simply called "a charnel." The word may sound lurid or gothic to us, but for medieval and early modern cultures the charnel was a hallowed place. The dead and the living were more fully integrated into a single community in this period than in later times; indeed, the dead played such varied and "vital" roles in everyday life that they represented, in Natalie Davis's wry phrase, one of the core "age groups" of early modern society.[3] They were by far the most populous one. In such cultures, where past generations were kept close in local cemeteries of limited size, the charnel house was something of a practical necessity. However, its utilitarian spatial economy had ethical and spiritual dimensions as well. It was here that the bones of the dead, removed from the ground to make room for more recent arrivals, were relocated and displayed with a new form of reverence, one no longer strictly conditioned by the immediate bonds of kinship. Ranged at large on open shelves, no longer set apart by names inscribed on tombstone or brass plate, "the inhabitants of the charnels" were mingled with one another and allowed to form new associations with neighbor and ancestor and stranger alike, in a newly sanctified but more anonymous congregation.[4] In the grave, the dead still bore their family names; in a charnel house of the type common in England, they were released from this last individuation.[5]

Dedicated to the slow, millennial purification of the flesh, the charnel served as a kind of way-station for the dead as they made their slow progress from this life to the next, from one dust to another. For relations and neighbors, the charnel was a destination and an origin, a future and a past, a place to which they themselves were bound as well as a place where their ancestors, those who gave them life, could be located, housed, and cared for. It was a concrete and material form of social memory, a sort of archive whose volumes, composed of bone rather than vellum, recorded the deep structure or genealogy of feelings in the city, the social and familial integuments of its long history. Late medieval and early modern societies were the products of a social memory system whose past tense had moods and inflections different from our own; the charnel house belonged to this grammar of felt history. It was a place where the past and the loved ones who embodied it were granted a lasting habitation in the affective landscape of the city itself.[6]

It was the Duke of Somerset, Lord Protector of the Realm, uncle to the boy-king Edward VI and radical promoter of the Protestant cause in England, who issued the order for the emptying out of the great charnel at St. Paul's. His goal was an evacuation in the most visceral sense of the word: a purging of the social body that could only be accomplished, it would seem, by the consignment of a significant remnant of the city's past life and, more importantly, its present affections, to the rudest of annihilations. The scale alone is shocking—400 years of kin and kind, numbering in the tens of thousands.[7] It makes the extremity of these last rites, the awful, cloacal violence done to the memory of so many generations of English women and men—"soylage of the citie"—all the more unsettling. We desecrate—we only feel the need to desecrate—what we also hold dear. What took place on this night in 1549 was an ambivalent ritual for a dark purpose. It was an effort to dislocate the dead from human feeling as well as local habitation; to root them out of the hearts and minds of their survivors, just as they were rooted out of the underground chambers at St. Paul's; to convert "them" into "it," vital memories into mere refuse or garbage, fit only for a macabre and disenchanted landfill at Finsbury Field.

Cities of the dead, as Joseph Roach reminds us, are primarily for the living.[8] The needs of the living change over time, however, and in times of cultural crisis they can change abruptly, violently, and with harsh intent, especially when a decisive break with the past takes place or is sought and deemed necessary. The Reformation in England sought, as Keith Thomas once observed, to make the break with the past a felt as well as a preached or proclaimed thing, an affective distantiation that would make theological and political reform more lastingly effective. It sought "to sever the relationship between the dead and the living" and to create, as a result, a new generation that would be "indifferent to the spiritual fate of its predecessors."[9]

The assault on the dead of St. Paul's was a strategic success, we might say, but a tactical failure. It did not, in itself, cause or signal an epistemic break.[10] I begin with it because it is so haunting and so emblematic of the affective dimensions of reform. In *The Reformation of Emotions in the Age of Shakespeare*, it will serve as an emblem (as opposed to a symbol or an allegory) in a modal sense of the word. Emblems are more structured and less easily understood than an anecdote or a representative example. They are incomplete and even indecipherable without their accompanying poem, gloss, or riddle: a body (image) without a soul (words). "For the device does not exist for itself," as D. J. Gordon reminded us, "it has to be read; moreover, it has to be difficult to read."[11] My purpose in this study is not to provide the prose equivalent of such a verse or gloss as if it were missing from the period. Rather, my goal is to investigate the affective media and technologies, the arts as well as other means, that were used by the period itself in the effort to understand itself: that helped the Elizabethan present to understand its own shifting or ruptured relationship with the distant and immediate past and to address the affective consequences of even a partial severance from the past with all of its embodied and tangible memories. Some of these efforts were official, many more were unofficial; some took the form of the spoken word, some were written or printed, and others were experienced in and through a wide range of visual and aural media. Early modern popular drama, a melding of available media, was one of the more telling, unofficial responses. It produced not an answer but a multimodal space of engagement, I want to suggest: a public place where audiences could experience, investigate, exacerbate, or salve the cognitive and affective conditions of their own possibility.

Playgoers coming from certain parts of London would have walked over grounds of the former marsh at Finsbury Fields as they made their way from the city proper to the liberty of

Shoreditch, where James Burbage's Theatre had been purpose-built in 1576, expressly designed for new kinds of theatrical performance. Few if any would have been aware of what lay beneath their feet. Over thirty years had passed and, in the beaten way of everyday places and their shifting mnemonics, the former marsh had given rise to a set of mills and sheds. But the emptying out of the charnel at St. Paul's was only one example of a much larger and broader effort to reconfigure the affective relationship between past, present, and future generations in Reformation England, just as Burbage's Theatre was but one example of the ways in which English culture responded to such efforts. The path between the two topographical locations is short and easily charted.[12] In another sense, however, understood as a cultural rather than a physical itinerary, the path between these two places is quite challenging to map. It involves a less familiar kind of journey—one that runs from Moorgate to Shoreditch, as it were, by way of the Elizabethan social imaginary.

It is an informing belief of this study that our most lasting and moving works of culture, especially but not exclusively those we call works of art, are what they are—lasting and moving—in part because they are so deeply and complexly engaged with what is at risk in the historical moment, unsettled in the collective identity, or unmoored in the cognitive and imagined and emotional communities that constitute the social body. This is especially true of theater, one of the most social of the arts. Theater is acutely local in its investments, figurative as well as literal. It is deeply rooted in the peculiar soil of its own historical moment. As a consequence, new forms of theater sometimes emerge at times of historical and cultural crisis. According to Jean-Pierre Vernant, the genre of tragedy first appeared at such a juncture in fifth-century Athens, when "a gap develops at the heart of social experience":

> It is wide enough for the oppositions between legal and political thought on the one hand and the mythical and heroic traditions on the other to stand out quite clearly. Yet it is narrow enough for

the conflict in values still to be a painful one and for the clash to continue to take place. . . . The particular domain of tragedy lies in this border zone.[13]

As a public and performative art, theater provides public and performative cultures with a means of thinking about themselves, especially when confronting their more painful or irresolvable conflicts and contradictions, or when other methods and media fail. Theater is a form of embodied social thought, we might say. It is a critical phenomenon in the way that theory, an etymologically related term for seeing, is critical: a far from harmonious and not always therapeutic way of thinking, by means of actual bodies on stage and in the audience, about the larger—and largely virtual—social body.

Introduction: Structures of Feeling and the Reformation of Emotions

I

The Reformation in early modern Europe left few communities untouched. Most if not all, large and small, experienced their own indigenous disaffections and suffered their own damaged social relations among kin and kind, stranger and neighbor, the living and the dead. And like Tolstoy's unhappy families, each community was different, each unsettled in its own way. Most of the forces of disintegration or dissociation—I use these words like disaffection, in a rooted and visceral sense—were doctrinal in motive and justification. Others were social or cultural, born from more secular reformations of public and private relations. All served to make uncertain, at the least, what we might call the affective core of individual and collective identities. The religious crises of the Protestant Reformation fractured and transformed Western Christianity, but they also precipitated other, less well-documented crises—crises of social identity as well as religious belief, cultural cohesion as well as church doctrine, felt relations with the past and present as well as eschatologies of times to come. The Reformations of faith coincided with a great many other changes, and these included reformations of the heart.[1] Structures of feeling, to invoke Raymond Williams's necessary concept, were reformed as well as structures of belief—or so I will be suggesting in the pages that follow.[2]

If the English Reformation was a period of significant historical trauma, as I think it was, the trauma was of a peculiar sort, easily overlooked by a number of twentieth-century historians. The English Reformation has sometimes seemed most remarkable for all that didn't happen during its erratic course, given the one big thing that eventually did—namely a relatively stable and relatively Protestant state. There were no immediate civil wars (but many skirmishes), no divisions of the kingdom (but many fractures), no pogroms (except against the dead). Most prominently, there were only limited outbreaks of the kinds of popular violence suffered by countries like France.[3] The absence of religious wars or widespread popular violence has often been taken as a clear sign that the English experienced relatively little disjunction as a society.[4] More recently, however, historians have drawn our attention to another, more costly English Reformation.[5] This Reformation was marked by "moments of rupture," in Peter Marshall's terms, that were "abrupt, traumatic," and long-lasting in their effects: "moments" that were felt far beyond their initial occurrence, in other words, "ruptures" that would raise the "emotional temperature of the growing fissures within English Protestantism in the early seventeenth century."[6] Faultlines opened up, to continue Marshall's geological metaphor, in the social, emotional, and cognitive landscape of early modern England.[7]

II

Some of the fissures and faultlines were created by explicit policy; others, including some of the most lasting and traumatic, were the unintended consequence of historical forces beyond the control or determination of individuals or institutions. In the space of a single generation, from 1530 to 1560, England officially adopted and officially abandoned no fewer than five state religions: five different and competing monotheisms, five incompatible versions of the one God, the one faith, the one truth, the one absolute.[8] The persistence of the absolute gave way, under a kind of historical deconstruction, to the insistence of the relative: what one monarch declared to be sacred and timeless, the next declared to be heresy or worse, in a Reformation and Counter-Reformation by state decree. One of the results was a lasting sense of unsettlement. Roger Williams, he of Rhode Island fame, captured that feeling when he reflected back (in 1645) on the odd process by which England became a Protestant nation:

> What lamentable experience have we of the *Turnings* and *Turnings* of the *body* of this Land in point of Religion in few yeares? When *England* was all *Popish* under *Henry* the seventh, how esie is conversion wrought to half Papist halfe-Protestant under *Henry* the eighth? From halfe-Protestantisme halfe-Popery under *Henry* the eight, to absolute Protestanisme under Edward the sixth: from absoluer [*sic*] Protestation under *Edward* the sixt to absalute Popery under Quegne *Mary*, and from absolute Popery under Quegne *Mary* (just like the Weather-cocke, with the breathe of every Prince) to absolute Protestanisme under Queene *Elizabeth*.[9]

The lament—and the image it conjures—is an extraordinary one: the body of the land turns and turns, at first suggesting a field being plowed up or graves being uprooted. Then the same figure is converted to the turning of "the Weather-cocke"—a precisely mixed metaphor that aptly conveys, in form as well as substance, the dizzying kind of cultural vertigo that could be felt nearly a century later. As Williams's caustic irony suggests ("how esie is conversion wrought"), people did not always change faiths like hats with each new proclamation. It is hard to imagine that anyone's conscience could be quite *that* adaptable. And yet, as each new regime declared and mandated its newly incompatible version of the absolute, most of one's neighbors managed to pass as true believers, most of one's family too, even a part, perhaps, of one's self.[10] It is difficult to know how deep the cultural confusion or skepticism or schizophrenia went, just as it is difficult to know what to call it, but it opened fissures of doubt everywhere: in the familial and the social, the secular and the religious, the intellectual and the physical as well as the affective domains of daily life.

In the course of the English Reformation, the English people did not become indifferent to the fates of their predecessors; they did not cease to feel the loss of loved ones or to mourn their passing in public and private rituals and in other, less codified expressions of grief. Feeling for the dead was still embedded and distributed across the sensible world, in names on gravestones, in the graves themselves, in monuments, portraits, biographies, and so many more private and personal ways, like the lingering smell of a father or mother or dear friend in a shirt or jacket or shawl bequeathed in a will.[11] Ossuaries were not eliminated everywhere in England after 1549. The campaign against charnel houses was limited in scope: there was no Dissolution of the Ossuaries, in other words, nothing on the scale of the Dissolution of the Chantries, the denial of Purgatory, and other efforts to sever the link between the living and the dead. But the affective landscape of community was profoundly altered nonetheless, sometimes in a quite literal sense. The fissure or faultline at St. Paul's was a tangible emptiness, an abscess in the ground that had previously been filled by an embodied, material, and concrete form of social memory. Social or collective memory resides in the lived landscape as much as it dwells in commemorative monuments or in the recesses of individual hearts and minds.[12] The expanse of property seized by Henry VIII in the Dissolution of the Monasteries was huge, not to be equaled or surpassed historically until the Louisiana Purchase. Henry's motives were political, economic, at times religious—not, in other words, directly concerned with affective reform. But the properties seized were also places of long-standing occupation, structures used by many generations and imbued with a many-layered patina of feeling and meaning. The boundary lines and property markers erased in the Dissolution possessed virtual dimensions as important as their actual ones; they had functioned as crucial sites in the social memory, in the imagined as well as the visible and sensible communities of the commonwealth, for such a long time. Yet even the Dissolution of the Monasteries, massive though it was, represents at best only one aspect of the broader affective reconfigurations of the period.

The "rage against the dead," as John Weever called it in 1631, was pervasive in unofficial as well as official forms.[13] In a number of towns and villages, the names of the dead, whether they were affixed on brass plates or incised in stone, were stripped or effaced from gravestones and tombs in the dead of night. Entire cemeteries were thus rendered mute, indecipherable, and anonymous, no longer capable of doing what cemeteries are designed to do—which is to locate loss in a public place, attach a name to that place and to the absence it incorporates, and so to release memory and feeling from the private recesses of the self and into the public realm. Naming the dead has a long history, of course. It continues to provide access to collective as well as individual feeling—witness our contemporary experiences of the Holocaust museum, the Vietnam Memorial, the AIDS quilt, the 9/11 memorial. Naming the dead has even been linked to the mythic birth of the art of memory itself. The poet Simonides of Ceos, as the story goes, was one of many guests at a lavish banquet. He was the sole survivor of the feast when the banqueting hall collapsed, catastrophically crushing to death all else who were there, including many of the town's most prominent citizens. The bodies of the dead were so mangled and mutilated, in fact, that their families could neither recognize their faces nor identify their remains. The survivors were unable to hold funeral rites for their loved ones, as a consequence: unable to bury the dead without identities and unable to mourn them as well. But Simonides was able to restore the dead to their families by remembering where each individual had been sitting at the banquet table. Attaching a name to each place in the hall, he used the literal *topoi* of the dead as mnemonic and rhetorical *topoi* or devices, enabling the entire community to carry out its maimed rites, negotiate its grief, and begin the longer, posthumous processes of mourning. To re-form, as it were, into a community.[14]

Iconoclasts who effaced the material artifacts of Catholic worship regarded the statuary and paintings they destroyed as idols, false objects of worship.[15] The radical reformers who raged against the dead by stripping graves of their identities and purging charnel houses did not imagine that the material remains of the past were being worshipped as relics.[16] On the contrary, they understood those remains precisely as what they were: the stuff of feeling and the bones of memory, sinews of the heart rather than idols of the spirit. Their goal was a kind of "counter-memory," in Michel Foucault's sense of the term: the creation of a new structure of historical consciousness that could delegitimize "the claims on the memory of the community by known individuals, neighbours and kin, parents and grandparents."[17]

Many of the starkest acts of counter-memory belonged to the reign of Edward VI, when the Book of Common Prayer was issued for the first time. In the new, reformed mass for the dead, the deceased was no longer to be addressed as a person or spoken to as if present but was to be addressed—or rather, identified—by the neuter relative pronoun, to be placed in the past tense and treated by the priest and congregation alike as an object, a thing of corruption, a mere corpus, an "it."[18] The radical nature of reform during Edward's reign has seemed to many an anomaly, uncharacteristic of the relatively moderate tenor of the English Reformation as a whole. Peter Marshall has argued, however, that the period should be viewed as something more, emblematic in my sense of the term rather than exceptional or singular. The Edwardian campaign against the dead was "one of the most audacious attempts at the restructuring of beliefs and values ever attempted in England, a kind of collective cultural de-programming." It marks the English Reformation itself as "an undoubted climacteric—something fundamental had been loosened, broken, and reset."[19]

III

The resetting took more than one generation. Patrick Collinson is quite emphatic about the Elizabethan aftershocks. "Shakespeare and countless others of his generation," he suggests, "did not know what to believe."[20] It might seem odd to highlight the challenges faced by this generation, born as it was into the relatively stable world of the Elizabethan compromise, rather than the challenges faced by their parents or grandparents, who had lived through the upheavals and martyrdoms of the previous thirty years. But Collinson is, as usual, a shrewd observer of sixteenth-century tensions and dilemmas. Shakespeare's generation inherited and had to learn to live with a profoundly dissociated sense of its world. Its spiritual alienation from previous generations—if not Catholic parents, then Catholic grandparents—was never as extreme or entire as radical reformers would have liked. But for many if not most, their conflicted emotions, including the anxieties produced by the loss of Purgatory and the denial of any earthly power that could affect the spiritual fate of their loved ones or themselves, would have been troubling, producing a deep and daily ambivalence at the affective core of the self. More concretely and less speculatively, they were more likely to be socially alienated from neighbors and acquaintances, since the religious identities of others around them could no longer be presumed or taken for granted and no longer verified by their outward signs of worship.

What does it mean, then, to say that Shakespeare and his generation did not know what to believe? Some were confused, some were conflicted, and others, to be sure, were committed and eager to share their zeal, but not always to good effect. "What manner of religion we have here in England I know not," declared one of Shakespeare's contemporaries, a tailor from Finchingfield, in 1577, "for the preachers now do preach their own inventions and fantasies, and therefore I will not believe any of them."[21] Fifty years ago, many historians were confident that the English Reformation was an accomplished fact by 1569 or 1570. More recently, they

have stressed the need to speak in the indefinite plural, and some
have argued that such "Reformations" were still ongoing well beyond the 1590s.[22] Local archives reveal a complex interweaving of
many if not all manners of Christianity, coexisting in a state that
was one of licensed pretense rather than communal tolerance.[23]
In Protestant Amsterdam, religious tolerance was "complicated"
but also official and explicit. The Elizabethan compromise was,
by contrast, a religious version of a "Don't Ask, Don't Tell" policy:
behave like an Anglican once a month by attending religious ser-
vices and (for the most part) we'll not inquire further. This does
not mean that most Elizabethans dissembled their actual faith,
only that the outward signs of faith had been rendered unreliable
and even indecipherable. It implied and would produce a culture
of marked social skepticism and suspicion about others, since
any given individual might well be something other than what
he or she had professed under the new dispensation. When Elizabeth was crowned, England was already a nation of converts,
some of them serial offenders. It was also a nation of "coverts":
a nation of hidden or impersonated or at least *suspect* identities,
ranging from priest-hole Jesuits to church papists, from church
Anglicans to Familialists to Anabaptists, and so on. It is often
hard for us to discover who believed what, or when the English
Reformation(s) came to something like completion. My point is
that it was hard for Elizabethans, too.[24]

What was in doubt for them was any reliable sense of a collective self, a phrase that sounds more paradoxical than it is.[25] A collective self might be thought of as a "where" rather than a "what,"
a set of places configured as an inhabited social network rather
than an ontological or anatomical autonomy. The collective self
is where an ontological, anatomical being enters into all of the
familial, social, cultural, religious, and political spheres that com-
municate with it, sometimes to enable, sometimes to repress, and
sometimes to re-interpellate an individual's orientation within
the social. It is a matrix held together by affective and ideational
and ideological bonds of all kinds, many of them in contradiction
with one another. In this sense, "collective" should not be con-

fused with the communal, the seamless, the harmonious, or the otherwise utopian. A collective self is composed at least in part by its flaws and fractures—its faultlines, to return to our geological metaphor again, this time in the more ideological sense that Alan Sinfield has explicated so well.[26] The faultlines that Sinfield defines and explores are the product of ideological contradictions in and of themselves, however; I want to expand the term, open it out a bit, in order to include other sites of stress and conflict in the early modern habitus and social imaginary. The faultlines I wish to examine are cultural as well as ideological; they are the product of a significant conflict *between* an ideology and something else, whether that "something else" is a particular and idiosyncratic affective investment or a larger, shared structure of feeling. Like geological faultlines, cultural faultlines are sites of tension and potential upheaval. They are also, unlike geological faultlines, sites of cultural contestation and production—where a culture defines itself and works itself out by working through (or alternately, burying more deeply) its informing and enabling contradictions.

The effects of this unsettled and uncertain relation to previous generations are evident even among otherwise devout Calvinists. What did it feel like to be a sincere Calvinist and contemplate the everlasting fate of one's mother or father or brother or sister—who was a papist?[27] Was it hard to escape a sense of guilt—theologically preposterous but affectively all too real—over their presumed damnation, *as if* it were the result of one's own reformed faith, *as if* one's own redemption was purchased at the cost of theirs? In other contexts, we would call this a form of "survivor's guilt." Such guilt seems to have played a role in the emergence of "applied rather than theoretical" Calvinists, as Linda Pollock has suggested.[28] Grace Mildmay provides one example. Lady Mildmay kept a written diary of her own generational anxieties. According to her account, she had spent her life in godly deportment, firmly convinced that she was one of the elect; yet she was also deeply troubled by the thought that others, especially Catholics like her own parents, would not be saved.

So she salved her spiritual and emotional torment by cheating a bit, easing out of strict Calvinism and into a form of covenant theology that allowed her to imagine that her parents too might see salvation, since they had always lived (or so she believed) *as though* they too were among the elect.[29]

Others were troubled at the thought of revising God's will on the basis of their own or their parents' best practices. Shakespeare gave us a typically "two-eyed glimpse"[30] of this in *Hamlet* by incorporating two incompatible cosmologies into a single play, brought into a face-to-face confrontation when Hamlet returns from his respectably Lutheran college in Wittenberg to discover that his father has been less comfortably lodged in what seems to be a Catholic Purgatory. It is a place that Hamlet the Younger knows does not exist and, furthermore, has always and already not existed: its nonexistence having been created by the Creation, as it were, rather than by the Protestant Reformation. Yet Purgatory is where his father resides, undergoing a long, painful, and searing penitence. He inhabits a papist lie, an imaginary afterlife where he nonetheless suffers actual and excruciating pain.[31] The two Hamlets and their eschatologies are impossibly and simultaneously embodied on the Elizabethan stage, in all their incompatibility and mutual exclusivity.[32] The audience is left to decide what to make of the incongruity—a challenge that audience members encountered regularly in day-to-day life as they interacted with the people around them, including many who embodied their own contradictions of faith and culture.

To revise Collinson slightly, let us say that the generation that was born Elizabethan—I would stretch the dates slightly to include Thomas Kyd, baptized two weeks before Mary Tudor's death—did not know what to *believe*, whether in terms of their own faith or the spiritual identities of those around them, and that they also, perhaps even as a consequence, did not know what or how to *feel*. Throughout Europe, the Reformation and Counter-Reformation were never limited to contestations of theology or politics, even when they operated at the most erudite levels of ecclesiastical doctrine or on the most unadorned and brutal scaffolds and pyres of power. Which brings me to the unanswerable but necessary question that haunts the present study: what did it feel like, to be an Elizabethan?

IV

Like monarchies or religions or ideologies, human emotions have histories. They are culturally inflected, shaped by family, kin, and a great many other private and public spheres where our social identities, our roles as collective and individual selves, are given form and life. Emotions would seem to be hard-wired into us as potentialities, but they are unlocked, learned, calibrated, developed, and modified in specific times, places, and spaces, in dynamic interaction and even experimentation or play with others. According to Clifford Geertz,

> We acquire the ability to design flying planes in wind tunnels; we develop the capacity to feel true awe in church. A child counts on his fingers before he counts "in his head"; he feels love on his skin before he feels it "in his heart." Not only ideas, but emotions too, are cultural artifacts in man. . . . In order to make up our minds we must know how we feel about things; and to know how we feel about things we need the public images of sentiment that only ritual, myth, and art can provide.[33]

To a significant extent I agree, but not everyone does. According to Sir Edmund Leach, *éminence grise* of social anthropology, Geertz's emphasis on the cultural and social construction of emotions is "complete rubbish."[34] Others might be more temperate of expression, but many social scientists of the past fifty years would side with Leach, arguing that emotions are universal rather than constructed, genetic rather than sociocultural, physiological ("feeling") rather than cognitive ("meaning"), transhistorical aspects of human nature rather than affective barometers of historical specificity or historical change.

What we call the emotions (or feelings or passions or affects) have been the subject of inquiry at least since Plato, and the questions asked of them—what are they, where are they, how do they work, and inevitably, are they to be trusted or not?—have always been of great consequence. One of the few certainties that emerge from such inquiries, from Plato to Galen to Rousseau, from Geertz or Paul Ekman or Catherine Lutz to Gail Kern Paster, is that answers to our questions do not come easily. Emotions are notoriously difficult to talk about, not merely in a personal sense ("he doesn't open up very much") but in an epistemological sense as well. They were equally difficult for the Greeks and the Romans and for the early modern English; they continue to be problematic for contemporary anthropologists, historians, psychologists, and interpreters of literature and other artistic media. When our questions are historical—lodged in the past—and phenomenological—what did it feel like to be an Elizabethan?—the methodological plight is exponentially worse. Anthropologists and psychologists have access to living subjects of study, whether they are members of an Ifaluk village or people of Polish descent or patients on a couch in Chicago or New York. Our local informants reside in archives or monuments or paintings or in the populated yard and gallery of Elizabethan theaters. The affective lives of others are difficult to understand even when they are the lives of those we know best, such as immediate family. When such cultural or historical proximity is lost, when our informants can no longer respond to our questions, the challenge is immense.

In "Meaning and Feeling in the Anthropology of Emotions," a comprehensive overview of the state of division in anthropology, history, and psychology in 1996, John Leavitt suggests that our discursive and theoretical trouble with emotions lies not in their primitive nature but in their alternative character. They are forms of communication and experience that are not inherently linguistic and not necessarily evident in outward signs like facial expressions. They have an intimate relationship with other, differently structured systems of meaning such as linguistic or discursive or gestural modes, yet do not lend themselves as well or easily to formal analysis. "Faced with the difficulty of conceptualizing a phenomenon we constantly and naively assume to involve both mind and body," suggests Leavitt, "[we] reduce it to only one side of this dichotomy."[35] We know better—"naively" is *good* in this quote, to be recommended—but we dichotomize them nonetheless. Such "biological reductionism" and "cultural reductionism," to borrow Leavitt's terms, record but fail to recognize the inherent, epistemological, and ontological hybridity of the emotions, casting their compound nature as an apparent problem rather than an actual resolution. Leavitt proposes that emotions provide ways of "feeling" that allow us to "think" about our social lives without the exclusion of middles or the consignment of nuance to the merely secondary or supplemental:

> It is their bridging character that makes emotion concepts both constantly apt and useful in our everyday lives and language and simultaneously "hard to think" in most theoretical discourses. . . . The "idiom of expression" [of emotions]—which differs from society to society (not to mention among classes, genders, regions, and linguistic and ethnic groups)—is more than a mere overlay: it is involved in the emotional experience itself. (516, 519)

Leavitt's own analytical terms are pointedly capacious, most insightful when they are careful not to mistake sharpness of definition with accuracy.

Emotions are boundary phenomena. They are prismatic aspects of somatic and sentient life, hard to contain in rigid or exclusive categories because they are, by their very nature, things that happen betwixt-and-between rather than here or there.[36] Emotions apprehend aspects of our lives that are "hard to think" in disciplinary and theoretical discourses, which suggests that emotions are themselves a form of lived theory, a way of seeing or understanding the world around us that can't necessarily be accomplished by any other means.

Attending only to the words that might identify a particular emotion cannot adequately apprehend their historical expression and inflection. This does not mean that language doesn't resonate with feeling in complex and recursive ways; nor does it suggest that language is an impediment or prison house, something to overcome or escape rather than a necessary tool for transcultural or historical analysis. The idioms of affect include everyday language, metaphors, gestures, unvoiced physical responses (or their absence), and a rather dense host of other, more complicated idioms. At times, those idioms take the form of poems or plays or the many kinds of stories we tell to ourselves, about ourselves, and for ourselves when we want to make sense of our collective as well as individual selves. Nonetheless, those who argue that human emotions are universal would prefer to bracket language and narrative altogether, reducing "emotion" to something that can be perceived in fleeting facial expressions and other visual, bodily cues. Paul Ekman used photographs of facial expressions to show that various cultures in various geographies could accurately identify cardinal emotions such as anger, grief, sadness, and so on, when expressed on the faces of far distant, Other tribes and peoples whose language, culture, politics, and history were equally remote. There are methodological concerns with Ekman's work—his photograph of an angry Maori proves instead to be the photograph of a Maori who has been told to mime or perform anger—but the most egregious flaw may be the degree to which Ekman allows his methodology to define his object of inquiry. "Love," he announces, as if stating the obvious, "is not an emotion."[37] The reason? Love, it seems, is too complex, too much influenced and altered by its modes of expression, too enduring and long-lasting (at least in some cases). It cannot be reliably identified with a fleeting and easily recognized facial expression, and so, by definition, does not qualify in Ekman's procrustean terms. Even though love is a kind of affect that is among the most commonly felt, desired, talked about, written about, and fought over in the history of humankind, it is not an emotion. Contra Ekman, I would learn from everyday language rather than overrule it, especially when dealing with such a "universal" emotion as love. There is indeed a "look of love," as the song would have it, but the face is not necessarily where we find it. It is in the song and not only, or not necessarily, in the facial expression. Whatever we call it, a feeling or an emotion, there is an art—let's say a need for an art—to find the heart's construction in the face, and this makes the science as well as the history of emotions problematic.

"Not everything that can be counted, counts," as Einstein purportedly and daily reminded himself with a posting above his own desk in Princeton. "Not everything that counts, can be counted."[38] In recent years, early modern studies have sought to determine what "counts" in the study of early modern emotions by means of a detailed and long overdue recovery of Galenic thought and its physiological, psychological, and geohumoral dimensions. The groundbreaking work of Gail Kern Paster and other scholars such as Katherine Rowe, Mary Floyd-Wilson, Michael Schoenfeldt, and Douglas Trevor has illuminated many of the complexities of the humoral system and has contributed a great deal to our understanding of the "psychological materialism" of sixteenth- and seventeenth-century thought.[39] I would hesitate, however, to regard Galenism as one of the early modern "idioms of expression" for early modern feelings and emotions. When Galenic physiology is asked to provide a key to the *lived* and *felt* past—to the phenomenology of early modern emotions—I remain skeptical, unable to understand how an etiological theory of the passions could become the basis for a phenomenology of emotions.[40] Whether an etiological theory is humoral, neurological, or hormonal, it has little to tell us about emotional experience. Does my sadness differ from my daughter's because I think emotions are neurological in their physiology and she has never heard of that? Such contemporaneous theories have a great deal to tell us about the history of ideas but their application to the way things felt—a phenomenology of Elizabethan emotions—seems, to say the least, problematic.

My own interests are no less material or historical those of my Galenic colleagues, but they are more transactional in a social sense of the word and hence, to my mind, more recognizably phenomenological. The social and the material, in my own understanding, are inseparable from one another.[41] If I am right and there was indeed a reformation of emotions in the early modern period, it took place most significantly in the domain of what we might call the social emotions, in the social and hence the lived world of feeling, as opposed to the theoretical or polemical discourses of medical treatises. When Michelle Rosaldo characterized emotions as "*embodied* thoughts," she didn't have in mind Ilongot *theories* about the physiology of grief.[42] Rosaldo's understanding of the "life of feeling" is close to my own:

> Feelings are not substances to be discovered in our blood but social practices organized by stories that we both enact and tell. They are structured by our forms of understanding. . . . The life of feeling is an aspect of the social world in which its terms are found. (143, 145)

Feelings are "*embodied* thoughts," as Rosaldo continues, "steeped with the apprehension that 'I am involved'" (143).

V

In Rosaldo's terms, feelings are social as well as individual in their embodiment. The apprehension of involvement, the social element of an emotion, is also the moment of embodiment. This is a functional rather than ontological understanding of "social" emotions. Traditionally, the study of "social" emotions assumed a fundamental division between society and the individual and understood "social" as opposed to "basic" or "cardinal" emotions. The latter are commonly said to be evident in newborn infants, who are unacculturated ("*infans*," without speech) yet exhibit what are arguably the visual and auditory signs of anger, fear, and so on.[43] More recently, however, social psychology has adopted a more functional model. "All emotions are sometimes social," as a 2008 survey described the consensus of social psychologists. "Some are social by their very existence and hence more consistently social than others."[44]

We are always negotiating where we stand in relation to others, which means that we are always reconceiving and redefining our sense of what we mean when we say "we" or "us."[45] These are such deceptively simple-sounding terms. A great deal of human history—the good and the bad, the enlightened and the barbaric—has been devoted to their clarification, to the effort to solidify their fluid nuances, fix their mobile boundaries, and enforce their many exclusions. They are among those "big words" that Stephen Dedalus feared, "which make us so unhappy."[46]

What did it feel like, to be an Elizabethan? The emphasis should fall equally on "feel" and "Elizabethan." The question concerns identity as well as affect, in other words. The point of asking it is to realize that Elizabethans asked it of themselves daily, as all cultures must do, and that the asking was especially difficult and even painful for them, as it is for other periods and cultures whose religious, social, and emotional communities have become radically contested, conflicted, fragmented, shattered, or sundered. When the "social practices organized by the stories we enact and tell" are out of order, the stories—what Milton Singer called "cultural performances"[47]—shift and multiply accordingly. Cultural performances can be conservative or critical, naturalizing or deconstructing. In times of crisis like the Reformation, the forms and modes of cultural performance proliferate. Interesting times may be a curse, but they are also rich with cultural merchandise. In the second half of the sixteenth century, in varied forums and a wide range of media, Elizabethan cultural performances provided Elizabethans with a way to realize how they had lost, to recall Geertz's image, something of the capacity to feel "true" awe in the church.

Some of the stories enacted and told in this context were in print, some delivered from the pulpit, some by storytellers, some by painters, and a great many by actors who performed them on the Elizabethan popular stage. When social media function in this fashion, they become what I would call "affective technologies."[48] They are "equipment for living," as Kenneth Burke would say.[49] My focus on amphitheater drama in the pages that follow is not meant to suggest that it was unique as such—as an affective technology. It was, however, an especially deep, sensitive, and probing instrument, as theater tends to be in times of crisis.

Michael Macdonald, an early modern historian, has similarly stressed the need to treat early modern narratives of various kinds, imaginative as well as nonfictional, as primary rather than secondary resources for the recovery and understanding of historical structures of feeling. "Stories are really all we have to reconstruct the inner lives of people in the past," as Macdonald suggests. "Stories are what they were made from in the first place."[50] The story he offers is an extended and wide-ranging example, a never-finished narrative that was told and retold by emotional communities scattered throughout early modern Europe. It is the tale of Francisco Spiera, an Italian Lutheran who was tortured into recantation by the Inquisition. He died in prison in the year 1548, in occlusion as well as seclusion, so that his dying state of mind and belief was difficult if not impossible to know. He may have died a Protestant and a martyr, having recovered his faith sometime after his recantation; he may have died in despair over his loss of faith, committing a kind of suicide (it was rumored that he starved to death) in prison. The unknowable conclusion to his story posed a question that many felt compelled to answer, which is one reason why his life and death were rendered in so many different vernaculars and reiterated in so many genres and modes of inquiry, whether in argument or art. For Macdonald, such a phenomenal appetite for the story of one Italian Protestant's ambiguous fate is significant in and of itself. All the stories told over—the overall process of the telling—provided access to something that was in doubt in every life, that might even be, like Spiera's fate, inaccessible in and of itself. For contemporaries, the indecipherability of the life and death resonated with other uncertainties and indecipherabilities of the period. For us—twenty-first-century literary and theatrical investigators, social historians, historians of emotions—such compelling stories and such compelled processes of storytelling can provide a limited but invaluable access to the social life of feeling and felt history.[51]

It is important to note the difference between narrative *representations* of emotional states—whether descriptions, depictions, or enactments—and the narrative process and phenomenology that Macdonald has in mind. In the one, the reader or viewer is presented with an example, a model, or an illustration of an affective state. In the other, the reader or viewer is being modeled or shaped or reconfigured as much by his or her own reading and viewing as by a represented state of being, capable of imitation. It is the reader's or viewer's own engagement and dialectical involvement with the media that catalyzes such affect in discourse and performance as well as everyday life itself. The affective life of storytelling is a matter of nuanced connotation and felt response rather than plot or representation alone. Stories are all we have to reconstruct the inner lives of people in the past: this is not only or even primarily because of the ways in which they *represent* faith or despair or anger or melancholy. It was through the telling—the affective, experiential process itself —that the inner lives of people were formed and reformed in a manner that could never be uniform or fully scripted. Such stories are among the places where the syntax and connotative nuance of social emotions are first developed, and they are one of the places we can still visit in order to learn something about what it felt like to be an Elizabethan, or an Italian, or a German, or a Spaniard, or a French woman or man.

One English retelling of Francisco's story suggests that the most compelling stories can only be retold, that their lowest common denominator is always more than one. In 1581 Nathaniel Woodes published *The Conflict of Conscience*, a morality play based on Spiera's life and death. Despite widespread English and continental familiarity with Spiera's biography, Woodes expressed his fear that the "vices of one private man" would not be able to touch or move a reader or audience as deeply as they should:

> The vices of one priuate man, to touch particulerly,
> Againe, nowe shall it stirre them more, who shall it heare or see,
> For if this worldling had ben namde, we wold straight deeme in minde,
> That all by him then spoken were, our selues we would not finde.

"Our selues we would not finde." We do want to find ourselves, Woodes assumes, but he speaks from the theatrical semiotics of the morality tradition, in which the concrete particularity of a man named Spiera—his historical actuality—would occlude our ability to do so. As Aristotle counseled, the particular cannot touch or move large and diverse audiences or resonate with as many kinds and classes of people as can the general or the universal. Worried that his play might not engage the needed structure of feelings in 1581, Woodes felt it would be better to adhere to late medieval practices rather than experiment with emergent early modern uses of the particular. He chose to abstract the historical figure, whose particular life and unknowable fate had already been so compelling to so many, into a personification of learning named Philologus. Woodes published two editions of the play in the same year, identical except in their concluding verses: in the one, Philologus dies a martyr; in the other, he dies in despair. If nothing else, the dueling editions remind us that the morality play remained a complex cultural form well into the sixteenth century. It had always been an effective embodiment of affective crisis, capable of a profound and even, as here, a textually embodied ambivalence.

Woodes's late morality play, the new forms of narrative historiography developed by Foxe and Holinshed and others, the new modes of popular, professional, amphitheater drama—all are examples of the kinds of affective technology that emerged and developed in the critical years of the English Reformation. All of them occupied quite different places in the Elizabethan social imaginary. They are all forms of cultural performance, deeply rooted in the period yet never merely topical in their relations to it, and each of them sought to engage different structures of feeling in their readers and their audiences.

VI

John Foxe included theater in his Protestant trinity of weapons against Rome. "*Preachers, Printers, and Players,*" he declared, would serve "as a triple bulwarke against the triple crown of the Pope, to bring him down" (1570: 1562).[52] His emphasis was not limited to the message or lesson preached from the pulpit, delivered by the book, or represented by the play. The power of these affective technologies lay not in their authors but in their congregations, readers, and audiences.

An example from *The Book of Martyrs* might clarify the probing and diagnostic dimensions that Foxe had in mind for his own monumental book. In an immolation for heresy that took place on Guernsey in 1556, three women of the Massey family—the mother and two of her daughters—were put to death but not before an especially horrifying event took place. As flames licked at the women's feet, one of the daughters (Perotine Massey) gave birth to a child. Officials in charge pulled the newborn child from the flames. They debated their next course of action and finally resolved to cast the infant back onto the pyre. Foxe describes the deaths with an unsettling degree of detail, as he does the many other gruesome deaths of Protestant martyrs/heretics in his massive and exfoliating *Actes and Monuments*. Nonetheless, the death of the Massey family—and three rather than two generations of it—is singled out by Foxe as one of the most "Tragical, Lamentable, and Pitiful" (1583: 1967) histories in the entire *Book of Martyrs*.[53] Not everyone agreed, however. The veracity of the account was challenged at length, most notably by Thomas Harding, who charged the death of the child to Perotine's soul rather than the bailiff, the Church, or the queen.[54] She had failed to invoke her childbirth rights, he said, out of shame for the sin she carried, unmarried as she was. Foxe countered all of the charges (even producing a husband) and expanded his account to include his rebuttal and more documentary support. He reiterated his assertion that this immolation was exceptionally unchristian: "a rueful sight, not only to the eyes of all that there stood, but also to the ears of all true-hearted Christians that shall read this history" (1583: 1969).

It might seem that the willful and deliberate immolation of Perotine's infant son would repel and horrify any and all readers; that anyone who saw it or read it or heard it read out loud could not fail to be moved and would perforce feel a sympathy and alliance with the suffering and the sufferer—a sympathy implicitly realigning his or her individual self with the Protestant rather than the Catholic point of view toward such an unspeakable horror. Such an assumption would miss the point of the narration, however, as a story intended to be told and retold. Foxe's motive is rhetorical—he uses language to convey the horror—but it is also diagnostic. As he well knew, many shared Harding's harsh counter-sympathies, from the bailiff and other secular and church officers to some of the witnesses in the crowd and even an uncertain number of his readers.[55] Their unsympathetic response was part of the design, the diagnostic axis of the text, and it tells us a great deal about everything that Foxe's own experience had taught him about the phenomenology of social emotions.

We, as twenty-first-century eyes and ears, are not part of that design. This does not mean that modern readers of whatever faith are not (most likely) distressed at the barbaric deaths. Whatever our own reactions, however, whether pity or horror or the kind of revulsion we reserve for the "inhuman" or the "unimaginable" or the "unspeakable"—words we use to inoculate ourselves against what we know to be all-too-human, all-too-readily-imagined, and always being realized in the actual world—what we feel is not the same as the pity or horror or revulsion that contemporaries would feel. Foxe characterizes the scene as a "rueful *sight* . . . to the *ears* of all true-hearted Christians that shall read this history" (emphasis added). The synesthetic rhetorical maneuver is an aggressive one in its own historical context. In ours, no matter what our own religious persuasion or lack of it, we twenty-first-century readers are, to a significant degree, excluded by it. We are not and never could be what Foxe means by "true-hearted Christians." Even if we *were* sixteenth-century English men or women—that is, the audience Foxe addresses at the same time that he calls it into being—our affective response would still be something less than automatic and far from predictable. It would not, could not, go without saying. Insofar as our ears—our sixteenth-century ears—viewed this account as a rueful sight, we would be accepting and embracing our identities as "true-hearted Christians." We would feel as if we were members of a social body newly composed of other like-minded and like-hearted individuals, and our feeling would go a long way toward making it so. But if, as sixteenth-century English men or women, we disagreed with Foxe's idea of a "true-hearted Christian"—if we did not subscribe, that is to say, to the emergent Protestant hegemony—we might be less sympathetic, even deeply conflicted. We might feel troubled yet duty-bound and constrained by faith when confronted with an unhappy need to respond to the event—as perhaps the bailiff felt. Or we might not feel troubled or conflicted or even confused, but instead feel a kind of righteous satisfaction at the enactment of God's will on earth. Some of us might find ourselves so far removed from any sort of horror or ambivalence as to feel a kind of joy. We might even feel like dancing in the streets.

Our grief or sympathy or conflict or holy zeal would be lodged in a place where affect and ideology, feeling and faith and other systems of belief or thought, are deeply interwoven; where the claims of the heart, to use a language less anachronistic, and the claims of the head are so mutually interdependent as to be hard to distinguish from one another. In Reformation England, writers like Foxe wrote in an effort to locate and chart such intersections between affect and various systems of belief, making the reader locate him- or herself in them. Such diagnostic trials of affective resonance were by no means unique to the Reformation. In all its different forms, media, and genres, social discourse often works to orient individual and collective identities and to discover or paper over the gaps and faultlines that may have opened up in them. What sets the social discourse and affective technologies of the Reformation apart was, in part, the nature and severity of such disorienting rifts in the social fabric.

Is it valid to talk about social emotions in these terms, as an intersection of affect and a system of belief or ideology? The early modern period did not, of course, have the term "ideology" at its disposal—"ideology" is one of our inheritances from the eighteenth century—but the period nonetheless understood the concept quite well. For example, here is Thomas Heywood's description of the ideological power of an English history play on the early modern stage:

> What English blood, seeing the person of any bold English man presented and doth not hugge his fame and hunnye at his valor, pursuing him in his enterprise with his best wishes, and as being wrapt in contemplation, offers to him in his hart all prosperous performance, as if the Personator were the man Personated, so bewitching a thing is lively and well spirited action, that it hath power to new mold the harts of the spectators and fashion them to the shape of any noble and notable attempt.[56]

An ideology is something that makes us hug its fame and hunnye (or whinny) at its valor: something that has the power to new-mold our hearts as well as our minds and to refashion them both. To be effective, in other words, an ideology must also and simultaneously be affective. We have to feel it—and feel it strongly—in our hearts *and* minds. To take an example—the one broached by Heywood above—consider the case of nationalism.[57] One of the distinguishing characteristics of nationalism as an ideology, according to Benedict Anderson, is that people are willing to die for it.[58] What makes an ideology "to die for?" Clearly, it is not only a matter of abstract ideas or the imaginary representation of social relations, whether those representations are true, false, mystified, or otherwise constructed. To do its work, any ideology needs to be felt as well as acknowledged (at the moment of interpellation) if it is to be embraced in a political or intellectual sense.[59] Ideology wants to move us—in an affective as well as a performative sense of the term.

What a writer like Foxe can teach us about the history of emotions goes beyond the strangeness of the past or the relative incommensurability of other cultures. Such differences are real and important aspects of any history or phenomenology of emotions. More startling, however, is the strangeness that inhabits the here and now of Foxe's England, for Foxe and his contemporaries—the affective and ideological alienations of community, evident most publically in matters of life and death, as in spectators' contradictory responses when they witnessed English subjects burning English subjects at the stake. Affective technologies like the *Actes and Monuments* seek to catalyze, inspire, or produce social affects, and at the same time, to sound out and probe the internal disjunctions and disaffections that impeded or prevented their embodiment in an imagined community. In this fashion—indirect, transactional, relational—Foxe framed his own version of the question before us, but in the present tense. "What *does* it feel like," as succeeding editions of *The Book of Martyrs* continued to ask in the editions of 1563, 1570, and 1583, "to be an Elizabethan?"

Does our own alienation or exclusion from a text like Foxe's imply that we can have no access to historical emotions, even when they have the same names—pity, horror, joy—as twenty-first-century emotions? That is not, I think, a necessary conclusion. We cannot experience historical emotions in the way they were once experienced, which should come as no surprise; we can't experience the emotions of our own children, loved ones, or neighbors in such a way. We might be able to feel and understand them in other ways: as Gloucester says in *King Lear*, we sometimes see them feelingly. But our embodied thoughts are most accurate and profound when they include a humble realization of their own inadequacies.

VII

In Polish, there is a form of sadness known as *tęsknota*. It seems to be a kind of homesickness in reverse, since you feel it (if you are Polish) when you are still at home but have been left behind by a loved one. You miss him or her, whether you are Polish or English speaking—but *tęsknota* is colored by a strong sense of alienated place as well as an absence of person or community. It is a deep, sometimes visceral longing for a person or persons who are missing and also for the place they are missing from, even though that place would seem to be where you are, where you have been, where you will remain. There is a gap, a lack, a hole in your familiar world, making you feel as if *you* were the one displaced. A landscape once familiar no longer feels like it is yours, even though you have never left it; "home" has grown strange and unhomelike. *Tęsknota*, as I understand it, is a sadness and longing deeply seasoned by the uncanny, a peculiarly Polish form of *Unheimlichkeit*.

According to Anna Wierzbicka, a cross-cultural linguist who has spent much of her career in the study of emotions—and who is also of Polish birth and descent—*tęsknota* is untranslatable. Whether this means that the feeling does not exist in our own repertoire of emotions, that it cannot be felt by you or me (assuming we are not Polish), is debatable. I might be able to *know* what a Polish man or woman feels when that person feels *tęsknota*, at least in a general, cognitive, yet sympathetic sense, to understand *how* that person might feel and yet be unable to feel it myself. However, the problem is not merely a matter of paraphrase or translation but one of collective identity and shared structures of feeling. *Tęsknota* is something I can describe more or less well using the tools of thick description, well enough at any rate that a Pole might say yes, your words capture some part of it fairly well. But I cannot reproduce it as my own social experience. I can understand it like an American, but I cannot feel it like a Pole.

I dwell on *tęsknota*, a modern Western emotion, rather than an early modern English example or one drawn from the ethnography of non-Western cultures, precisely because it is a modern, Western, and European emotion. We can consult a living expert and a living local informant, whose testimony is all the more reliable because Wierzbicka can double in both roles. She can study the feeling *in situ*, so to speak.[60] Furthermore, as a modern Western European emotion, the strangeness of *tęsknota* cannot be ascribed to significantly different conceptions of the individual, the subject, etiological theories of the emotions, or any of the other means we use to distinguish between peoples then and now, here or there, "advanced" or "primitive." And finally, *tęsknota* took on its contemporary, deep resonance at a certain moment in the past—a moment of cultural crisis, when a gap opened in the affective and geographical landscape that swallowed the Polish nation itself.

According to Wierzbicka, *tęsknota* acquired its modern, untranslatable dimensions in the first half of the nineteenth century, specifically in the period of the Great Migration that began in 1831. Tens of thousands of Poles were forced to flee the country, which was subsequently partitioned between Russia, Prussia, and Austria. Poland ceased to exist as an independent nation or state and would not regain its independence or its place on the map of Europe until well into the next century. *Tęsknota* is, for Wierzbicka, a collective as well as individual kind of longing, the register of a loss much larger than more familiar or private bereavements, no matter how devastating, can be. *Tęsknota* involves a loss and a longing that is material as well as metaphysical, one that is entirely tangible and specific but also deeply historical, a matter of real estate as well as emotional states, involving the social body as well as or even more than the individual one. It is political and emotional, collective and personal, a recollection of wholeness that hurts like the phantom memory of an amputated limb. It is a kind of scar tissue on the national or ethnic or cultural soul, as deeply affective as it is cognitive and ideological.

We don't have cross-cultural linguists of Wierzbicka's caliber and qualifications to tell us about emotions-as-felt during the Reformation or to identify those that were qualitatively different from what we can feel in our own twenty-first-century lives. We do have words used in context, however. What Wierzbicka found untranslatable in *tęsknota* was the historical syntax and grammar of the word, its deep situation and relation.[61] Wierzbicka felt *tęsknota* before she studied it and arrived at her historical hypothesis. The word—*tęsknota*—is a memory, in and of itself, of a historical moment of rupture and trauma. It is a compact and felt history, nestled in the symbolic imaginary as well as the word. For modern Polish, it seems to be still in partial solution, not yet fully precipitated out of its deep historical and collective structures of feeling.

The power of words to signify and evoke emotions is not necessarily negated, however, if the word for a particular emotion does not exist. As embodied thoughts lodged at that uncertain intersection of feeling and ideology or belief, social emotions are quite often hard to articulate, even for a native and contemporaneous affective subject. The lack of a single word that defines what we feel or want to convey is a strength as well as limit in language, however. The relationship of language to emotion is dynamic and processural rather than static or definitional or merely nominative. The power of words is not to reduce feeling to a specific term, to affix a label to it, but to trace and enact the syntax of a feeling. Their power lies in layers and accretions of connotation and in the rhythms and prosody of language. One word won't do, if you will, when more words will suffice. There is a reason why Rosaldo, Leavitt, and other theorists of embodied thought turn to story and poetry and other cultural performances rather than a dictionary or thesaurus. The power of words lies in their capacity for indirect articulation, nuance, and inference, as much as in their capacity for signification in the Sausurean sense of the term. Their capacity may be most fully embodied in literature and drama and other verbal arts. We may not have a word to identify what Anna Karenina feels as she returns to the train station at the end of Tolstoy's novel. But every detail of the description and narration of her progress toward death—indeed, every word of *Anna Karenina*—conveys and embodies a fuller, more accurate, and more moving sense of what she feels than any glossary of affective terms could possibly do. Whether we call emotions a kind of language or not, a language of the heart rather than the tongue or ear or head, their relationship with words is symbiotic rather than merely semantic.

VIII

Wierzbicka could well be wrong about the historical cause: what counts in historical structures of feeling can't always be counted. We can trust her expertise as a historical linguist, however, when she tells us that the historical resonance of *tęsknota* shifted soon after the period of the Great Migration. In the opening lines of *The Merchant of Venice*, we encounter a different kind of sadness and a different kind of uncertain resonance. When Antonio announces that he is sad and lays such peculiar emphasis on the mystery of his sadness, neither of his audiences, on stage or off, can be anything other than perplexed. He himself does not know what he feels or why he feels it. This unknowability might even be a key to the feeling, but all we know for sure is that we share his confusion:

> In sooth, I know not why I am so sad.
> It wearies me, you say it wearies you,
> But how I caught it, found it, or came by it,
> What stuff 'tis made of, whereof it is born,
> I am to learn;
> And such a want-wit sadness makes of me
> That I have much ado to know myself. (1.1.1–7)[62]

Like us, Shakespeare's audience is also kept in the dark. Neither the imagined audience of the past nor the imagined or actual audience of the present has what is needed to understand or feel a sadness so opaque—not even the merchant can discover the context of his own sadness. We have a name, but not a local habitation for it. The play opens with a "known unknown," then, and some members of the audience will be compelled, like Salerio and Solanio on stage, to speculate on Antonio's apprehension of his self. Is it because he is melancholy by nature? As understood in this period, melancholics were often unable to say why they were sad. Their affective perplexity had little to do with circumstance and much more to do with a general and temperamental condition of their character: not repression but constitution. Or is it because Antonio is waiting for Bassanio and anticipating the impending loss of *his* affections? He knows Bassanio wants to talk to him about wooing a lady in Belmont; he is waiting on the Rialto because Bassanio has already promised to tell him, at this specific time and place, about the lady and his impending pilgrimage. They have an appointment, to which Bassanio is characteristically late. Does the realization that he is about to lose his dear friend to another—and to a woman, too—induce in him a specifically homosocial sadness? In the first instance, an inquiry into the philosophical and physiological implications of "melancholy" in the early modern period might shed some light on Antonio's affective travails, here and throughout the play. In the second, an inquiry into male-male relationships might broaden our understanding. One of the functions of Antonio's indecipherable sadness is to compel these kinds of speculation and inquiry. The audience, then or now, cannot feel Antonio's sadness, but it can and does share his experience of affective uncertainty and indetermination.

Marlowe taunts us with a different kind of sadness in *Edward II*, when he asks the audience to witness the capture of the king through the eyes of a sympathetic abbot. An affective point of view is established on stage; whether we adopt or reject it as our own, the abbot's sadness has spatial as well as social dimensions. Edward has sought refuge in the abbey of Neath but Leicester and his men are not far behind; the "lamentable death" of the king, announced in the full title of the play and anxiously anticipated by the audience since Galveston's opening speech, is about to begin its extended progress toward its appalling conclusion.[63] Despite Edward's earlier contempt for and abuse of the clergy, the abbot seems sincere when he announces his loyalty and service to the king. Edward, however, is uncertain at first:

> Father, thy face should harbour no deceit.
> O! hadst thou ever been a king, thy heart,
> Pierced deeply with sense of my distress,
> Could not but take compassion of my state.
> . . . .
> Yet, gentle monks, for treasure, gold, nor fee,
> Do you betray us and our company.

He is being betrayed as he speaks these lines, of course, but the betrayal takes place off stage and isn't the one he fears. It is a "gloomy fellow in a mead below" who reveals the king's sanctuary to his pursuers and not the abbot or any of the gentle monks. The abbot confirms his loyalty to the king in the profound dismay he feels, as he witnesses Edward's capture:

> My heart with pity *earns* to see this sight;
> A king to bear these words and proud commands!
> (19.70–71; emphasis added)[64]

"To earn" is to be "affected with poignant grief or compassion" (OED): it is exactly the kind of affective identification and fellow-feeling that the king had hoped to find in the abbey. Modern editions of the play regularly note this archaic term for grief and caution that the abbot's "earn" has nothing to do with something deserved, worked for, or legitimately achieved. However, the early modern "earn" was amphibolic in another sense, and by definition. "To earn" also meant "to desire strongly, to long" for something keenly (OED). As it happens, "earn" sounds out an ambivalence located at the core of early modern feeling. If we translated this other dimension of the abbot's "earning," we would hear him "yearning" for the spectacle of a derogated majesty.[65]

A complex set of ambiguities is introduced in this single word. Neither audience, Marlowe's Elizabethan nor an informed modern one, can be entirely certain that the abbot's feeling is a purely empathetic or sympathetic response to the king's misfortune. Everything in the context of the scene suggests an unmixed pity and empathy. Only one register of "earn" should be heard in the abbot's voice: he grieves to see Edward captured. Nonetheless, the word he uses is one that lodges two contrary feelings within it, making it an Elizabethan example of those antithetical words that Freud found so fascinating.[66] Why does he *earn* at the sight if what he meant to say was that he *grieves* at it? Is it possible that he intends to express the latter alone, that he believes he is grief all the way down, but that his choice of words is telling, that it hints at an underlying ambivalence that he himself is unable to acknowledge? Perhaps, perhaps not. It would make little dramaturgical sense for Marlowe to introduce a minor and fleeting character at this point in the play to make him the vehicle of such a profound equivocation of emotions. But without some confirmation one way or the other, perhaps a word or two from the abbot after Edward has been dragged off stage, a residue of uncertainty remains for the Elizabethan audience, who would have registered the ambiguity or ambivalence of "earning" more immediately than a modern audience could. What is the emotion being invoked on stage? What does the *abbot* feel or not feel?

The more important question, of course, has to do with what members of the audience feel at this moment, in response to both the capture and the abbot's "earning" over it. Do we (either then or now) earn or yearn to see the downfall, humiliation, and death of this king? The abbot's grief has the peculiar effect of alienating us from its eloquent expression, if we ourselves are of two minds and two hearts when it comes to the play and its impending *dénouement*. And we are of two minds, two hearts, aren't we? Whether we are Elizabethans or postmoderns, isn't this exactly what we came to the theater to see, in this and many other English history plays—the lamentable but compelling and avidly anticipated death of an English king? The abbot's "earning" does not cause or induce our own imitative grief *or* yearning. Rather, it exposes a queasy underside to what we feel. It momentarily brings out of solution an affective precipitate— "earning" in both of its senses—that resonates with all that is unsettled elsewhere, off stage in the audience and outside the theater as well.

This puts a lot of interpretive pressure on a single word and a single moment. In defense, I should point out that I am hardly the first to think that "earn" plays a significant role in Marlowe's scene. Shakespeare responds to *Edward II* in remarkable ways throughout his own play *Richard II*. He echoes Marlowe's abbot with his own moment of "earning" a king's captivity, but it is to a quite different effect. Just before the murderers enter to kill the king, Richard's former Groom of the Stable visits him and describes Bolingbroke's coronation procession. The new king rode

Richard's favorite horse—the pride of the groom as well—quite masterfully, as if it were his own steed:

> O, how it *erned* my heart when I beheld
> In London streets, that coronation day,
> When Bolingbroke rode on roan Barbary,
> That horse that thou so often hast bestrid,
> That horse that I so carefully have dressed! (5.5.76–80)

The groom feels and expresses pity for Richard throughout this scene. He's sorry that his old master is no longer in the saddle, literally and figuratively. This is what grieves him at the sight of a new king and master, whom even Barbary seems to accept with grace. However, the groom is also glad to see the horse again—and glad to see him looking so good, prancing so well and so proudly. He yearns to see Barbary at her best, yet grieves the fact that Richard no longer is the one who commands her. He is a divided subject embodied for us on stage, but the lines of his multivalence—pity for Richard, delight in Barbary, grudging admiration for Bolingbroke—are distinct, clear, and certain.

In Marlowe, it is the *audience* who is the divided subject. His scene holds a mirror up to an affective ensemble, located off stage and in the playhouse, which is dissociated, doubled, and divided. In Shakespeare the division on stage relieves the audience of its own contradictory perspectives; Shakespeare responds to Marlowe with a sentimental version of what it means to "earn" the dismantling of the sacred and the majestic. It is not accidental that the deepest focus of the groom's ambivalence is on the horse rather than the two monarchs. Remembered rather than enacted, the scene shifts the "earned" from the human to the equine, lending an endearing but also comic tone. As with Aumerle's plot against Bolingbroke's life in *2 Henry 4*, Shakespeare's earning is "altered from a serious thing." It can be touching, but it doesn't touch as keenly or probe as deeply as Marlowe's earning.

Marlowe uses one affective point of view, embodied on stage—the abbot gazing on Edward's capture with grief—to locate in the audience a doubled, contradictory set of emotions. Not everyone will be as aware of his or her own compromised affections. The shifting degrees of awareness, the differently embodied thoughts and feelings of each audience member, run through what is, after all, an artificial social gathering, brought together briefly as a performative community. In this kind of theater, this performative social space, the characters, actors, spectators, and auditors all perceive the reactions of their others. During a performance, any view of the action on stage will include a view of some of the other spectators and their reactions. An amphitheater audience was in its nature an audience-oriented heterogeneity, self- and other-aware; a transactional dynamic structured the "playing" space—the gallery and the pit as well as the stage—and expanded the threshold where drama and everyday life overlapped and merged and complicated one another. In its own theatrical apparatus, amphitheater performance included entrances and exits, trapdoors, balconies, encoded zones like the *platea* and *locus*, mechanical machinery and devices, walls, roofs, actors, and the auditors and spectators themselves—along with their various, never quite synthesized, and sometimes incompatible points of view and lines of hearing.[67] The social body gathered together in the Rose Theatre in 1592 or 1593, when Marlowe's play was first performed, was a dystonic one, rooted in its own divisions as much as in its wholeness or harmony or sense of community. It was this aspect that allowed it to function as a simulacrum of the larger social body, the Elizabethan habitus, which was itself an imagined community and, as a consequence, entirely real. Indeed, I would go so far as to say that the social can't be real *unless* it is also virtual or imagined. It exists, to paraphrase Craig Calhoun, precisely *because* it is imagined.[68]

Marlowe's audience lived in a world where the sacred and the absolute had grown clouded and unsettled, not necessarily secular or disenchanted but subject to many doubts and qualifications if they were to be collectively tenable. Structures of feeling were no longer held in suspension and were coming out of solution. "Earn" is the name of one of the affective precipitates. Marlowe rehearses a historical ambivalence as a theatrical and performative ambivalence. Using a single word to create a dia-logic affective gaze, a synesthetic paradox of eye and ear, he tests the mettle of his spectators and exposes their own divided selves in Edward's fall, making the audience feel, or rather, *earn* the queasy underside of a specifically Reformation form of empathy.

IX

What is the relationship of "structures of feeling" to social emo-tions, or to the finely nuanced, indefinable yet powerfully felt and realized, emotions of a character like Anna Karenina? If "struc-tures of feeling" is a *necessary* concept, as I called it earlier, what makes it so? Contemporary critical social thought has often *be-haved* as if it were an unavoidable concept, judging from the fre-quency with which "structures of feeling" have been invoked. But this is at best a symptom of a critical, social, and literary need for theoretical terms of such capacity. At worst, it is the symptom of a new jargon and nothing more.

The usefulness if not the necessity of Williams's concept stems from its deep focus rather than its sharp definition. Ac-cording to Williams, who introduced the concept and used it in a number of his own cultural and literary studies, structures of feeling are components of the social that are by nature dif-ficult to articulate—or rather, they are by definition impossible to articulate, insofar as they remain structures of feeling rather than other kinds of cognitive and affective experience. Like Nor-bert Elias, Cornelius Castoriadis, Pierre Bourdieu, and Anthony Giddens, Williams was keenly interested in what goes without saying in a given community or culture, and he regularly sought ways to conceptualize the forms and domains of "non-discursive consciousness" without reducing it to an ideology, trivializing it as merely a form of common sense, or equating it with repressed knowledge.[69] Structures of feeling are modes of thinking as well as feeling that are inseparable from lived experience. They are historical and culture-specific rather than universal. They are in operation all the time, yet can only be accessed or understood to

a limited extent and by indirect means. For Williams, literature
and theater are among the more roadworthy vehicles for such
partial and indirect access. Williams understood literature itself,
as Catherine Gallagher has noted, as a kind of counterhistory
that allows us to apprehend nondiscursive as well as discursive
forms of consciousness. He read literature as the history of "the
not-quite-said":

> Like other counterhistorians (Nietzsche, Foucault, and et. al.) he
> haunted the borderlines where dissonance and incoherence are
> registered, and stressed that modern social experience is replete
> with cognitive and affective discrepancies, which rarely find direct
> expression.[70]

Literary, theatrical, and other forms of art go beyond the pale of
articulation when they cross over into these borderlands of lived
experience, which is where "structures of feeling" are located.
One of Williams's lasting strengths as a Marxist theorist was his
recurrent turn to literature as a resource and not merely a misrep-
resentation of real social relations or an ideological device that
needs to be corrected or scolded. For Williams, literature was
also, and more importantly, a cultural performance of a less hegemonic kind—a way to learn about the past in its own uncertain
terms, when we want to know more than paraphrasable content.
He had a lifelong trust in the capacity of art to think beyond the
terms of its explicit means of representation and provide quite
complex forms of indirect, critical social thought.[71]

Gallagher misunderstands Williams, however, when she re-
lates structures of feeling to structures of repression.[72] Williams
himself took great care to divorce the former from the latter. As
a social theorist, he was wary of the concept of repression just as
he was wary of the ways in which canonical historical materialism had marginalized cultural dialectics and cultural modes of
production such as literature and drama. Structures of feeling
are not social experiences that have been repressed. Rather, in
Williams's own, carefully chosen metaphor, they are "social expe-

riences *in solution*, as distinct from other social semantic formations which have been *precipitated* and are more evidently and
more immediately available."[73] Structures of feeling are not buried or denied or felt only in distorted or neurotic ways. On the
contrary, they function as aspects of lived and embodied social
experience precisely because they *are still* in solution and *not yet*
precipitated out into articulation or discursive knowledge. Most
emphatically, structures of feeling are not related to a political
unconscious, whose horizons of ideology were best articulated
by Fredric Jameson in *The Political Unconscious*.[74] Unlike structures of feeling, the political unconscious lives in and thrives on
repression: it swims in the waters, to adapt Foucault's comment
on Marx and the nineteenth century, of post-Freudian theory.

Understanding what Williams meant by "structures of feeling" is made difficult, I must acknowledge, by the fact that a definition has to be extracted from a series of tantalizing references
and uses of the phrase that are scattered throughout his work
and only occasionally punctuated by a partial gloss or example.
How such structures differ from, intersect with, or are otherwise related to ideology is unclear; how they operate in the social imaginary, submerged and solvent but not repressed, is never
adequately addressed. However, there is a "fuzzy logic" to the
concept, properly speaking. Fuzzy logic is not a vague, inexact,
or messy logic. In higher mathematics, it is an immensely useful
tool for thinking about uncertainties and probabilities. In day-
to-day life, we use it regularly: fuzzy logic is what allows a video
camera, for example, to adjust its focus and its exposure continu-
ously as it pans or zooms in and out of a scene.[75] "Habitus" and
"symbolic imaginary" share a similar logic and similarly allow us
to avoid confusing precision with accuracy.

It is because of its "fuzzy logic" that Williams's concept is *necessary*, as I claimed earlier. It provides a way to talk about the
social emotions of everyday life in the past without inevitably
thinking in terms of repression. One of my hopes in what follows will be to flesh out certain dimensions and dynamics of

Elizabethan structures of feeling as they came under pressure and reformation. Such an enterprise will involve, of necessity, a dialectical approach and methodology:

> Methodologically . . . a "structure of feeling" is a cultural hypothesis, actually derived from attempts to understand such elements and their connections in a generation or period, and needing always to be returned, interactively, to such evidence.[76]

Methodologically, as Williams implies, such attempts to understand are more often oblique than direct. By indirection, as it were, we seek to find directions out.

X

It was Brecht rather than Dryden, despite the historical distance of the first and the historical proximity of the second, who best understood early modern theater. This is emphatically the case in his understanding of the dialectic or dialogical structure of many of its plays and their consequent affective strangeness:

> Take the element of conflict in Elizabethan plays, complex, shifting, largely impersonal, never soluble, and then see what has been made of it today, whether in contemporary plays or in contemporary renderings of the Elizabethans. Compare the part played by empathy then and now. What a contradictory, complicated and intermittent operation it was in Shakespeare's theatre![77]

Brecht's Elizabethan drama is a dynamic, critical, and necessarily refracted mode of theater. It is a mode that is finely tuned, whether by design or effect, to sound out a Reformation culture in crisis. Such negotiations and reformations of the heart could not be performed without the aid of such refractions—without the "internal distantiation," in Althusser's terms, that certain forms of artistic endeavor make possible.[78]

When Walter Benjamin proposed that "even the dead" are not safe unless the historian is capable of "fanning the spark of hope *in the past*" (emphasis added), he had in mind a committed form of engagement by the historian.[79] But the responsibility toward the past is first felt by works of art themselves. Works of art can reveal a "contradictory, complicated and intermittent" sympathy with their particular pasts and presents, engaging in a kind of reading or critical social thought that can be valuable, even enlightening, to their own particular present.

Sometimes a complex form of cultural performance and production—Elizabethan popular drama was certainly a prominent example—can serve as a primary rather than a secondary forum for social thought. Sometimes—and my premise is that Reformation England was one of those times—theatrical performance and reception enable and constitute a significant form of analysis and inquiry in and of themselves, a kind of critical social theory conducted by other means. This is what Tadeusz Kantor seems to have had in mind when he described theater as "an answer to, rather than a representation of, reality," and suggested that "theater takes place when life is pushed to its final limits, where all categories and concepts lose their meaning and right to exist."[80] This is of course too broad, too hyperbolic, and too catastrophic to apply to the conditions of possibility for all theater, in all of its modes and specific historical instantiations. But Kantor's theater resonates with the theater that emerged in Reformation England. For Kantor, theater of this order doesn't simply happen when you bring together a script, a stage, some actors, and an audience. It takes place—emerges and unfolds—when a culture is in crisis. It is a remarkable response to historical trauma, as Benjamin himself discovered in his early treatise on Reformation *Trauerspiel.*[81]

If space is a social production, as Henri Lefebvre has argued, then the social and the spatial are codependent, part of the same dialectical processes of production.[82] When Marlowe highlights his audience as a divided subject, it is not to deconstruct that audience or to remind it, in an overly simplified metatheatrical sense, that it is merely an audience. On the contrary. It is to clarify the fractal complexities of the audience *as* a subject, a social *individuum* in action, always more than one in its singularity and sometimes embodying those fractures, faultlines, and incompatible points of view. Elizabethan amphitheater playhouses produced new kinds of plays but they also produced a new kind of cognitive and affective space, one that was by nature dynamic, interactive, highly experimental, and inherently theatrical. It was a space expressly designed to resonate with an audience newly uncertain of its individual and collective identities—custom-built, in other words, to plumb and sound out the gaps that had been opened in the Elizabethan social body as a consequence of the English Reformation.

XI

All societies negotiate and reconfigure, on a day-to-day basis, the ties that bind them together as societies. They do so in times of relative calm as well as times of crisis or social trauma, and they do so with the aid of a wide variety of nondiscursive practices of everyday life in addition to the discursive forms and media that are available to them. A great deal of what goes without saying in a given culture, the diurnal rhythms and everyday activities of heterogeneous individuals—buying the morning paper, shopping for a salad, taking the kids to school; walking to St. Paul's for the latest word on the Lopez case, picking up daily victuals and neighborly gossip in Eastcheap, taking in the latest offering at The Theatre—such routines play a role in the constitution of collective identities and the development of one's understanding of their vernacular nuances. They keep members of a cognitive and affective community up to date with themselves.[83] Such ties are also regularly renewed, revised, challenged, or derogated by and through a wide range of discursive, mixed, and nondiscursive media, which sometimes take the form of what I have called "affective technologies." In the early modern period, these included a host of ritual practices, running the gamut from the secular to the religious, and an even larger range of oral practices. They included new forms and modes of communication and new developments in historiography, theater, and other narrative forms and cultural performances, through which Elizabethans told the story of themselves, to themselves and for themselves.

My own examples in the chapters that follow are limited to the early modern stage, which means that they are limited in more than one sense of the word. They are not intended to be representative, especially not in the sense that they codify these forms and modes. They are certainly far from exhaustive, even in terms of the stage, even in terms of Shakespeare. However, they are meant to be suggestive beyond their immediate concerns and specific arguments. My hope is that these inquiries might prove useful to others in their own efforts to comprehend the period in question, perhaps even to those whose concerns lie in other historical periods. I do not seek merely to illustrate the ways in which theater reflected or represented social events, issues, or transformations that were taking place elsewhere. The relations between media and world examined in *The Reformation of Emotions* are more complex, more mutually dependent, more dynamically recursive, than reflection theory would recognize, given its emphasis on social mimesis and secondary, derivative forms of representation. The media and practices I want to clarify are refractive, unsettling, and creative or world-making; they are social productions, dialectical rather than reflexive or didactic in their relation to their readers and audiences and worlds, both old and new. The texts and cultural performances examined here are processes as well as products of thought and feeling—and the "mind" that is thinking and feeling is a social one, a collective self and not merely an individual author or reader. Such forms and media are "equipment for living," in Kenneth Burke's terms, and the tools they provide are affective as well as cognitive.[84]

In times of relatively moderate change, the kinds of cultural work performed by social media and practices will be moderate as well. But in times of more radical disruption, when the past—always a scarce resource, as Arjun Appadurai reminds us—is contested in ways that threaten to undo long-standing values and beliefs, then the arts and practices of social identity can also undergo radical transformations.[85] New modes of historical thinking and consciousness, new tools to grapple with new or newly fraught problems, can and do emerge. Their emergence has less to do with causes and effects than with responses, whether direct or indirect, implicit or explicit. They are questions posed for their various audiences, challenging as well as constructive, not so much to be answered as to engage with and even be discomfited by.

The next chapter, titled "Affective Irony: Toward an Emotional Logic of the Elizabethan Stage," argues that the social logic of emotions in the period, as opposed to their physiological or etiological explanations, is crucial to the historical study of Elizabethan emotions, especially insofar as they were under pressure of reform. To begin, I consider Thomas Wright's *The Passions of the Minde in Generall*, frequently cited in recent years to argue for a humoral phenomenology of early modern emotions. The distinct structure of the treatise in its successive sections, focused as they are on somatic, social, and spiritual arenas of both temperament and emotion, reveals an understanding of the passions in Wright's treatise that is more social and less humoral than has been assumed in recent years. Wright's model of social passions is an oratorical one, however, and limited by its insistence on the mimetic sociality of emotion. Such a Ciceronian understanding proves inadequate to the early modern stage, as I show by examining a series of Elizabethan revenge plays—one of the most popular genres on the amphitheater stage. From Fredson Bowers to recent scholars, the popularity of revenge plays has regularly been regarded as an example of social mimesis: if revenge was so prevalent on the Elizabethan stage, then it must have been a prevalent problem in Elizabethan society. What you see on the early modern stage, however, is not what you get.[86] Despite the claims of reflectionist scholars, Elizabethan England was not a "revenge culture" and had not been one for many decades or even centuries.[87] The affective embodiment of characters on stage was both transactional and intersubjective in its relation to the audience. The shift from complex allegorical embodiments of affective character, as in the morality tradition, to the more psychological (but by no means more complex) dimensions of character, suggests that the drama of post-Reformation England served as a kind of affective laboratory in both design and function. It was designed to test and explore the affective faultlines that ran deep in its large and diverse audience.[88] In *The Spanish Tragedy* Kyd employed the affective architectonics of the new amphitheater playhouse to cast a shadow of dramatic irony over the entire audience, paradoxically creating a kind of antimimetic semiotics at the heart of his drama. Shakespeare's *Titus Andronicus* builds upon Kyd's use of social emotion as a form of social cognition and imbues its transactional relation to its audiences with an "affective irony" (we saw an early example in Marlowe's staging of "earn"). A history of "theatrical" emotions that limits itself to the ways in which they are represented or described on stage can easily overlook and obscure this other, antimimetic resource and dialectic. The audience's affective reactions are often catalyzed—induced, felt, and experienced as emotions—most effectively when they are alienated from the emotions expressed or represented on stage. The chapter concludes with an extended examination of *The Merchant of Venice*, a play of remarkable cognitive and affective acuity.

Chapter 2, "The Wreckage of History," focuses on Shakespeare's first history tetralogy, made up by the three plays devoted to the reign of Henry VI and *Richard III*. These plays explore the complex relations between historical memory and historical forgetting. Drawing on work by Edward Casey and Cathy Caruth, I argue that forgetting can sometimes be a necessary component of memory, something that becomes especially evident in times of collective social trauma. "Historical trauma" manifests itself in two distinct forms, each of considerable and real consequence. The loss of eucharistic thought in Reformation England structures the historical consciousness of these four plays, but their evocations of loss should not be mistaken as collective nostalgia or evidence of Shakespeare's "Catholic sympathies." They are explorations, often probing and discomfiting, of the affective and cognitive gaps that haunted many dimensions of day-to-day life in Shakespeare's world.

Chapter 3 is titled "What's *Hamlet* to Habermas?" It draws together the preceding considerations of Elizabethan and Jacobean drama and expands them to analyze the relationship of theater to the early modern public sphere. A corrective reading of Jürgen Habermas's flawed narrative of a "bourgeois public sphere" clarifies the affective sociality and dimensionality of amphitheater drama and explores the ground it shares with other instantiations of theatrical performance. Performance in the presence of an audience—a theatrical production as well as a performance of the play—was understood to be a form of "publication" in its own right, and there are pressing reasons to recover this performative sense of publication. Making ideas and affective actions public by theatrical performance renders them in a substantially different form than other modes of publication, including oral, visual, scribal, and printed forms. "Theatrical publication" is at once a mode of production and a mode of consumption; the play is produced and consumed by an audience in collaboration with a playwright and a company of actors. The play is not embodied on the stage or the page: such embodiment is a process rather a presentation, and it takes place within the architectonic sociality of the playhouse or theater itself.

In a brief epilogue, I return to the dead with a brief meditation on what it meant to think and feel with, to think and feel through, historical things, including the bones and skulls of loved ones. Throughout the book, I have invoked in passing the language of cognitive ecology to make sense of the social and intersubjective dynamics of early modern performance. Bringing the dead of St. Paul's together with the bones of the graveyard scene in *Hamlet*, I make explicit some of my earlier references to the concepts of distributed cognition and extended mind, and I offer some concluding thoughts on the affective tools and technologies that Elizabethans used in their own efforts to understand what it felt like to be an Elizabethan.

1

Affective Irony in *The Spanish Tragedy*, *Titus Andronicus*, and *The Merchant of Venice*

"He which will make me weepe," claims Thomas Wright in *The Passions of the Minde in Generall*, "must first weepe himselfe."[1] With later help from Cicero as well as Horace, he goes on to argue that emotions felt (and well expressed) by an orator will also be felt by his audience. The speaker's passion resonates in his auditors with a kind of tonal sympathy, so that they are moved to imitate the emotion they witness and to experience it for themselves and in themselves.[2]

Tears are complicated things, social as well as material, and this can make them difficult to understand: like the difference between a twitch and a wink, what we see on the face looks the same whether they are tears of joy, sorrow, or a sign that one has been chopping onions. Historical tears are even more problematic. These we encounter only indirectly, in one kind of archive or another—a treatise on the passions, a playscript, a lyric poem—and have to do our best to understand them, whether we have sufficient context or not.

But the social and transactional semiotics of crying, including the response of the person witnessing it, are complicated even when the tears are visible and tangible on the face and supplemented by the sound of laughing or crying. Tears can be feigned as well as truly felt, as Wright acknowledges. He is careful to stress that the orator should actually feel the passions he wants to stir in his audience. But the need for authenticity is not entirely transparent, since Wright does not assume or claim that only "real" or authentic tears can move auditors "to weep themselves." His own immediate cultural milieu, including as it did the popular and highly affective drama of the Elizabethan and Jacobean stage, argued otherwise. Elizabethan stage players, he acknowledges, can "act excellently"—so much so, that they can also move us to fear or anger or mirth or sadness. But they also "act fainedly" and do not genuinely feel the emotions they cause or induce or persuade us to feel:

> and this the best may be marked in stage players, who act excellently; for as the profession of their exercise consisteth in imitation of others, so they that imitate best, act best. And in the substance of external action for most part orators and stage players agree: and only they differ in this, that these act fainedly, those really; these only to delight, those to stir up all sorts of passions according to the exigencie of the matter; these intermingle much levitie in their action to make men laugh, those use all gravity, grace, and authority to persuade: wherefore these are accounted ridiculous, those esteemed prudent. (179)

Left unclear is the affective nature of the tears wept by a theatrical audience, whose members are not pretending to feel what they feel. Are such emotions the same as everyday emotions? Do they feel or look the same? Do plays, it might be asked, make us dream real or theatrical tears?

Such questions have a long history in Western culture. From Plato to Augustine to Stephen Greenblatt, the relation between what an individual might feel at the performance of a play and what that same person might feel in response to similar "real-world" experiences has troubled theatergoers, philosophers, psy-

chologists, and anyone else who has attempted to understand
the affective experience of an audience. Most discomfiting are
the moral incongruities that can haunt that experience. We take
pleasure, in a sense, in watching and empathizing with tragic suffering. Why does it feel so good to feel so bad about Gloucester's
blinding or Cordelia's death? Some modern explanations have
turned to psychoanalytic theories of sadomasochism to explain
why theatrical suffering can be so satisfying. Some have turned
to the evident artificiality of theater, suggesting that the aesthetic
realm provides a kind of quarantine from reality, a space that is
safely and even comfortably walled off and protected from everyday concerns. Others yet, to theories of Winnicottian play
or an atavistic need for the ritual release of a tragic catharsis.[3]
Wright's advice is more practical: since feigning is not honest,
orators rather than actors should provide the model for right
rhetorical feeling. If the orator himself feels the need for a mentor or model, then he should look to the preacher, who is the
"glass for every orator" to imitate, rather than the Elizabethan
actor, whose affective powers might be effective but are also, in
the final analysis, "ridiculous" (179).

Wright assumes, and many—including myself—would agree,
that the passions or emotions are social things, distributed across
social bodies in many different forums that range from the family to the sermon or speech to the production of a play. However,
Wright's oratorical model—his Ciceronian template for social
emotions at work, in what he defines as their most exemplary
setting—encourages him to frame his argument in terms of a
mimetic dynamics of feeling, which are not, or so I would argue,
always adequate to comprehend the *social* dynamics of emotions,
which are more dialectical and recursive, interpersonal, intersubjective, and inherently transactional. These social dynamics
are *sometimes* mimetic but not always or essentially so. Affective
resonance or sympathy becomes a great deal more problematic, as
I hope to show, when our paradigm shifts from the monological
dynamics of the podium or pulpit (at least as framed by Cicero
and Wright) to the dialogical dynamics of theatrical performance.

I

Before I can continue, however, there's a question that needs to be addressed. Where's Galen in this picture? Given the "humoral turn" of recent studies early modern affect, why have I so notably left humoral theory out of my initial overview and critique of Wright's views?[4]

When discussing the affective work of the orator, the preacher, and the player, Wright does not turn to Galen or the Galenic theories of the humoral body. Indeed, humoral thought is largely absent from most of his treatise, with the exception of its two initial "books" or chapters. The structure of Wright's treatise is instructive in this regard. Its six chapters fall into three distinct groups. In the first section, focused on the physiological imbrications of the passions, Wright discusses the relationship between the humoral body and the passions of the mind—the relationship, I would stress, and not the identity. In this section, Wright makes it clear that humors are not the same as passions and, furthermore, he emphasizes that the relationship between the humoral and the emotional is ambiguous and multivalent in many senses. Sometimes passions engender humors or alter the humoral balance; sometimes humors engender passions.[5] But there is not a consistent relationship between the two, neither a causal nor a catalytic one.[6] The first section of the work could be read as a limited etiology of the passions, the equivalent of a modern hormonal or neurological explanation, if one keeps in mind the ambiguities of cause or catalysis that I have just noted. Wright provides an account of some aspects of the physiological production of emotions, but he does not equate or merge such aspects with the experiential, observable, or interactive operations of the passions—the phenomenology, as it were, of social emotions in everyday life.

In the central and longest section of *Passions of the Minde*, from the third through the fifth books, Wright addresses the social dimensions of the passions.[7] They operate as a kind of language, made up of internal and variously embodied feelings and the words and gestures or outward signs that can accompany them, at varying degrees of intentional and involuntary expression, whether these signs of affect are visual, auditory, or verbal. Social emotions are in some sense innate, something we are born with, but they also develop and change from infancy to maturity, conditioned as they are by formal and informal kinds of social interaction. And of course, they are capable of being further refined and calibrated through explicit training and practice. In the final, third section of the treatise, where Wright considers the spiritual aspects of the passions, neither Galen nor Cicero is any longer relevant. Here, Augustine and scripture guide Wright's discussion—aptly and predictably so.

The somatic, the social, and the spiritual. My terms are meant to be heuristic. They correspond, roughly speaking, to the three distinct objects of Wright's inquiry: to the province of the humors; the province of the social, including feeling, language, rhetoric, expression, and a great deal else; and finally, the province of the soul. For Wright, as for most of his contemporaries, this sequence would be read as an ascending order, a rising progression from the material to the immaterial, from the flesh to the spirit. The passions are neither separate from nor identical to either extreme. They "stand betwixt these two extremes," as Wright tells us, "and border upon them both" (7), so that they "inhabit both the confines of sense and reason" (8). They are betwixt-and-between phenomena, according to Wright, grounded in the social *mise en scène* in ways that might recall Michelle Rosaldo's description of emotions as "embodied thoughts, thoughts steeped with the apprehension that 'I am involved.'" As I emphasized earlier, Rosaldo had the social body in mind and not merely the corporeal bodies of the Ilongot tribes she studied. She was very careful not to reduce affective embodiment to the somatic, and it seems to me that Thomas Wright—and Timothy Bright and a long list of other early modern explicators of the passions—shared her caution. "Feelings are not substances to be discovered in our blood, but social practices organized by stories that we both enact and tell."[8] Not substances in the blood: in other words, neither humoral nor hormonal, even though humors and hormones have often been thought, at different historical moments and regimes of medicine, to play a role in the workings of the emotions.

In *Humoring the Body*, Gail Kern Paster disagrees quite emphatically: "For early moderns, emotions flood the body not metaphorically but literally, as the humors course through the bloodstream carrying choler, melancholy, blood, and phlegm to the parts and as the animal spirits move like lightning from brain to muscle, from muscle to brain."[9] In the traditional understanding that Paster means to correct, the humoral self was understood quite differently. It was fixed, rigid, and intransigent, characterized by obdurate temperaments that were caused by imbalances in the humors that could not be seen or measured in themselves.[10] The temperament of any given individual was an observable symptom of an otherwise inaccessible and opaque inner state. Temperaments then and now were understood to be extremely resistant to change. In humoral medical practice, an overly dominant humor might be brought into balance by purging the appropriate fluid or substance or spirit from the body—by bleeding, administering laxatives or emetics, and so forth. Fevers, rashes, and other outward signs of illness could also be caused by temporary imbalances of the humoral system and were treated as such.[11]

Paster recognizes that humoral theory "is often identified with typologies—the four temperaments, the four complexions," but in her "own reading of humoral discourse [she] finds a much greater emphasis on change and penetrability, on a way of inhabiting the body with keen attention to the winds and waters of its internal climate."[12] Those winds and waters are to be understood, as she suggests above, not metaphorically but literally. The humoral self is pre-Cartesian, an epistemic distinction in Paster's terms. She suggests, for example, that our own distinctions between the figurative and the literal, the inner and the outer, as well as the body and the mind, are dichotomies of the modern, post-Cartesian age. They can make it hard to realize that early modern emotions are, properly understood, quite beyond our understanding. They will remain so, until we recognize the humoral flux of early modern emotions and realize how radically strange this makes the Elizabethan world in comparison to our own affective worlds:

> The passions are like liquid states and forces of the natural world. But the passions—thanks to their close functional relation to the four bodily humors of blood, choler, black bile, and phlegm—had a more than analogical relation to liquid states and forces of nature. In an important sense, the passions actually *were* liquid forces of nature, because, in this cosmology, the stuff of the outside world and the stuff of the body were composed of the same elemental materials.[13]

We move with ease from "close functional relation" to "more than analogical" to a heavily emphasized identity (passions "actually," passions "actually were," passions "actually *were*"). An identity is never directly asserted between the passions and the humors. However, we seem to move from passions that were *like* liquid states to passions that "actually *were*" liquid states— seeming identical, but only at an elemental level. The impression left, however, is that anything said about the humors in a Galenic text is implicitly yet literally being said of the passions, too.

I am wary of collapsing the distinction between the literal and the metaphorical in this way. One of the things it obscures is the oscillation between literal and metaphoric, actual and virtual, real and imagined, that is basic to much of social life and essential in theatrical performance. Such fluidity of critical terms is crucial, however, if one wants, as Paster explicitly does, to use Galenic humors and many other kinds of liquids or spirits or waters or winds as a literal articulation of how it felt to be an Elizabethan. A proper understanding of the humoral system, she writes, will give us access to "the phenomenological character of early modern life."[14]

Paster proposes an extreme and epistemic break between the humoral past and its post-Cartesian successors. This sense of what it means to historicize the emotions is not shared, it should be noted, by other key participants in the humoral turn.

In their own readings of humoral theory and embodiment, such a strong relationship or identity between humors and emotions is not claimed. Indeed, a number of other humoral theorists are also wary of treating humors as a guide to emotions, as such. They focus instead on the undeniably strong relationship between fixed temperaments and humors.[15] The geohumoral system brought to our attention by Mary Floyd-Wilson in *English Ethnicity and Race in Early Modern Drama* is an excellent example. Floyd-Wilson situates Galenic thought in a climatology and ecology that is indeed quite strange to us; she demonstrates, quite persuasively in my view, how pervasive this geohumoral system was in the construction of premodern racisms as well as premodern temperaments. But in her study, the ecology between the humoral self and its climatological environment locks the former in place, so that place determines temperament (in early modern terms) or ethnicity (in modern terms). The humoral self is remarkably fixed in this cosmology, set in affective concrete rather flux and flow. Climate was believed to a strong determinate of shared ethnic characteristics of entire peoples, producing fixed and hard-to-change ethno-environmental temperaments. Northerners' cold and wet climate explained why they were so brutish in body and mind and so lascivious; the hot and dry climate of southerners (meaning, e.g., tropical, sub-Saharan) produced hot and dry bodies rather than cold and wet ones, resulting in an overly *intellectual* temperament that was also slow to be aroused sexually or emotionally. "I think the sun where he was born," as Desdemona says when jealousy is first raised to explain Othello's behavior, "Drew all such humours from him" (3.4.29). The perfect balance of humors, the golden mean of innate character, was found only in people of a Mediterranean climate—unsurprisingly, since humoral theory and its Greek and Roman physicians were native to such a clime.

The iconic choler of Pyrrhus, as described by the visiting player in *Hamlet*, is obviously not environmental in this sense of human geography. The description of Pyrrhus has often been understood as a clear but parodic manifestation of the rigidity of humoral temperaments:

The rugged Pyrrhus, he whose sable arms,
Black as his purpose, did the night resemble
When he lay couchéd in the ominous horse,
Hath now this dread and black complexion smeared
With heraldry more dismal. (2.2.432—436)

Paster suggests that the description of Pyrrhus, overstuffed as it is with the language of choleric humor, is far from parodic. It exemplifies what she calls the "emotional intelligence" of the Elizabethan stage: "What I will argue is that, far from being only a set-piece occasion with hermeneutic value because of its metaphorical mirroring of Hamlet's circumstances, Shakespeare's representation of Pyrrhus's wrath here is fully cognate with his representation of affect and interiority elsewhere in the play."[16] As she acknowledges in passing, this is a minority view. For other commentators, the language, imagery, and prosody of the player's description of Pyrrhus's choler separate it from the emotional intelligence of Hamlet's world. Given the metatheatrical dynamics of the scene, Pyrrhus's wrath also has been understood as the echo of older modes of affective drama, designed to sound archaic and anachronistic in a play that otherwise negotiates so flexibly between formal and casual discourse ("But in the beaten way of friendship, what brings you to Elsinore?") and devotes itself so entirely to the question, What does it feel like to be Hamlet the Dane?

By many accounts, Hamlet is a mercurial character, which I mean metaphorically and not literally. He is ambivalent and duplicitous, but it's not always possible to determine when he's feeling something, when he's acting as if he did, and when he himself isn't sure of which is which. He is highly susceptible, of course, to modern psychoanalytic and psychiatric diagnoses, if one is so inclined. Instead, Paster explains his metamorphic qualities and the play-world itself with a "humoral diagnosis." Accordingly, she treats the ghost of Hamlet's father as a humoral rather than a spiritual or demonic manifestation. It is an aspect of Hamlet's own humoral ecology, the sign of his own "emotional inconstancy." In his worries over the "ghost's" validity (2.2.575–80), for example, he sees himself as too open and vulnerable to influences brought in and through the air, a victim of the pneumatic character of life. But such vulnerability is a constant peril for—indeed almost a natural outcome of—early modern conceptions of subjectivity dependent on the ceaseless interactivity of fluids, spirits, and world to explain behavior and affect. The resulting construction of subjectivity is prone to continual emotional transformation, thanks to the ongoing tumult or even just the continual movements of inner bodily fluids and their exchanges with the world.[17]

I would agree that there is a characteristic "emotional intelligence" to the player's Pyrrhus. In my view, however, it is located in what is being performed as opposed to what is being described. Pyrrhus's choler is not, after all, the focus of Hamlet's attention; it is not what he is disturbed by. He reacts entirely to the *player*'s theatrical tears, which are "real" despite the fact that they are feigned. Hamlet's affective reaction culminates in the soliloquy that concludes act 2, but the undertone affects everything he does and says in the scene with the player. An expression of feigned grief so "real" that it produces "tears that be wet," as Lear says to Cordelia, contrasts starkly with Hamlet's ostensibly "real" but wayward grief, his own melancholy, his own nonhumoral angers and rages and his prolonged inaction. The point of comparison between the two expressions of grief is not the tears that Hamlet does or doesn't shed, but the revenge he hasn't taken. For Hamlet, revenge is the equivalent of the player's tears, the only apt embodiment and expression of his own grief. Other modes of expression—tears, unpacking his heart, taking on a frantic disposition—cast doubt on the authenticity of his own grief. Is his grief real or sincere if he can't respond appropriately—by killing Claudius? Does he even *feel* what he *should* feel? Does he feel it enough? How can he know that he does, as long as his vow to avenge his father's death remains unfulfilled? What is he to his father, or his father to him? These are the issues he has grappled with from the beginning of the play. They are all non-humoral articulations of the difference between what is felt and what is communicated or shown, whether by suits of solemn black or tears or revenge. Hamlet's affective response is relational and social even when the relation is between feigning and feeling, real or artificial tears.[18]

How can we know what an Elizabethan audience thought or felt as they watched, heard, and responded to any given performance? The blunt answer would be "we can't." That does not mean, of course, that the question should not be asked. We cannot know what a modern audience is thinking and feeling either, even when we are seated in the midst of one ourselves. Emotions are difficult to talk about and resistant to verification (at times, even to the person feeling them) or definition because they are nondiscursive as well as discursive, psychological as well as physiological—and, as both Wright and Rosaldo remind us, never reducible to one extreme or the other. Due to their hybrid, amphibolic nature, in other words, their phenomenology resists our methodologies to a great degree. In a phenomenology of historical or theatrical emotions, it might be tempting to limit evidence to the explicitly articulated, reported, or theorized. If we do, however, are we producing a history of emotions or a history of ideas about emotions? Aren't we confusing evidence with the explicit as well as the extant?[19] Aren't we producing an inherently false history by accepting only that which was recorded in the past, whether in print or manuscript, has survived the vagaries of history, and has been catalogued and hence made accessible? Not everything that counts can be counted. What I take away from Michael Macdonald's brilliant study of the life and death of Italian Protestant Francesco Spiera—briefly discussed in the introduction—is an encouragement to embrace formal literary and theatrical analysis as a useful tool for the study of early modern emotions, not merely in terms of what characters and plays say or explain or represent but also, and more crucially, in terms of what theatrical performance makes happen in and with its audience, beyond the discursive and mimetic dimensions of the stage. Elizabethan popular drama, perhaps all theatrical performance, is a hybrid of semiotic and affective layers. By its very nature, theater is not only performative but also transactional.

The significance of Elizabethan amphitheater drama for the reformation of emotions, its role in conditioning and dissecting and exposing affective as well as cognitive states of mind, will not be adequately understood if we limit our analysis to the realm of representation or mimesis. What counts most in a theatrical performance cannot be confined to what the stage represents, what it shows to us, embodies, enacts, or otherwise makes manifest, or to what the playtext and dialogue articulate, whether on the stage or on the page. Like any performative mode of production, early modern drama was a distributed phenomenon in an affective as well as a cognitive sense. It extended beyond the acting space or scaffold to take place in and with the audience, its necessary participant and dramaturgical collaborator. Theatrical performance in production is, in fact, a quite unusual form of commodity. A play in performance before an audience brings production and consumption together as one process, coincident in space as well as time. It is in some respects a perfect commodity form, or at least a transitory and effervescent image of the thing itself.[20]

How can we know what an Elizabethan audience felt? It is here, at the threshold of a profound methodological aporia, that Wright's rhetorical tears need to become historical ones. Do we weep when we see others weep? Of course we do—sometimes. We do, unless we live in a time or place where "we" has become a vexed question rather than a social given. When a culture's sense of collective identity is unsettled in more than customary ways, its cultural performances take on new forms. In England in the second half of the sixteenth century, the Elizabethan stage was one of those emergent forms: one that profoundly complicates Wright's confidence in a kind of affective mimesis, just as his own brief consideration of Elizabethan actors complicated his faith in the sincerity of real tears.

II

Halfway through *The Spanish Tragedy*, a boy enters carrying a small box and speaks briefly to the audience. Identified only as

"Page," he is new to the play; his monologue will be his only speaking part. In the scene immediately following, which takes place in the duke's prison, he will perform a bit of silent mumming, pointing to the box he carries while winking at Pedringano, a murderer on the threshold of either pardon or execution, misleading him to think that the box contains the order for his release. But as the audience knows, having been shown by the boy in the previous scene, the box is empty.

In terms of the plot, the pointed dramatic irony is superfluous. In a paradoxical sense, however, it is a signature aspect of the play, making the execution scene a kind of synecdoche for the play as a whole and its relation to the audience. Here is the Page's first scene in its entirety:

> Enter BOY with the box
>
> *Page:* My master hath forbidden me to look in this box, and by my troth 'tis likely, if he had not warned me, I should not have had so much idle time: for we men's-kind in our minority are like women in their uncertainty, that they are most forbidden, they will soonest attempt: so I now. By my bare honesty here's nothing but the bare empty box: were it not a sin against secrecy, I would say it were a piece of gentlemanlike knavery. I must go to Pedringano, and tell him his pardon is in this box, nay, I would have sworn it, had I not seen the contrary. I cannot choose but smile to think, how the villain will flout the gallows, scorn the audience, and descant on the hangman, and all presuming of his pardon from hence. Will't not be an odd jest, for me to stand and grace every jest he makes, pointing my finger at this box: as who would say, "Mock on, here's thy warrant." Is't not a scurvy jest, that a man should jest himself to death? Alas poor Pedringano, I am in a sort sorry for thee, but if I should be hanged with thee, I cannot weep.
>
> *Exit* (3.5.1–19)[21]

Encouraged to assume that the box contains the warrant for his pardon, Pedringano will indeed jest himself to death and neglect to make the final confession that might have saved his soul.[22] The Boy pities him—"I am in a sort sorry for thee"—but the only way he can express his sympathy for Pedringano and weep for him would damn the Page himself. If he reveals the scurvy jest of the empty box, his master will put him to death—which will also make it impossible to express his sympathy. Dead boys don't cry. It's either tears now and no tears forever after, or no tears today but tears tomorrow and tomorrow and tomorrow.

Like the wheel or the inclined plane, dramatic irony is a simple device with complex uses. It is a narrative and situated form of metadrama, native to an art form—theatrical performance— that is inherently metadramatic. Theatrical representation is sometimes confused with spectacle ("theatricality") or what is shown on the stage, but in the semiotics of performance, as I said earlier, what you see is rarely what you get. If there is a stage— any empty space that has been designated as such—there will always be a signifying gap, a space for ironic understanding, an incongruity between the means of representation and what is represented.[23] There is always a disjunction between levels and kinds of knowledge, of being, and of worlds. Dramatic irony embodies and spatializes such disjunctions, and it is important to note that this form of embodiment takes place in the audience as much as the stage. This is especially evident in the spatialization of perspective—in cognitive, affective, and literal points of view—that takes place between the audience and the stage.

As Michael Hattaway has noted, Kyd's sense of theatrical space was architectonic.[24] He used the entire theatrical apparatus of the new amphitheaters–the scaffold with its platea and locus, its trap, its tiring room and exits and entrances, its balcony, and, most importantly, the encompassing auditorium and the social space of its occupants—to sound out the dimensions of cognitive and emotional dissonance in his audiences and to discover, at select moments, the seams of their occasional coherence. When the ghost of Andrea and his companion Revenge—should we call him a character, an embodied spirit of vengeance from Hades, or a personified allegory?—open the play, they enter from a place that anyone in the audience would be able to point to, whether they issued from a "hell-mouth" (a stage device familiar from the late medieval tradition), from a relatively unadorned trap, from the pit, down from the gallery or out of the tiring

house. But the place they come from is also impossible to locate: it is nowhere, a classical Hades whose coordinates cannot
be mapped onto any Christian cosmology, whether Protestant
or Catholic. Where do the two figures sit down after Andrea's
Virgilian address to the audience? It is unclear in the play-text
but any production must resolve the question in some fashion.
We know they sit down somewhere—on the stage itself, among
the audience, or (my architectonic preference) on the balcony
that over-peered the playing space—and that they watch over
the action, since they comment on it after each of the four acts.
"Here sit we down to see the mystery, / And serve for Chorus
in this tragedy" (1.1.90–91). From this moment forward they are
ostensibly on stage, overseeing the entire play, commenting on it,
and even, according to the intimations of Revenge, directing its
action: "Be still Andrea, ere we go from hence, / I'll turn their
friendship into fell despite" (1.5.5–6). The entire play becomes a
play-within-a-play, producing a kind of dramatic irony gone viral. But the immediate question for any acting company with
limited funds—that is, most if not all—is also inescapable. Is the
effect worth the expense of committing two actors to largely silent parts? Why did Kyd choose this kind of metadramatic effect
when it was such a *costly* one to produce?

In the performative economy of the stage, assigning two accomplished actors to largely nonspeaking roles would render
those actors incapable of doubling; with a company of fourteen
or sixteen actors, it would be an unusual as well as noteworthy
expenditure. Michael Boyd solved the problem by masking Revenge's face in his 1997 RSC production and veiling the balcony
from which he and Andrea watched the play, making it possible
to substitute stage dummies or understudies for the characters,
thus freeing two accomplished actors to perform other parts
on the main stage.[25] Boyd's solution could have been adopted
and would have worked well when the play was first performed
at the Rose Theatre and in its subsequent revivals. But there is
a danger that such solutions might eliminate one of the crucial dimensions of the performed play—perhaps even the most

crucial one. Watching and listening can be an action of some consequence. When Andrea and Revenge are masked, as in the 1997 RSC production, two actors are made available for roles in the main play, but their eyes as well as their faces are hidden from sight; their focus of attention is not evident to the audience, and this occlusion of the gaze renders active watching into something passive. If the audience is instead allowed to see Revenge and Andrea observing, listening, responding, even falling asleep at one point, what is gained? My point is not to invoke an authoritative or Elizabethan version of the play or to give the playtext, with its implicit and explicit cues, an overriding authority. The question is not "did an Elizabethan production do this or that?" but rather "was this or that possible for an Elizabethan production?" Is it not only possible but also in tune with other aspects of the play in performance? If so, would the play thus performed gain access to different critical, affective, or even confessional dimensions of its audience? What does the nonspeaking presence of an unmasked or unobscured Andrea and Revenge accomplish?

The felt and lived experience of the play would change dramatically. Hieronimo's reiterated expressions of grief over his son's death are conveyed in an affective rhetoric more formal but no less effective than Shakespeare's:

> Oh eyes, no eyes, but fountains fraught with tears,
> O life, no life, but lively form of death;
> O world, no world, but mass of public wrongs,
> Confused and filled with murder and misdeeds! (3.2.1–4)

Do we weep if we see and hear Hieronimo weep in this extended and brilliant soliloquy? The answer will be conditioned by many general factors: an audience's time and place in history, its familiarity with and accommodation of a more declamatory style of dramatic verse, the emotional and cognitive scaffolding of its everyday life, and, of course, the heterogeneous and inherently conflicted character of any actual audience, in any period, attending any specific play. But the mediated character of our sympathy or empathy or identification in Kyd's play also conditions it. We see and hear Hieronimo directly, through our own eyes and ears, from our own specific location in the theater, situated as we are in our row in the gallery or place in the pit of the Rose Theatre in early modern London or in the Swan in contemporary Stratford-upon-Avon. But we also see and hear his grief from the standpoint of Andrea and Revenge—through the virtual perspective of their eyes and ears.

Ghosts are to be expected in Elizabethan revenge plays, but Andrea does not haunt the Spanish or Portuguese courts in the way that the ghost of Hamlet *père* haunts the Danish court. No one on stage is ever aware of his presence. But he and his companion Revenge do indeed haunt the amphitheater, complicating the already complicated perspectives of the audience. Their visible surveillance creates a complex mediation of our own gaze and feelings. It establishes a spatial and perspectival irony that alienates members of the audience from their own affective responses, making them occupy multiple and contradictory points of view. No matter how moved or appalled we might be at Hieronimo's grief or madness or murderous violence past the point of vengeance, Revenge and Andrea are always doubling our point of view at the least, casting their ironic shadow on our most heartfelt and sincere responses. We do not watch them constantly, but when we do look their way, Revenge may be sleeping; he may be concentrating his attention on some aspect of the *mise en scène* and, in doing so, directing our own gaze to it. He could also be looking directly at a specific person in the audience, including one of the spectators who is, at that exact moment, looking directly at him. In the return of the spectator's gaze, the performative costs entailed in keeping the characters and their eyes visible throughout the play become worth the investment. The gaze of Revenge would convey more than a touch of the uncanny.

The setting is Spanish and hence Catholic; the afterlife, however, is a pagan Hades. This pronounced incongruity complicates the ethics of revenge considerably, as Hieronimo alternatively appeals to the angels in heaven and god of the underworld, quotes Seneca and the Bible. But his dilemma proves to be more difficult than deciding the cosmological parameters of justice and vengeance or identifying his son's murderers. If all is being orchestrated by Revenge on behalf of Andrea, then Hieronimo is an agent without agency in the play, deluded into thinking otherwise. Horatio's death is necessary for Andrea's revenge to succeed, since it provides the motivation for Hieronimo to act. He will only realize the extent of his disenfranchisement after the play and the epilogue are over, since he will learn the true cause of his loss—why Horatio had to die—only when he arrives in Hades. He declares himself to be "author and actor of this tragedy" (4.4.147), but there are three audiences to his pronouncement—the one on stage in the Spanish court, the one in the playhouse, and the one supervising from above or in the wings. Their perspective encompasses both Hieronimo's play—all that is framed by the prologue and the epilogue, all of Hieronymo's delusions of agency—and the audience with an ironic gaze that frames the otherwise actual audience in the playhouse. Framed by these points of view, the play has always and already been about Andrea's revenge; Hieronimo's moving and conflicted debates about justice and revenge, what Seneca or the Lord saith about the latter, are beside the point. He does not jest himself to death, but like Pedringano he doesn't know how empty and beside the point his agony really is.

It is "appropriately inappropriate," to borrow Jonathan's Bate apt characterization of a speech in *Titus Andronicus*, that the protagonist at the center of the play's impossible cosmology—Catholic, pagan, neither here nor there—resembles nothing so much as a conflicted Calvinist, whose agonies about what to do are also irrelevant. They presume a free will a Calvinist could never possess. In this respect, Hieronimo's closest analogue is the Elizabethan audience, most fully embodied in the spectator who glances up to feel Revenge's gaze directly—who has realized that she too is one of the abject preterite, the doubly predestined soul of His architectonic point of view.

III

"Appropriately inappropriate": I have borrowed the phrase from Jonathan Bate, who coined it to describe Marcus's speech in act 2, scene 4 of *Titus Andronicus*, delivered when he discovers Lavinia in the woods and responds to her awful devastation with one of the most excruciatingly indecorous speeches in the Elizabethan canon.[26] Earlier I described Elizabethan popular theater as a kind of affective laboratory, an instantiation of drama oriented toward the location, exploration, and exploitation of those faultlines and dissonances of feeling that characterized the emotional communities of post-Reformation England. *Titus* is an almost clinical example. Kyd's affective intelligence is fully absorbed into the play as a whole; act 2, scene 4 of *Titus* might be described as Shakespeare's objective correlative to *The Spanish Tragedy*. It acts out the "affective irony" everywhere implicit in the earlier play but never as fully realized in Kyd's own experiments with affect, cognition, and dialectically engaged points of view.

Act 2, scene 4 has long seemed to be an unplayable disjunction of eye and ear. Eugene Waith located the problem on the stage rather than the page. He loved the language of Ovidian transformation so much that he regarded the physical presence of Lavinia on stage as the problem, the source of what made the scene so impossible to stage. This flaw explained why the play could be such a theatrical failure yet capable of real poetic power if allowed to work its magic where it belonged, in the study.[27] Peter Brook cut Marcus's speech in its entirety and famously abstracted and aestheticized Lavinia's wounds with flowing swaths of red silk, reducing the incongruity between Marcus's flowered rhetoric and Lavinia's ruined body. The inappropriate beauty of Marcus's style was incorporated into Lavinia's mutilated body, producing an abstracted, aestheticized, and Ovidian representation of her wounds that might have been intended, in defense of Brook's abstraction, to give physical form to Marcus's metamorphic imagery. In her 1999 film Julie Taymor partly followed

Brook's lead. She cut thirty-one lines out of Marcus's fifty-eight-line address—all of its opulent imagery—and also cut back and forth from Marcus to Lavinia in sequential close ups, never letting us see them in the same frame except in one opening telephoto shot, where Lavinia is a distant figure out in the marsh, and one closing shot, at the moment when Marcus finally takes her in his arms.

It is an effective scene in the film but one that doesn't discover what the scene might accomplish if presented in full, not only textually but also spatially and perspectivally. For this we have to turn to two relatively uncut productions of the 1980s, each of them directed by women. Jane Howell, who directed the play for the BBC Shakespeare Series in 1985, gave us the first modern production that presented the scene in its entirety, retaining all of its performative dimensions. Deborah Warner followed soon after with her famous 1987 stage production for the RSC. The impact of Warner's better-known stage production has been considerable, even for those who have only read about it.[28] It taught an entire generation of playgoers that the affective intelligence of such scenes is lodged in the incongruity that develops from its contradictory internal and external points of view—in precisely what a long tradition has regarded as flawed and so to be downplayed as much as possible, whether by cuts in the scene or removing the entire play from the stage. In Warner's production, of course, no camera lens controlled or filtered the audience's gaze in order to reduce the inappropriateness of Marcus's words, which were always foregrounded by the mute and bleeding presence of Lavinia herself. Similarly, Howell included Lavinia and her uncle in the same frame while Marcus not so much addressed Lavinia but spoke about her *as if* she weren't there. She is immediately before and slightly above him in the forest, brought even closer on the screen by the camera angle. Lavinia and Marcus face one another directly, so that Lavinia hears Marcus's speech and Marcus sees Lavinia's absent voice, her silence materialized in the "crimson river of warm blood, / Like to a bubbling fountain stirr'd with wind" that flows from her mouth instead of speech. The breadth of the camera's gaze reproduces, in a flattened form, the view of an audience in a live performance:

> Who is this—My niece, that flies away so fast?
> Cousin, a word. Where is your husband?
> If I do dream, would all my wealth would wake me.
> If I do wake, some planet strike me down
> That I may slumber an eternal sleep!
> Speak, gentle niece, what stern ungentle hands
> Have lopped and hewed and made thy body bare
> Of her two branches, those sweet ornaments,
> Whose circling shadows kings have sought to sleep in,
> And might not gain so great a happiness
> As have thy love. Why dost not speak to me?
> Alas, a crimson river of warm blood,
> Like to a bubbling fountain stirred with wind,
> Doth rise and fall between thy rosèd lips,
> Coming and going with thy honey breath.
> But sure some Tereus hath deflowered thee
> And, lest thou shouldst detect him, cut thy tongue.
> Ah, now thou turn'st away thy face for shame. (2.4.11–28)

For shame? In Howell's film, Marcus's spear shifts from its resting, upright position to point at Lavinia when he speaks of "some Tereus," from an "at ease" posture to an attack mode, and his body shifts as well, from upright to a more aggressive crouch. Lavinia shrinks from the spear as it comes to bear on her. Marcus's imagined violence against a mythic rapist is explicitly aimed toward the victim and "her" shame, a vector that will be more explicitly enacted by Titus himself at Lavinia's death. Marcus strikes the first note of an intrafamilial aggression that Howell highlights throughout the production, tracking how often familial sympathy for Lavinia converges with a violent antipathy toward her, the shame of the Andronici clan.

In any filmed version, even one as low-tech as the *BBC Shakespeare Plays*, the use of close-ups will mean that we will not always be able to see Lavinia's reactions as we watch and listen to

Marcus, and vice versa—yet this binocular focus is crucial to the perspectival dynamics of the play. Howell and Warner refused to soften or filter the clash of eye and ear that had rendered the scene unplayable in the past, and with surprising results. According to Alan Dessen, who interviewed members of the 1987 (Warner) audience, many identified this scene as the strongest and most effective in the play. Because of the twofold consciousness that the offstage audience experienced, as Dessen hypothesized, they were made to "both see Lavinia directly *and* see her through [Marcus's] eyes and images."[29] This is a key if incomplete realization. Marcus's speech is not, in and of itself, so far removed from Hieronimo's quite moving yet rhetorically ornate and flourishing speeches of shock and grief, but in the latter case, Horatio, the object of his father's grief and the eventual catalyst of his revenge, has the decency to be dead. The dead Horatio behaves as the victim in a revenge play should behave, as a corpse or a ghost. As a consequence, he doesn't have to listen as his wounds and corpse are lavishly described or grieved. He is the one person in the playhouse who has no point of view on Hieronimo's grief.

There is no ghost in *Titus*. Instead, Lavinia haunts the play by violating the generic role of a victim in a revenge tragedy. Like a ghost, she is a boundary crosser and an uncanny presence, inhabiting a space she should no longer occupy, but her transgression is generic rather than metaphysical. She should be dead but is not dead yet.[30] This is so disturbing to Marcus that he repeatedly tries to naturalize her, as it were: her wounds are *martyred* signs to be *mourned*; she is no longer part of the family, no longer a present relation but a thing of the past. "This *was* thy daughter," as he says to Titus (emphasis added). She is addressed at such times in the third person, even though she is present and her hearing has not been affected by the violence she has suffered. She is, insofar as Marcus can rhetorically accomplish, in the position of the dead in a Protestant funeral ceremony after the reforms of Edward VI.

Jonathan Bate describes the language in an uncut staging of the scene as "a kind of bandage, life-preserving and wound-concealing," and argues that "a lyrical speech is needed because it is only when an appropriately inappropriate language has been found that the sheer force of contrast between its beauty and Lavinia's degradation begins to express what she has undergone and lost."[31] Dessen and Bate are insightful commentators on the Warner production and on the play as a whole,[32] yet both stop short of their own insights when they resolve the transactional dynamics of the scene in favor of Marcus's grieving point of view. Marcus's language is a bandage, yes, but it is a bandage for Marcus and *his* audience, it seems to me, rather than for Lavinia, her physical and psychic wounds, or *her* audience. Dividing the epistemologies and as well as the ideologies of the audience in this scene produces a different effect than Marlowe's "earn to see," touched upon earlier in this study—different and even more unsettling.

Alexander Leggatt suggests that Marcus "re-enacts the offense, eroticizing her body and making her bleed . . . repeat[ing] the atrocity in a different key," and his point is hard to argue against.[33] Dessen suggests that we are forced to see Lavinia directly and also to see her through the eyes and images of her uncle, but this overlooks the most important triangulation in the scene. We are also forced to see and hear her uncle through her own eyes and ears. She is not dead yet. The scene is constructed, in other words, around the brute fact that Taymor and others have cut from it: Lavinia herself has to listen to the narcissistic grief of patriarchal sympathy, to endure its concern with its own psychic wounds and suffering as embodied and projected onto "her" shame. In their multiplex point of views, some audience members will recoil from the self-regarding nature of such sympathy. Paradoxically, their revulsion from Marcus's tears brings them closer to Lavinia and enables them to feel a deeper sympathy for a more complex victimage—to see and hear it, as it were, from Lavinia's visual, affective, and cognitive points of view. It is perhaps impossible to allow the scene to remain in such suspension, in such an acute state of appropriate inappropriateness, whether in critical language or in theatrical performance; it is perhaps inevitable that we resolve the contradiction and incon-gruity into an emotional and cognitive synthesis. But even if we do, our perspectives are less comfortable thereafter if we have felt the disjunctions first.

If "dramatic irony" is what we call a situation when a char-acter is left in the dark but the audience is in the know, then "affective irony" seems an appropriate name for situations like this one, when a character's expressed feeling or "sympathy"—Marcus's Ovidian, narcissistic grief—is an object of irony for the audience rather than a model for its own sympathies. What the speaker feels is precisely *not* what we feel: on the contrary, it is what alienates us from his or her expressed feeling. It is not that we feel the opposite—this is not Brecht's epic theater, in which the spectator says, "I laugh when they weep, I weep when they laugh."[34] But then, Brecht's epic theater in practice wasn't quite as binary in its emotional logic as he sometimes made it sound. Irony is not a reversal of meaning or feeling: it marks a range of available alternatives by marking one possible meaning as exactly not what is meant, not what should be thought or felt. What moves us most profoundly about Lavinia's plight begins in our recoil from Marcus's sympathy. Sympathy or empathy for La-vinia becomes entirely and ironically different from what Marcus embodies and expresses. Such affective and perspectival identifi-cation grows in direct proportion to the strength of our revulsion at Marcus's own, thoroughly self-centered, honor-based horror at Lavinia's "shame."

Lavinia's undead role in *Titus* is the generic equivalent of the uncanny. Her mute presence adumbrates and disturbs Titus's grief as well as her uncle's, clarifying the degree to which their expressions of sympathy mar themselves in expression, in the speaker's own articulation of them. Titus later imagines sitting with his daughter at "some fountain, looking all downwards to behold our cheeks," wet with tears,

> And in the fountain shall we gaze so long
> Till the fresh taste be taken from that clearness
> And made a brine pit with our bitter tears? (3.1.123–29)

Missing from his fantasy but captured in the logic of its imagery is the effacing effect of his grief on its ostensible object of grieving. The tears shed over the image of poor Lavinia in the pond destroy the water's reflective qualities, so that the grief expressed in those tears occludes any sight of Lavinia's face, the ostensible object of that grief.

Our point of view is refracted into a dramatic irony of cosmological proportions by the supervising presence of Andrea and Revenge in *The Spanish Tragedy*. *Titus* refracts our affective point of view whenever Lavinia is on stage. No matter how well one tries to keep her in mind as a witness to all the scenes she mutely occupies, doing so while reading the play is a considerable challenge, requiring a regular and constant effort. On the page, Lavinia fades away from our attention when she is not speaking or reacting to the people around her. On stage, we can't escape from her or forget she's there. "What the playtext decorously conceals," as Pascale Aebischer put it in her study of the play's stage and screen history, "performance shockingly reveals."[35]

Affective irony of the sort that I've been outlining is not limited to this play or genre or even to this historical instantiation of theater, but I do think it defines an emotional logic characteristic of the Elizabethan popular stage. The newly formalized playing space and theatrical apparatus of the London amphitheaters clearly allowed for complex and contradictory forms of affective cognition, distributed between on- and offstage points of view. The most significant performative changes fostered by the new playhouses took place not merely on stage but in the architectonics of the entire theatrical apparatus. The audience was more fixed in its relation to the performance than it had been in previous forms of popular drama. Its literal points of view and audition were more fixed than they were for an inn-yard or street-corner audience, and, equally important, the audiences themselves were more stable, more attuned to the architectonics of performance and their role in its production, more consistent from one week to the next. Playwrights could write with them in mind and companies could rehearse and perform with them in mind, as contributing members of the theatrical production. This spatial and demographic regularization is often regarded as a reduction of agency for the audience, but the amphitheater playhouses functioned to enhance rather than suppress that agency, insofar as it was the agency of an *audience* as opposed to a less focused gathering. The professionalization of actors in the economies of early modern popular drama required a "professionalization" of the audience as well, evidenced not only in the price of admission but also in the development of their auditory and spectatorial literacies. This fixing or settling took place, moreover, at a time when social and cultural points of view had been radically unsettled and had grown extraordinarily heterogeneous.

Perspective by incongruity, as Kenneth Burke taught us, is an inherently *dramaturgical* way of glimpsing something that might otherwise be impossible to apprehend.[36] The more formalized space of the new amphitheaters lent itself to many different experiments in the dialectics and incongruities of affective points of view. Like "feeling," a word that nicely bridges the physical, affective, and cognitive realms, "point of view" is a hybrid or amphibious concept. These are the words we often think to police, trying like Humpty Dumpty to teach them who is master. They are not only hard to manage—all words are so. But these are also words that are wiser than their users sometimes are, reminding us that accuracy and precision are not always synonymous. Words like "feeling" and "sense" bridge the somatic and the nonsomatic worlds, and neither world—nor the words themselves—can or should be reduced to one or the other. "Point of view" similarly bridges the spatial and the ideological and the affective in a way that enables rather than confuses our thinking about what happens when we see things with a different set of eyes or hear things echoed through the responses of another. Emotions or feelings are also, perhaps always, points of view.

IV

Charles Macklin is playing Shylock at the Theatre Royal, Drury Lane. Shylock is no longer the comic, burlesque, *commedia dell'arte* figure created by George Granville half a century before, when he rewrote Shakespeare's play and called it *The Jew of Venice* (1701).[37] Macklin is a frightening Shylock, a character capable of engaging darker ranges of feeling and bias than Granville's burlesque had ever done. This is the authentic Shylock, as Alexander Pope has reportedly pronounced: "This is the Jew / That Shakespeare drew."[38] London audiences have not been able to get enough of him. Tonight, as expected, the applause at the end of act 1 is enthusiastic and delighted.

However, one young man finds his enjoyment dampened, the confidence of his "direct and natural feelings" cast in doubt, when he notices a young woman, seated down the row in the box they share, who is in evident distress. On her face is an emotion "of great sensibility, painfully, proudly repressed"; the woman herself is strange in appearance but immediately alluring, striking, and "sympathetic." He finds her "uncommonly interesting, though with a peculiar expression and foreign air."[39] She is, he realizes at some point, a Jew herself and has been deeply disturbed by Macklin's Shylock. Despite what he feels and regards as a natural antipathy towards Jews, her person and her distress capture his own affective point of view, and for the remainder of the performance he watches the play through the young woman's eyes:

> I could no longer enjoy Macklin's incomparable acting; I was so apprehensive of the pain which it must give to the young Jewess. At every stroke, characteristic of the skillful actor, or of the master poet, I felt a strange mixture of admiration and regret. I almost wished that Shakespeare had not written, or Macklin had not acted the part so powerfully: my imagination formed such a strong conception of the pain the Jewess was feeling, and my inverted sympathy, if I may so call it, so overpowered my direct and natural feelings, that at every fresh development of the Jew's villainy I shrunk as though I had myself been a Jew. . . . I was so placed that I could see her, without being seen; and during the succeeding acts, my attention was chiefly directed to the study of all the changes in her expressive countenance. I now saw and heard the play solely with reference to

her feelings. . . . I saw that the struggle to repress her emotion was often the utmost she could endure.[40]

His "inverted sympathy" marks a decisive turning point in his life, as he will later realize. It is a moment of conversion from one racial, religious, and affective identity to another: from an unquestioning anti-Semite with a visceral fear of Jews—instilled when he was a boy by an unscrupulous house-maid—to an enlightened individual who will eventually marry the woman he first sees *entr'acte*, in the audience. It is seeing the performance through her eyes, shifting his perspective to her point of view and imagining community with her, which produces a profound and lasting alienation of his own affections.

This epiphanic moment is drawn from Maria Edgeworth's novel *Harrington*, first published in 1817 and set in London of the 1760s. The novel is a *roman-à-clef*, written in response to a reader who had been unhappy with the anti-Semitic portrayal of Jews in *Castle Rackrent* and Edgeworth's other novels. Shakespeare's play (or rather, Macklin's variation on it) is the occasion for a complex and edgy *apologia*: Edgeworth's former, now unpalatable prejudices are projected onto the iconic Bard as well as her fictional protagonist, allowing her to participate in the enlightenment of them both and remind her readers that even Shakespeare was flawed in some respects. Some twenty years before the publication of *Harrington*, Richard Hole imagined a similar kind of affective estrangement but suggested it might be a paradoxical aspect of the play itself in performance, a metadramatic rather than extra-theatrical dimension. In an essay published in *Gentleman's Quarterly* in 1796, Hole acknowledged that much of the play engaged the racial, religious, and cultural prejudices of its audience quite directly, but he also argued that these "prepossessions" of the audience, embodied and enacted by that audience, could be alienating rather than gratifying for any given individual. Shylock's mistreatment by Solario and Solanio "always excites, as was intended, laughter," but the laughter can also catalyze a radically different response, conflictual if not antithetical. They laugh, and we are silenced by it. Those around us suddenly feel more like a crowd or a mob than an audience. "We" are no longer a part of the community that surrounds us but apart from it, in a state of internal distantiation. All that is required for this to happen is that we glimpse a crucial scene, passage, or character from "a fair point of view," even if it is only for a single, isolated moment.[41]

What is curious is the fact that both Edgeworth and Hole imagine a moment of distraction *from* the play, an interruption of the dramaturgical impetus that is felt as a shock of disorientation and re-cognition. The question is whether such an experience belongs to the design of the play or not: whether it is something integral or extraneous to it, metadramatic or extratheatrical, appropriate, inappropriate, or an oxymoronic combination of the two. Is it the work of the viewer during a performance, in other words, or the work of the play in performance? Or quite possibly, both?

In a self-reflective coda to his own discussion of *Merchant*, C. L. Barber was candid enough to confess that the best answer might be elusive. What distracts him from his own interpretation of the play as one of Shakespeare's successful festive comedies is a conflict between form and affective consciousness, the determinates of genre and the particularities of character. The "difficulty" of the play stems from the fact that Shylock seems to be integral to its design and yet, at one and the same time, to exceed that design, and to do so in a way that cannot be ignored but must nonetheless and finally be forgotten:

> About Shylock, too, there is a difficulty which grows on reflection, a difficulty which may be felt too in reading or performance. His part fits perfectly into the design of the play, and yet he is so alive that he raises an interest beyond its design. I do not think his humanity spoils the design, as Walter Raleigh and others argued and as was almost inevitable for audiences who assumed that to be human was to be ipso-facto good. But it is true that in the small compass of Shylock's three hundred and sixty-odd lines, Shakespeare provided material that asks for a whole additional play to work itself out.

The figure of Shylock is like some secondary figure in a Rembrandt painting, so charged with implied life that one can forget his surroundings. To look sometimes with absorption at the suffering, raging Jew alone is irresistible. But the more one is aware of what the play's whole design is expressing through Shylock, of the comedy's high seriousness in its concern for the grace of community, the less one wants to lose the play Shakespeare wrote for the sake of one he merely suggested.[42]

One of the admirable things about this passage is Barber's honesty. If his terms are not adequate, they are accurate: experiencing something similar to what Edgeworth and Hole describe, he has the courage of his contradictions. How can we resist the irresistible, as he says we must do? How can we accept the high seriousness of community at the expense of the human? Should genre dictate the limits of affective and cognitive engagement, despite the contextualized and phenomenological facts of our feeling and thinking, or vice versa?

Framed in terms of intentionality, these are insoluble questions. Insoluble is not the same as invalid, however. Genre and character are certainly in uneasy relation to one another in *The Merchant of Venice*. It is hard to know what "kind" of play it is meant to be and what its "kindness," in the generic as well as the affective sense of the term, might mean:[43]

I am a Jew. Hath not a Jew eyes? hath not a Jew hands, organs, dimensions, senses, affections, passions; fed with the same food, hurt with the same weapons, subject to the same diseases, healed by the same means, warmed and cooled by the same winter and summer, as a Christian is? If you prick us do we not bleed? If you tickle us do we not laugh? If you poison us do we not die? (3.1.49–55)[44]

An unforgettable assertion of common humanity, the speech in its entirety is also an assertion of the right to exact bloody and exemplary revenge:

And if you wrong us shall we not revenge? If we are like you in the rest, we will resemble you in that. If a Jew wrong a Christian, what is his humility? Revenge. If a Christian wrong a Jew, what should his sufferance be by Christian example? Why, revenge. The villainy you teach me I will execute, and it shall go hard but I will better the instruction. (3.1.56–61)

In Harold Bloom's uncompromising gloss, the speech as a whole is not a claim "to respect or compassion, as the critics for a century have had it, but to revenge."[45] And for Bloom, it goes without saying that a desire for revenge is damning, something that could only alienate the audience from any sympathy it might otherwise be inclined to feel. Shylock may claim that his vengeance will be an act of *imitatio Christianorum*, an imitation of the Christians around him and thus an act of human kindness in the categorical, not necessarily humane, sense—but why believe him? Shylock is a bloodthirsty villain, after all. Who but a villain could embrace such vengeance with such a passion?

The list of others who could do so, who actually do so yet remain sympathetic, is an extensive one. Elizabethan popular drama had a deep appetite for revenge plays like *The Spanish Tragedy*, *Titus Andronicus*, and *Hamlet*. However, characters who crave revenge on this stage are typically not inhuman or unsympathetic figures; by definition, they are protagonists who commit bloody deeds rather than villains who commit bloody deeds. Whatever Harold Bloom might claim, revenge is at the heart of all of these protagonists, who make strong and strongly ambivalent affective claims on the audience. Shylock's justification of revenge complicates his character, to be sure, but in the way that genre or role complicates characters rather than determines them. This was a theater that experimented with a wide range of allegorical, iconic, and affective forms of theatrical persons, each with its own way of making claims on the theatrical audience; it also experimented with a remarkable range and mix of genres, and these can also be surprisingly difficult to assess from a historical distance.

Genre is always mixed, as we know. A genre exists only in its own violation; its singularity as a recognizable form is born of its multiplicity rather than the reverse, which means that it is always "more than one," always a surprise, always less familiar than what we had in mind.[46] Historical or cultural distance means that we have to grapple with anachronistic forms of strangeness and with false cognates of familiarity. The Elizabethan revenge play has proved especially difficult to locate in its own vernacular and its own time and place. The problem is not merely a formal or literary one, however, and the difficulty is certainly not a sign of modern and post-modern enlightenment grappling with early modern barbarism. Genres are affective devices as well as cognitive ones. They identify the community of other works to which a play might belong and the kind of play we might expect, but they also identify the communities of emotion that we might be asked to bring to bear on it: what structures of thought and feeling, which aspects of the many affective worlds of our everyday lives, might come into play. Elizabethan audiences had a better ear for Elizabethan genres than we could ever have, which is why we need to historicize those genres as much as possible if they are to be felt or understood in all their contradictions. Genre does not resolve questions of character, theme, ideology, prejudice, and so forth. Rather, it is a way of asking such questions— and not necessarily answering them. Genre works to unsettle our initial premise about what kind of play or novel or poem we have entered into—in this case, to unsettle what Barber called the "design" of the play: its structure as a romantic comedy. What if the "distraction" of Shylock is included in that design? What happens to this comedy's high seriousness, in Barber's terms, if we take it to be concerned with the failure of community—the opening premise of any Elizabethan revenge play—as much as, if not more than, the grace of community? What kinds of "kindness" might be involved, to use the language of the play, if a member of an Elizabethan audience, well versed in the ambiguities and ambivalences of Elizabethan revenge—a native speaker of the genre, as it were—shifted her perspective and did indeed regard Shylock as a revenger rather than "a thoroughly conventional villain," as the critics for quite a bit more than a century have had it?[47]

V

In *Elizabethan Revenge Tragedy* (1940), Fredson Bowers offered a sociological explanation of the Elizabethan revenge play that is still regularly invoked to explain the prevalence of the genre. The premise of the study was that the popularity of revenge tragedy on the Elizabethan and Jacobean stage can be explained by the ubiquity of revenge practices in Elizabethan society. According to Bowers, early modern England was a revenge culture in an anthropological sense of the phrase, albeit a culture in transition and no longer sanguine about the ethics of vengeance or the ideology of *lex talionis* or the cycles of reciprocal violence produced by such structures. In Bowers's account, revenge plays addressed this residual moral dilemma in a largely didactic and corrective fashion, showing their audiences that the "wild justice" of vengeance, as Francis Bacon called it, is inherently counterproductive. Revenge inevitably reproduces the injustice it abhors; in the end, the revenger resembles his or her own opponent, the villain who prompted the need for revenge in the first place. Private revenge always "ends unfortunate," to quote Bacon again.[48] Or as Vindice says in *The Revenger's Tragedy*, announcing his own cue: "'Tis time to die when we are ourselves our foes" (5.3.109).[49]

Bower's guiding assumption, that theater is a critical social phenomenon as well as an aesthetic or ludic experience, is commendable. The problem with his answer to the question—why so much revenge?—is methodological as well as theoretical. His claims about the direct social relevance of the genre assume revenge to have been a significant concern or common occurrence in early modern England, and as he discovered, there is no evidence (beyond the stage) to support such a view.[50] An anthropologist or historian in search of an early modern revenge culture would never think to fix upon Reformation England; the archives of Italy or Spain yield more plentiful and convincing fruit than any local records office in England. Early modern England was a violent society, to be sure, as were its European contemporaries. It was also a highly litigious society, comprising a people who were (arguably) a bit more inclined than their continental counterparts to take their injuries to court rather than settle them in the street or on the tavern floor, to argue or sue under provisions of English criminal or common law rather than to plot assassinations or vendettas. This doesn't mean that people didn't talk about avenging wrongs or even take what they called "revenge," whether on the streets or in the courts. In sociological terms, however, early modern England was not a revenge culture, despite Bower's claims to the contrary. It is no accident that stories from Italy and Spain, for example, were so frequently borrowed by Elizabethan playwrights for the plots of their revenge plays. Revenge as such is hard to find in England—or rather, it is hard to find outside of the Elizabethan playhouse. On stage, revenge is almost impossible to avoid.[51]

What is most striking, in fact, is the *inverse* relationship between revenge off stage and revenge on stage in Reformation England. Bowers's question, recast in my terms—what kind of social work were these plays doing?—remains a valid one. It becomes all the more compelling once we realize that social mimesis of such a literal or thematic kind—if revenge is a constant on stage, it must have been a problem off stage, too—was not the dominant mode of representation in Elizabethan amphitheater drama. It is the lack of direct relation between social structures and dramaturgical form—in a certain sense, the irrelevance of revenge—that makes the genre so relevant, useful, and even necessary. Like Hamlet, its best-known example, revenge on stage lacks an objective correlative, but the lack in this case profits rather than deprives the audience. By indirections, the Elizabethan stage found directions out. Revenge plays allowed Elizabethan theater to "talk" about something else, including pressing and genuine social issues and contradictions—which is no small achievement.

Elizabethan England was not a revenge culture: it was an

otherwise-preoccupied culture that found something it needed in stories borrowed from revenge societies on the continent. These were stories about social systems that were dysfunctional or broken and unable to fix themselves anymore: societies in which the desire to put things right, the need for justice, has become inseparable from the need to violate what's right, the dictates of law and social order. A number of recent studies, informed by a more dynamic sense of the relationship of theater to society, have begun to clarify the genre as a significant kind of social thought—a phenomenal, affective, and embodied form of social cognition. Revenge plays grappled with social contradictions that were epistemic rather than merely local or topical, problematic junctures in which, as Katherine Maus suggests, the "entire society, or some large subsection of it, participates: points at which its self-conception is perniciously inconsistent, and at which it makes conflicting demands upon its members."[52] Linda Woodbridge has surveyed the genre most thoroughly, putting to rest a great many received but misleading critical ideas and demonstrating that a broad, inclusive sense of the genre—one that recognizes, for example, hybrid forms like revenge comedy—is needed if we are to understand "the cultural work that literary revenge performs."[53] Revenge tragedy rehearsed, in Huston Diehl's terms, "the drama—and the trauma—of reform."[54] The Reformation sought, as we have seen, to render succeeding generations indifferent to the affective claims of the past. Revenge tragedy "spoke to the anxieties produced by this painful transformation in relations with the dead," as Michael Neill has suggested:

> Revenge tragedy, at the deepest level, is less about the ethics of vendetta that it is about murderous legacies of the past and the terrible power of memory. If English Renaissance tragedy played out society's effort to reach a new accommodation with death, the drama of revenge showed how that must be contingent on the struggle to accommodate the dead themselves. . . . [The revenger] is the agent of that remembrance upon which a restored social order is felt to depend; but he has ceased to be a social man, for in his willed surrender to the claims of the dead he invariably "loses" or "forgets" himself.[55]

Neill suggests that revenge tragedy spoke to one of the central traumas of the Reformation, the one caused by efforts to dissociate the present from the immediate and still-affective past. As Natalie Zemon Davis remarked, the effort to banish certain forms of affective memory, especially those that recollected the dead, could be counterproductive:

> Especially, the living were left with their memories, unimpeded and untransformed by any ritual communication with their dead. Some memories bite the conscience. Paradoxically, in trying to lay all ghosts forever, the Protestants may have raised new ones. . . . The ending of Purgatory and ritual mourning, whatever energies were thereby freed for other work, may have left Protestants . . . less removed from their parents, more alone with their memories, more vulnerable to the prick of the past, more open to the family's future.[56]

Revenge plays were alternately compelling, entertaining, and horrifying; sometimes tragic, sometimes burlesque and self-parodic, like *The Jew of Malta*; always significant, perhaps even necessary forms of social and affective thought.

Natalie Davis, Peter Marshall, Patrick Collinson, Norman Jones, and Michael Neill share a fundamental assumption: that the damage done to historical consciousness in the Reformation was historical, complex, and social or collective as well as individual. The "terrible power of memory" included Protestant efforts to achieve social and historical forms of amnesia, but the result, as Davis notes, could be counterproductive. The dead return to haunt the present when they are unaccommodated: out of place like the ghost of Hamlet's father, placeless like the ghost of Andrea in *The Spanish Tragedy* or the bones of St. Paul's. If remembrance is the prick of the past—"Remember me," says the ghost of Hamlet's father—it is because that past has been fractured, split, or dismembered in everyday life. Not all agree, I should point out. Cynthia Marshall reverses this formulation in *The Shattering of the Self*. In an astute application of Freudian and post-Freudian psychoanalytic understandings of sadomasochism, Marshall posits an Elizabethan subject who has already been consolidated by the "nascent ethos of individualism" but at such an expense of psychic spirit that he or she feels the need for a "temporary respite from the accumulating pressures of individual selfhood." Violent theater like revenge tragedy and horrifying histories like Foxe's *Book of Martyrs* provided respite by exposing audiences to "an experience of psychic fracture or undoing," which can be a relative and apparent pleasure in the post-Freudian terms she explicates. Marshall recognizes that a fundamental paradox structures the Freudian or Lacanian self, due to the "contradictory, self-canceling nature of subjectivity"; in this, her views are accord with my own sense of subjectivity in general. However, I disagree that the "early modern *impulse* to undo or negate the self"—the disintegration of societies and selves enacted on stage or gruesome descriptions of dying Protestant martyrs—was a "wish-fulfilling" impulse and fantasy rather than a historical inheritance and reality.[57] In my view, the shattering had already taken place: it was the historical trauma we call the Protestant Reformation. In Marshall's formulation, the trauma on stage is imaginary rather than historical, providing a kind of holiday from autonomous selfhood. I'm uneasy about the shift out of a more historicized understanding and into a self-oriented, psychologized one, given the evident trauma to the collective self in the period of the Reformation. Rather than providing a relief from the pressures of a new and psychically demanding autonomy, an asserted but undocumented "*ethos* of individualism," the represented traumas of theater and other affective technologies worked to probe and anatomize the violence that had already been done to the social *individuum* and had yet to be fully accommodated.

VI

Hath not a Jew eyes? The fact that Shylock's speech begins and ends with revenge does not identify him as a bloody Elizabethan *villain* who plots and schemes criminal acts, including murder.

Villains in revenge plays are concerned to keep their crimes secret and hidden away from public view; Shylock's concern in his revenge against Antonio is just the opposite. He is not Lorenzo, he is not Claudius, he is not Iago. Rather, his "course of justice" identifies him as an *exemplary* Elizabethan revenger. Shylock plots and schemes to make the "wild justice" of revenge operate within rather than without the strictures of formal justice. His "private revenge" is meant to be open, public, and endorsed by the laws of Venice. "Hath not a Jew eyes" is indeed a justification of revenge as well as an appeal to a common humanity, but it is also a generic claim, Shylock's embrace of the revenger's familiar if ambivalent role on the Elizabethan stage. This does not mean that we grant his claim or entirely reorient our affective point of view. Genre neither dictates meaning nor guarantees response. Shylock is not Hieronimo, nor is he Hamlet. His vengeance seeks and finds, or seems to have found for much of act 4, what these other revengers seek but cannot find: a court of law where the enactment of justice fully coincides with the satisfaction of revenge. A generic cue like this defines a horizon of expectation rather than a categorical solution; it indicates a community of other works to which this one belongs or corresponds, from which it will also diverge in unexpected ways. An Elizabethan audience would make the generic connection more immediately and viscerally than a modern audience could do, in which case, the surprise of such an incongruous congruity would be all the more powerful. Moments like this are designed to arrest the attention and give us pause. They can act as *distractions* from the impetus of the play, in other words—and that is precisely their function.

"Distraction" is not a necessary term. Other terms would suffice: "interruption," "puncture," "displacement," as well as "estrangement" or "alienation." However, "distraction" has a history in twentieth-century theater and theory—a history worth noting, if only because it begins in a surprising disputation. According to Brecht, "Reception in Distraction" (*Die Rezeption der Zerstreuung*) was a negative and unwanted thing;[58] he uses the phrase to refer to the complacent and even hypnotic diversions of bourgeois theater. It was not a synonym for estrangement but precisely the kind of audience complacency that the Brechtian *gestus* and other forms of *Verfremdungseffekt* (the alienation or estrangement effect) were designed to overcome.[59]

Walter Benjamin turned Brecht on his head, however, when he argued for the dialectical nature of Brechtian distraction and its strong relation to *Verfremdungseffekt*. In "The Work of Art in an Age of Mechanical Reproduction," Benjamin's seminal essay on media and culture, distraction is a productive process as well as a potentially negative one: it is the problem and the cure, the thesis and the antithesis.[60] In his own descriptions, in theory if not in practice, Brecht's epic theater can seem distressingly didactic, programmatic, and even antitheatrical. The alienation effect can sound as if it is all cognition and no affect, a critical intervention from outside the work of art. Benjamin describes a multiphased distraction that engages, in Howard Eiland's useful phrase, the "whole sensorium" of the audience:[61]

> And their reception in distraction, like that of the movie audience, is not merely visual but tactile or visceral; it involves their whole sensorium, as illuminated by memory (for the experience in "intoxicated experience" is long experience [*Erfahrung*]). Their struggle against dispersion succeeds only by dint of studious abandonment to it, and this is the source of their presence of mind as something bodily.

Like other forms of affective irony, the surprise or shock or alienation-effect of productive distraction does not deaden the dramaturgical impetus but deepens and multiplies it: distraction draws us further into the affective dimensions of the play by making possible another view, which "impels us back and forth between two levels [or layers] of 'reality.'"[62]

Harrington's experience at the Theatre Royal also involved the discovery of another level of reality, even an entirely different play, when he was impelled to view Macklin's performance from a different perspective. Edgeworth located the discovery outside of the play and its "design," to use Barber's term. Like many a modern literary critic, she understood her task to be the demystification of the aesthetic object, a symptomatic reading and correction that also allowed her to establish her own, now ethically superior, point of view on anti-Semitism. The transactional dynamics of Harrington's "distraction" in the theater are wonderfully described. But analogous critical distractions—the discovery of another, incongruous yet internally distantiated perspective—are to be found in the play, in its design and in almost every scene. Some appear in the form of unexpected genre cues that have surprising implications. Some are thematic and woven throughout the play: our felt difficulty with Shylock's character or Antonio's many hypocrisies or Portia's own, more honestly admitted prejudices, would enter here.[63] Some of the most powerful are embodied in an absent stage prop, like Leah's turquoise ring, the bond and memories and love it embodied, all defiled by his daughter when she traded it for a monkey.[64] One of the most surprising is embedded in Shylock's name. Generations of scholars have sought the imagined Hebrew roots of "Shylock" but failed in the effort. They were looking in the wrong place, as Stephen Orgel has recently rediscovered. Shylock, the alien inhabitant of Shakespeare's Venice, has a name that is notably English, dating back to Saxon times. It means "white-haired." In sixteenth-century England, it was hardly uncommon. Indeed, a study of its relative frequency, conducted by someone with the suitable database and computer skills, might even allow us to determine the statistical odds of a Shylock—an English-born, Protestant or Catholic individual—in the Elizabethan audience. In Shakespeare's play, Shylock's name is also *uniquely* English—the only English name to be found in Venice or Belmont.[65]

What might this mean? Those Elizabethans who recognized the name from everyday life would hear, at least for a brief moment, the native and familiar speaking from the place and in the voice of the foreign and the other. Even if no one ever heard "Shylock" as his or her contemporary, the name remains in the air, an estrangement by familiarity that would have been so easy for a playwright to avoid. It is an "inherent, objective feature" of the play, and as Kiernan Ryan has stressed, such features "should not be dismissed as *imputed* properties [emphasis added]" or as overly inventive and anachronistic critical ingenuities.[66] They are concrete registers of past conditions of possibility, in understanding and in performance. This particular example, like many of those surveyed by Ryan, includes an inversion of sympathies among its possible effects—and one that does not depend, as it did in *Harrington*, on the accidental presence of an alluring and mysterious young woman in the audience. Such distracting elements—Ryan's inherent, objective features—produce a great many difficulties for modern directors, audiences, readers, and professors of English studies. Like Barber, we insist on a design—we know the villain when we see him—even when our sense of design is contradicted by one of the inherent, objective features of the play. Our difficulty should be taken seriously, since the true "design" of the play lies in its deviations from genre as much or more than its adherences. Seeing and hearing differently is precisely what we are meant to do in response to a play like *The Merchant of Venice*.

Differently but not, I would stress, either unanimously or harmoniously. A guiding premise of this study has been the primary status of theatrical performance before an audience, the actual production of the play. Performance is not a secondary phenomenon, the presentation of a text on stage; a playscript or printed text is not "the play" but a metonymy for it. Implicit in such an assumption is the agency of the audience and its role in the production, as both producer and consumer. The playing space, in a sense, extends beyond the actors on the stage to include the audience as well, as if it were an onstage audience of the kind that Beaumont so beautifully materialized in *The Knight of the Burning Pestle*. The reactions of others in the audience, unvoiced as well as audible, were also part of the *mise en scène* being produced; the amphitheater design built these relations and dynamics into its architecture, guaranteeing that any view of the action on stage included a view of the audience and its varying reactions. Edgeworth's "correction" of Shakespeare's play was insightful beyond its pretensions of moral superiority; however, her assumption that a shift in point of view like Harrington's could only take place outside of the play is too limited in its understanding of where the threshold of performance is located. Distraction-in-reception is not as extra-theatrical as she believed; what Harrington unwittingly discovered in his affective reorientation were the metatheatrical dimensions of *The Merchant of Venice* rather than its extra-theatrical correction.

The Merchant of Venice is not an enlightened defense of religious freedom or a subversive critique of anti-Semitism or an exposure of the ethnic and religious hypocrisies of Christianity, although it can be viewed from all of these perspectives. It is inextricably implicated in the prejudice and hypocrisy with which it works and on which it depends. It immerses itself in the destructive element, as Conrad's Marlow advises in *Lord Jim*. It prompts unsavory responses from some in the audience and allows and even induces pleasure for those who are entertained by Shylock's abuse. It also prompts and induces distractions, discomforts, and ironies as well as sympathies of affect. As Benjamin stressed, a "studious abandonment" is needed for the dialectic of productive distraction to work; a full and embodied rehearsal of what we hope to transcend may be necessary for the shock of re-cognition to be affective as well as cognitive, effective and not merely self-confirming.[67] *The Merchant of Venice*, like any cultural artifact that depends upon the agency of its audience, cannot be as innocent or exemplary as we might think we prefer. If any document of civilization is also a document of barbarism, as Benjamin also taught us, then there is indeed a dark side to affective irony and other forms of productive or dialectical distraction, a dark side to any form of empathy or sympathy.[68]

Elizabethan amphitheaters were designed to make productive use of conflict as well as consensus, contradiction as well as resolution. They were more explicitly dialogic than the proscenium stage or the fully darkened auditorium that migrated from Wagnerian opera to dramatic theater, which reconfigured the theatrical apparatus in an attempt to flatten perspectives and dampen down the sometimes-paradoxical effects of affect. Audiences are networks as well as groups, collective but not always communal entities in their intersubjective relations with one another. "Collective" is a word for conflict as well as community: for multiple and not necessarily compatible points of view, perspectival ways of thinking with and through performance that were, in this kind of theater, remarkably interactive and open-ended.[69]

This kind of theater offers a messy, speculative, and necessarily inexact way of thinking about feeling, but this is its strength rather than its failing as a cultural and historical resource: such thinking and feeling were messy and interpretive and conditional processes for Elizabethans, too. Early modern amphitheater drama provided a kind of inhabited or at least regularly occupied affective technology, a place where players, playwrights, and their audiences could explore the social imaginary they shared, in all its faultlines and gaps and dissociations—could probe and feel and even touch some of the crucial integuments and sinews of the social body that had become disarticulated in the upheavals of "embodied thought" that constituted the reformation of emotions in early modern England.

The Wreckage of History: Memory and Forgetting in Shakespeare's First History Tetralogy

Ernst Renan once remarked that nations are born as much out of what we forget as what we remember. "Forgetting," he suggested, and even "historical error, is a crucial factor in the creation of a nation."[1] What is true of a nation is also true of many other kinds of imagined communities—those places none of us have been, that have to be believed to be seen—and collective identities.[2] Some errors and amnesias are of an accidental sort, but Renan also asked us to consider those that are, to put it mildly, more complexly motivated.

In Shakespeare's *Richard III*, Margaret forges an unlikely alliance of almost all the surviving women in Richard's world when she teaches the assembled women in the play, all of them grieving mothers and widows like her, how to curse. She counsels them not in witchcraft, which has played a regular part in Shakespeare's earliest history tetralogy, but in the arts of memory: how to regard the membrane between truth and lie, what we know and what we believe, how and what we remember and how and what we forget, as entirely porous:

Think that thy babes were sweeter than they were,
And he that slew them fouler than he is. (4.4.120–21)

It is commonplace to say that any act of memory is also an act of forgetting, but unless we have in mind something like a zero-sum game—I forget one thing to make room for another—it is much harder say what we mean or to provide examples.[3] Margaret's canny deconstruction of one of the affective cores of history—righting the wrongs of the past—provides a glimpse of one extreme. Know the truth, and believe otherwise; remember and forget at one and the same time.

It's an easy thing for Margaret to say. She can speak from a viewpoint that is internally distantiated from the world she occupies, at once inside and outside of ideology—grieving for her own dead babe, who both was and wasn't sweeter than he was—because she's not, after all, really there, from a historical as well as a theatrical point of view. The historical Margaret d'Anjou was still in France and, more to the point, had been dead and buried for three years by this moment in 1485, on the eve of Richard's downfall.[4] In order for her to haunt the play as its dynastic memory, she has to be brought back from the dead. The "ghosts" of Elizabethan popular drama violate different thresholds than the traditional revenant, who merely comes back from the dead. Andrea (with Revenge) haunts the playhouse rather than the play; Hamlet the Elder inhabits a quintessential nothing (Purgatory) and haunts the wrong Christian cosmology; Lavinia fails in her role as a revenge-object, with the consequence that she haunts the play-world and violates it, as it has violated her, from her rape to her death; Margaret crosses over from her death in history into an almost posthumous life in *Richard III*, an undead haunting conjured by the need to return across the English Channel to make an art of cursing. Shakespeare asks his audiences to "forget" history so that it can be remembered in the form of his play, in other words, and this is not something the playwright does lightly or merely for dramatic effect, at least in this instance. Margaret brings the past into the future, "ghosting" the present for the audience.[5] She is dehistoricized so that she can become an embodiment of the historical consciousness of this cycle of plays, which has from the first been about the complex algorithms that govern the relation between memory, forgetting, and the various forms of historical misrecognition or error that catalyze them both. Margaret is, in a sense, profoundly absent whenever she is present, a memory that recalls and embodies its own forgetting as well as others.

Before I can explore such a claim, however, I need to complicate things a bit further. We know that different cultures remember and forget themselves in quite different ways. The media they use as *aide-mémoires*—usually some combination of the oral, the inscriptive, and the performative—contribute to but do not fully determine those differences. Furthermore, we know that memory is not something that only happens in our heads: it is distributed around us in the form of cultural and affective artifacts, ranging from written texts and memory chips to public monuments or even the contours and byways of the lived space that we inhabit. Moreover, it is distributed in collective as well as individual forms.[6] So-called oral cultures sometimes manifest what J.A. Barnes described as a form of "structural amnesia."[7] Oral history, passed down from one generation to the next by memory and typically memorized word for word by a pupil at the feet of a master, professes to be unchanging. When the present circumstances or social structures of such societies change, however, so do their timeless narratives. The past exists in homeostatic relation to the present, in other words, with consequences that can best be illustrated if I digress for a moment into the colonial history of Northern Ghana and the research labs of the University of California, San Diego.

I

Early in the twentieth century, the history of a tribe in northern Ghana called the Gonja was written down for the first time—the Gonja had no written version of their language—by British officials on behalf of an empire that was extending its control over the area. Ages past, it seems, a legendary figure named Japka had invaded, conquered the indigenous inhabitants, and settled down to rule. He fathered seven sons and gave each of them his own chiefdom, decreeing that only his sons and their descendants— the future rulers of the seven provinces—could succeed him as supreme ruler of the land. At the time of the British survey, this long-remembered and foundational political structure could still be witnessed in, and brought to mind by, the physical land-scape of the country: there were still seven provinces, ruled by the seven lineages that descended from the original seven sons, with the current supreme ruler chosen from among these ruling families. The geographical topography of the kingdom served the Gonja as an embodied kind of collective memory.

Sixty years later, within the span of what we sometimes call "living memory," the history of the Gonja was recorded again, this time by a visiting anthropologist and his assistant. In the intervening years, however, British hegemony had encountered some hegemonic difficulties, and two of the seven provinces no longer existed. One had been abolished and absorbed into its neighbors in retribution for its resistance to its new masters; the other had vanished due to more mundane and bureaucratic needs, when two of the "original" provinces were combined to make the region more efficient for colonial administration. Nonetheless, the newly recorded story of the Gonja was remark-ably the same. The political structure and genealogy of the tribe still asserted itself in the physical landscape, so that the provinces of the kingdom still served as an embodied memory of the un-changing, immemorial, oft-told and retold past. Once again the legendary Japka came and conquered, and once again he divided his kingdom among his sons, whose descendants subsequently ruled each province in unbroken lineal succession from the dawn of remembered time to the present. The original sons and the exfoliating bloodlines and the chiefly provinces, however, now numbered five—just as they ever were.

For Jack Goody and Ian Watt, who relate this story in a sem-inal essay about the consequences of literacy, what the Gonja lacked—what literate cultures gain, from the power of the written word—was historical consciousness itself.[8] Literate cultures, according to the story they tell themselves, remember the past more accurately because the preserved, written record is always there to remind them about the ways in which the present differs from the past. This does not mean, I hasten to add, that such cultures never forget themselves. Literate cultures—or rather, more complexly mixed cultures, in which oral, written, and performative forms of memory have deep but interconnected roots—have a tougher time of it when they want or need to forget. Their acts of cultural memory can also entail forms of cultural amnesia but, according to Goody and Watt, they can never be as absolute or as fully oblivious to recent disturbances in the relation of past to present. The existence of the archive and other ways of storing and recording the past make its reconfiguration more difficult and incremental. Literate forgetting requires a different kind and degree of cultural labor and is never as far-reaching as it sometimes wants to be, no matter how harsh or extensive it becomes. Only in oral cultures, according to our anthropological informants, do we encounter true structural amnesia, with its startling absence of anything resembling historical consciousness and its radical and regular annihilation of the past.

Since I first encountered their story in Goody and Watt's essay, the Gonja have haunted my thinking about social and collective memory and the components and consequences of historical consciousness. As it turns out, the Gonja had belonged to a mixed "oral and literate" society rather than a strictly oral one—like almost all human societies of the past three millennia—even though their own language had no written form.[9] This had been true for centuries before the arrival of the British with their colonial administrators, anthropologists, and fledgling literary historians of the English novel.[10] Their own language had no writing but this did not mean that they were without writing. British pens had been preceded by Islamic ones in the form of resident Muslim scribes who wrote down records and communications—possibly even genealogies—for those who could afford their skills, operating much like clerks in medieval and early modern England.[11] But even if the world of signs that the Gonja inhabited had not included writing, the scale and nature of tribal amnesia in this story would be unsettling. Two entire lineages, made up of real people and real ancestors, were erased from the consciousness as well as the political topography of the tribe, and all within the space, as I have said, of living memory. Since Goody and Watt, more recent anthropologists and historians of orality have challenged such clearly demarcated lines between "oral" and "literate" cultures. The strict opposition of one and the other has come to be regarded by many as an ethnological fantasy; historical consciousness and its absence, the processes of remembering and forgetting, have become more complicated, even implicated in one another, as a result. It seems to me, in this vein, that something important was indeed recorded or remembered in the structural amnesia of the Gonja: that forgetting and remembering coincided quite acutely in their twice-told tale and in the affective and traumatized landscape it narrated.

When we speak of historical trauma, we usually have in mind a kind of trauma characterized by the unremitting return and involuntary reliving of the past. Cathy Caruth and others have ably explored this kind of trauma.[12] But there is another kind of historical trauma, I would suggest, marked less by an undesired return of the repressed than by active, often quite remarkable efforts to erase a previously acknowledged past. Whether such attempts fail or succeed, in whole or in part, they tend to occur on a large and collective scale, as do structural amnesia and historical consciousness itself.

In trauma of the first order, we don't recall the traumatic event in the normal sense of recollection but instead relive it: it occupies us not as a memory does but as a primary and unprocessed experience does, except that this experience happens again and again because it is never accomplished or completed as such. It has never really *been* experienced: it has never made the passage from present to past tense, leaving the sufferer trapped in the initial and seemingly forever-after encounter with it. Thus, a crippling paradox lies at the heart of this kind of historical trauma. We do not return to the event. Rather, we are (and were) never able to leave it, because we were never able to experience it adequately or fully in the past. This form of trauma might seem to be the symptom of an inability to forget, but the resemblance is a misleading one. We cannot forget what we have not yet adequately experienced, nor can we remember what we have not yet forgotten. What should have become the past does not so much return to haunt us as it fails ever to leave us, ever to make the crucial transition from "now" to "then"—to undergo the translation of living experience into lived experience that both remembering and forgetting require.

The oral histories of the Gonja exhibit a different kind of historical trauma or, rather, a different extreme on a spectrum defined by remembering and forgetting in their multifactored relation to one another. The violation of genealogy in order to maintain genealogy, the stark yet unacknowledged revision of the past in order to make it accommodate a colonially imposed present, might at first resemble an inability to remember, but I want to suggest that this resemblance is misleading, too. Traumas of the second order are in some ways the inverse of traumas of the first order. For Goody and Watt, the kind of collective forgetting illustrated by the Gonja demonstrates an absence of historical consciousness that is typically and exclusively exhibited by oral cultures. Rather than an absence of historical consciousness, however, "structural amnesia" seems to me to be a kind of collective forgetting—one that registers a particular kind of wound to the social, a traumatization *suffered by* historical consciousness rather than the consequence of its lack or absence. There was violence done to the social and memorial structures of the Gonja. It was not merely a symbolic or abstract violence, since it included the death, imprisonment, or disinheritance of a host of individuals from two prominent and revered families as well as the dissociation of those families from collective memory. If the effacement of two entire lineages—again, in the space of living memory—was only what it looks and sounds like, a total and absolute forgetting, it would indeed suggest the absence of any recognizable kind of historical consciousness, as Goody and Watt presume. Like individual forms of amnesia, however, structural amnesia clearly involves a kind of retention *in absentio*, a memory trace; inscribed on the land as an absence, it might be said to *embody* what it also (or thereby) disembodies. All forms of memory may involve a paradoxical game of *fort/da* that we, as historical creatures, must play with ourselves in order to become—and herein lies another paradox—historical creatures in the first place.[13]

"Remembering," according to Edward S. Casey, "is as much a withholding of the past as a holding of it in mind. We preserve the past as truly in *not* exhibiting it to ourselves or others in so many words or images as in re-presenting it in these ways."[14] The Gonja political and social landscape clearly holds something it also withholds. Their mutating yet never-changing genealogy is a troubled and compensatory response to a historical trauma perceived or at least felt as such, at some level of the social imaginary. The new story the Gonja tell themselves about themselves is not composed on an empty slate or impressed on a blank tablet of wax. It is at once a scar on the social body—and like scars on physical bodies, a somatic form of memory—and a pyrrhic effort to save the appearances. The trauma of colonization recorded in the landscape is also, or is instead—is also *and* instead—resolved in that landscape, projected as a timeless continuity that none-theless records "what has been lost" in the form of "what has never been."

My syntactic stutter and italics and scare quotes are poor reg-isters of the paradox involved when a culture has a "record" of something it never possessed, a "memory" of what it has also, to all appearances, entirely forgotten.[15] What has been lost so fully and so paradoxically? Not only the political autonomy but also, and more importantly, the cultural and historical integrity of the tribe—in other words, precisely what made it function as a tribe, a kind of collective social body that is also a kind of imagined community. The present, postcolonial situation, misrecognized as the memory-trace of the original division of the kingdom, is inscribed over the actual and recent trauma of that division, naturalizing but also embodying the violence done to the tribe in both its social landscape and its social imaginary. The new genealogy and new political landscape do indeed manifest the absolute and sheer absence of memory that Goody and Watt describe, but they also, and at the same time, embody the trauma involved in such deep forgetting and such paradoxical remembering. The missing sons and their extended lineages are gone but insistent, like phantom limbs that still have the power to cause real pain in the social body, just as they do in the physical and individual body.

II

One should be wary of analogies and metaphors like the ones I have just introduced (or rather, reintroduced). But the well-established, perplexing medical phenomenon of the phantom limb has something important to tell us about memory and forgetting in practice. An amputee who has suffered a loss of limb will sometimes feel a real and excruciating pain in the missing limb, the one that is no longer there. The absence of her arm or leg feels like its presence, in a maimed and damaged state; it is an absence that embodies, in a sensible if not literal or logical sense, what is missing. The body and the mind cannot forget the limb—yet they cannot properly remember it either, since this would require the synaptic acknowledgment that the limb has indeed been lost. The often-excruciating and debilitating pain that accompanies the condition has long resisted the capacities of medical science to cure or relieve it. It has typically been impervious to drug therapies, regimens of hypnosis, sessions of acupuncture and all other remedies that were attempted, until quite recently.[16] V. S. Ramachandran, a neuropsychologist in San Diego, decided to treat the body's memory (like the body's pain) as something real, whose somatic manifestations were both virtual and actual.

Ramachandran built a simple wooden box with a mirror inside that bisected it into two compartments . The top of one compartment was covered, but the top of the other was left open, so that the reflective side of the mirror could be seen by the patient, as one side of the open rectangular shape. Both the enclosed and the open halves of the box had an opening on the side that faced the patient. When the patient inserted her intact right arm and hand into the open compartment, she was told to "insert" her missing left limb into the other, covered compartment. What she saw in the mirror was a reflection of her undamaged arm and hand. However, it looked like a restored left limb, an intact, fully functional arm and hand in the place where her lost and painful phantom limb was "located." Told to perform a simple task with her virtual hand, she could only create virtual movement in the mirror by moving the undamaged limb; to her eye, it looked and eventually *felt* as if she were moving the missing, phantom limb as well. Her neural matrix and brain felt the virtual arm and hand in the mirror as an actual limb that was whole and without visible harm. After a few sessions, the pain and the phantom limb itself were gone, no longer felt in the patient's day-to-day experience of her own, re-incorporated body.[17]

III

Historical consciousness, modes of remembering and forgetting, categories of historical trauma, the insistence of things that aren't there anymore, the substantiality of the virtual: my excursus into anthropology and neurology is excusable only if it helps the reader as it has helped me, to think through the implications of absence, whether the absence is found in the historical consciousness of a people or the historical consciousness of a play on the Elizabethan stage.

There have always been things missing from our understanding of the English Reformation.[18] This is, at least in part, because something was missing for those who lived through it as well: missing yet felt, manifesting itself in a kind of structural amnesia that is easy to mistake for a simpler kind of absence, misrecognition, or lack of concern. The ways in which the Eucharist was felt and remembered by the social body in pre- and post-Reformation Europe provide an excellent example. Medieval scholars have clarified just how deeply eucharistic thought penetrated late medieval society. Miri Rubin has gone so far as to suggest that the Eucharist worked to "organize people's utmost feelings, thoughts, and actions."[19] Tracking what he calls the "public career of eucharistic ideas," Christopher Elwood argues that late-medieval eucharistic thought and practice affected "the way ordinary men and women conceived of political power, interpreted their social world, and established the relation between the sacred and society."[20] The Eucharist played a role, in other words, in the ways in which everyday people conceived of themselves, cognitively and affectively, as collective selves: how they thought and felt about themselves in relation to various different forms of collective identity, secular as well as religious. The pervasiveness of both of these dimensions, secular as well as religious, helps to explain why the demystification of the Catholic doctrine of transubstantiation was such a dominant concern for reformers. Indeed, it proved so fundamental to all branches of Protestantism that a consensus on the metaphysics of the consecrated but reformed Host was impossible to achieve. Lutherans, Calvinists, and other competing sects could agree on one thing: that what happens at the moment of consecration is of supreme importance in the material as well as the theological world. Studies such as those I have cited above, detailing how thoroughly eucharistic thought pervaded everyday life in the late medieval period, raise compelling questions for anyone studying the literature and drama of the Reformation and Counter-Reformation—questions about collective memory and forgetting as well as theology. How does one forget so thoroughly something that had been so thoroughly integrated in, and integral to, one's sense of self, in all its private and public, individual and social components? Or, if such a monumental act of individual and collective amnesia seems impossible, how can something that lies so close to the heart of the social imaginary, lodged in the affective core of social as well as religious life, be converted into something else, so that it can be, in a sense, forgotten and remembered at one and the same time, in the sometimes bloody and often traumatic process of reform?[21]

In sixteenth-century England, successive regimes attempted quite extreme and explicit pogroms against the past. They burned books and their authors, too. They effaced inscriptions and tore down or defaced monuments that memorialized past generations, and they did so even when such memory traces bore no doctrinal or explicit religious significance, no direct threat or even relevance to the newly reformed faith. They uprooted graves and emptied out their neighboring ossuaries in an effort to eliminate the physical presence of the past, which is to say, the material memories of the once-living in their most (dis)-embodied and all-too-human remains. These were acts of what was known as *damnatio memoriae*, a forced and often officially legislated forgetting exercised against words and things, people living and dead.[22] In Keith Thomas's terms, such a razing from the book or landscape of memory sought to bring into being a new generation that was affectively dis-affected in its relation to previous generations, one that was "spiritually indifferent to the fate of its predecessors."[23] Such extreme efforts to forget or make an entire society forget have rarely if ever succeeded in full, but the failures like the successes could be costly. In cultures of complex literacies, whose modes of oral, written, and performative signification can be quite densely interwoven, the effort to forget can be traumatic in itself. Somerset did not succeed in making Londoners unsympathetic to the spiritual fate of their predecessors when he emptied out and desecrated centuries of their dead in his dark-of-the-night evacuation of the ossuary at St. Paul's.[24] But he did eliminate a material form of social memory for a significant number of London's inhabitants, depriving them of one of the ways in which affective bonds with the past could be felt, expressed, maintained, and passed on to future generations. After the purging of St. Paul's, the integrity of the tribe, so to speak, no longer included a material element of the past, an extended and distributed affective relationship with history. The overt ideological campaigns of Edward's or Mary's reign were not significant in terms of any lasting changes they enforced or instilled in their subjects. They are, however, evidence of how deeply the roots of collective identity and social memory penetrated the affective landscape of sixteenth-century English culture—and how difficult and traumatic it could be to uproot the past or even attempt to do so.

Semantic shifts bear witness to other kinds of ontological and epistemological alterations in the long unfolding of what Christopher Haigh once called the *English Reformations*, in the historically indefinite plural.[25] This is the period in which "individual" began to lose its primary emphasis on the indivisibility of a compound or molecular identity (as in "the glorie of the hye and Indyvyduall Trinitie") and to develop its modern sense of singularity and, in terms of political or social subjects, its mystified presumptions of autonomy. Individuals, in other words, lost an important part of their social and collective identity—were no longer an *individuum*—in the period extending from the Reformation to the late seventeenth and early eighteenth centuries. Early in this period, terms like "real" and "substance" begin to migrate away from their Platonic and Aristotelian senses toward their modern, everyday or colloquial sense of things material in nature. "It is striking, and very confusing," notes Raymond Williams, that the classical concept of "realism" reversed itself almost completely, so that its dominant emphasis became the material or the actual, that which is fully accessible to the senses: for example, the stone that Dr. Johnson kicked to refute Bishop Berkeley's traditional sense of "the Real." In classical metaphysics, the Real was based on "an assertion of the absolute and objective existence of universals." "Reality" was something largely or fully inaccessible to the senses, lodged in what we cannot taste, touch, or see. In the early modern period, classical "realism" underwent such a sea change that it became, in Williams's terms again, "what we would now call extreme idealism."[26]

The Real had been anchored in what might be called the *virtuality* of a thing rather than its physical or material *actuality*. In the Catholic doctrine of transubstantiation, the sacramental character of the "Real Presence" had been the most *real* substance that could exist, since it transported this metaphysical paradox beyond its worldly limits. Protestant reformations of the Eucharist affected the vernacular and phenomenal aspects of everyday life, but the "Real Presence," once Real in its virtuality, became merely figurative, a metaphor for substance rather than the Thing itself. As Evelyn Tribble has argued, such radical changes bear witness to an epistemological and social crisis as well as a semiotic one, pointing "not only toward shifts in signifying practices, but also toward shifts in the entire way of conceiving human society."[27]

Theater bears witness as well; historically, this has always been an important part of its social function. Medieval theater played a crucial role in the medieval social imaginary, providing a means of exploring, exemplifying, celebrating, and even challenging aspects of the social body, including those imbricated in eucharistic thought and practice. Corpus Christi cycles, whether those performed at York to celebrate the Feast of the Eucharist or the religious pageant plays performed in other cities, were one of the more public and explicit ways in which medieval urban populations experienced the ambivalences and tensions of the Eucharist, of Christian history, and the social body itself, which were traced in the city topology, made flesh in the actors, the costumes, the pageants, and the spectators, alongside their sacramental orthodoxies. Medieval biblical drama enacted history in its figural (in Auerbach's sense of *figura*) and anagogic dimensions; the relation of then and now, there and here, Jerusalem and York, was embodied in the figural overlay of the historical past, present, and future.[28] Pageants cycles were a "bespoke" form of site-specific cultural performance. The biblical past was not so much represented on the pageant or stage as it was restored to its figural dimensions, manifested in an English here and now. York, Chester, London, and hosts of other cities produced site-specific cycles, each one different from the other, each one a distinct and differently performed instantiation of figural history. Religious pageants produced an entire physics as well as metaphysics of social and religious community. "This type of theater," as Peter Womack has suggested, "involved the urban community *as a whole.*"[29]

Pageant plays, enacted on city streets; morality plays, in a variety of sites including aristocratic homes; a vast range of secular drama and dramatic entertainments performed in town squares and inn yards and in motion along country roads—performance, whether theatrical, festive, ritual, or in some other form of "playing," was everywhere one looked in medieval English society. In other words, English society had been a performative culture long before The Theatre was erected in 1576. The emergence in the sixteenth century of yet more and new forms of theater, new modes of performance and new dramatic genres, was a sign of necessity as well as novelty: a sign that an already well-stocked performative culture was confronting new and rather complex demands on its collective memories and identities, feeling the need for new and sometimes paradoxical ways to forget and to remember at one and the same time. The history lesson I would draw from the Gonja is not that Protestant England suffered an equivalent form of structural amnesia. Rather, my point is that unsettling or traumatic alterations of historical consciousness do not always look unsettling or traumatic. Sometimes, in fact, they look like a cycle of English history plays.

The Elizabethan history play is hardly the only genre to grapple with the affective and cognitive challenges of the period, what Huston Diehl has felicitously called "the drama—and the trauma—of reform."[30] Nor was drama the only discursive mode—witness Foxe, Holinshed, de Bry, and so on—that invested itself so directly in the question of history. It may have been the one more likely to put history "to the question," in Michael Neill's sense of the phrase.[31] If Shakespeare's first history cycle is any guide, at any rate, this emergent genre was one of the more acute, self-critical, and self-aware examples of the Elizabethan inquiry into a no longer linear or complete past.

IV

When news of Henry VI's marriage to Margaret of Anjou reaches the English court, Gloucester's reaction is extraordinary. The immediate effect of such a union will be an erasure of history: not merely a contamination of the royal bloodline in the present but a retroactive annihilation of the English peerage, "undoing all, as all had never been":

> O peers of England, shameful is this league,
> Fatal this marriage, cancelling your fame,
> Blotting your names from books of memory,
> Razing the characters of your renown,
> Defacing monuments of conquered France,
> Undoing all, as all had never been! (*2 Henry 6*, 1.1.94–99)

Hyperbole, yes, but Gloucester's rhetoric also bleeds into a more paradoxical kind of forgetting. Blotting names, razing characters, defacing monuments: these are straightforward examples of *damnatio memoriae*, that arduous process of disremembering the past that certain kinds of cultures perform in times of crisis. But the caesura of Gloucester's last line marks a space where *damnatio* bleeds into a more traumatic and structural form of amnesia. "Undoing all || as all had never been." Undoing memory here is actual as well as figural: it undoes history in the act of rewriting it, so that "as [if]" becomes impossible to distinguish from "has never been." Whether written, oral, or something in-between, historical consciousness is a creature that eats its own tales in order to survive.

The young Margaret, who will serve as the aging but vital force of the rest of the tetralogy, enters only in the final moments of *1 Henry 6*. We end with a beginning, just as we begin with an ending. *The First Part of Henry the Sixt*, written and first performed (arguably) sometime in the late 1580s or early 1590s, opens with the epistemic death of Henry V.[32] Or rather, with the maiméd rites of his funeral procession, which is cut short by the news "of loss, of slaughter, and discomfiture" in France. Glouces-

ter bewails the situation by invoking a kind of preternatural or
haunted subjunctive:

> Is Paris lost? Is Rouen yielded up?
> If Henry were recalled to life again,
> These news would cause him once more yield the ghost.
> (*1 Henry 6*, 1.1.65–67)

Raised from the dead but deprived of life once again in the same
hypothetical clause, Henry's second death would be a willful one,
out of shame for the upheavals of the present. However, there is a
misprision in Gloucester's exclamation, a confusion of historical
cause and effect. News does not travel quite so fast; insurgencies
develop at a more labored pace than this. Paris and Rouen and
Rheims and Orleans had to have been rebelling while Henry V
was still alive, before the alterations of the present killed him a
second time. The cities were under siege already during Henry V's
reign; the dissolution of the kingdom began, had to have begun,
under Henry V's own watch. Gloucester's implication of cau-
sality, however, makes the catastrophe across the channel seem
sudden, abrupt, and, most important of all, portentous. It seems
to issue from Henry's death rather than precede it, so that it can
become a response to that passing—of a king, a father, a more
heroic age—and thus a comment on the new regime. We are to
blame, says Gloucester—and for a moment, the historical sense
of the audience is out of sync with diachronic sequences of cause
and effect.

Such violations of historical consciousness are typical.
Gloucester's collapse of history into the shock of the new is not
the most glaring example, merely the first. History on the Elizabethan stage often works to make familiar things strange and
to inculcate a curiously compelling kind of historical alienation
in its Elizabethan audience. Without taking poetic license with
the past, Shakespeare highlighted such alienation on stage with
the centripetal structure of this early history cycle. In the first
play, the enemy of England will seem to be reassuringly Other,
not only French but also female—as if to say, what could be

worse?—in the guise of Joan of Arc, *la pucelle*, and Margaret of Anjou. In the subsequent plays, chronicling the internecine War of the Roses, there will be a discomfiting narrowing down into people and places that are all too English and distressingly intimate, so that the action occupies ever tighter and increasingly claustrophobic circles of intrafamilial conflict and revenge. We have seen the enemy, and he is us.

"Why did the company," Peter Womack has asked, "in mounting this immensely ambitious national cycle a year or two after the Armada, choose the most inglorious and unsuccessful period of English history it could find?"[33] It is a necessary question and more complicated than it might seem at first. Womack's initial answer brings Benedict Anderson into conversation with Victor Turner:

> So long as the dynastic legitimation of the monarch and the nobility is more or less working, the stage does not afford any space for anyone else. The community of the nation is not needed, so to speak, and so there is no call to imagine it. It is only when that hierarchical order fails that the undifferentiated totality of the realm appears, as *that which is harmed by failure.* The theatre's obsession with the contentions of noble houses is not a reflection of contemporary political reality. . . . Rather, the *enactment* of such conflicts operates like a ritual, in which the degradation of the institutional forms of the realm generates a manifestation of the *comitatus*, the prior, underlying body to which all—characters and spectators—can feel they belong.[34]

Legitimacy is the issue, and an emergent form of popular sovereignty—the imagined community of the nation—is the answer. Out of the total failure of dynastic continuity, necessarily justified by lineage and divinity, comes something new, or rather, as Womack expresses it, something newly "remembered": a prior, underlying social body, the imagined community of the nation.

A community of *citizens*, let us say, as opposed to *subjects*.[35] The failure of dynastic or genealogical legitimacy creates the space for a countervailing sympathy, organized around a more collective legitimacy that returns to kings and queens but with a difference. It is a sympathy for something that recent studies of the Elizabethan history play have understood as a kind of early or proto-nationalism.[36] The answer to Womack's question seems to be manifested at the end of *Richard III*, with Henry Tudor restoring sanity to the realm but only with the participation of the audience in its restoration. The imagined community that we, characters and spectators, "remember" is not an alternative historical consciousness or a counterhistory but an interpellated one that operates, in Womack's terms, as a "constructed archaism." In order to be effective, as I argued earlier, any ideology—royalism, nationalism, socialism, and so forth—must first be affective. It must enter into our hearts as well as our minds, which is something the powers of state and church have always known. Monarchies and religious institutions and other hegemonic forms have always imagined their own communities, and they have typically, even necessarily, done so through their own subjects—who make their own history, as Marx noted, but do not make it as they think or please.[37] Machiavelli provides a host of early modern examples. Fulke Greville gives us a characteristically sharp exposé, in a characteristically concise couplet:

> For Power can neither act, work, nor devise
> Without the people's hands, hearts, wit, and eyes.[38]

Apt student of history that he is, Prince Hal, the once and future king of *1&2 Henry 4* and *Henry V*, structures his own path to the throne as a ritual process, a *rite de passage*, from which he will emerge as a much needed and earnestly wished-for savior capable of redeeming time when men least think he will.

Endings, however, do not always have the final word. One of the important contributions that Womack makes to our understanding of the Elizabethan history play, to my mind, grows from his realization of this fact. History on stage, he asserts, does not fall into a "neat teleology" or resolve itself into a redemptive progression from "divine cosmos to sovereign state."[39] The past and the present impinge and intrude upon one another; they are each made up of times, places, issues, and allusions that are not proper to them. These are the "*constructed* archaisms" that work, in Womack's terms, to bring then and now, medieval and Elizabethan into an open-ended dialectic with one another. The historical consciousness of these plays is no longer figural and, despite all the invocations of God, not particularly Christian. History in them is dialogic rather than figural, so that its linear progression, from "divine cosmos to sovereign state," is more apparent than real. Its progression from past to present, historical division to sovereign unity, becomes, in the moment by moment production of the plays, a mutually recursive and ultimately deconstructive conflict of critical simultaneities. Incongruity takes the place of teleology, in both discrete and comprehensive ways.[40]

In Elizabethan theater, constructed archaism becomes a structural as well as a thematic element:

> The relationship between the different versions of the realm—hierarchical and populist, "kingdom" and "commonwealth," the Queen's subjects and Christ's people—is not one of chronological sequence but of conflicting emphases within the frame of late-medieval *and* Elizabethan thought.
>
> These conflicts ran . . . right through the middle of the Elizabethan theater. As protégés of noblemen . . . the actors were firmly defined within the quasi-feudal structure of lordship and service. But as common players, "servants of the people," they were no less committed to addressing an unstructured and freely assembled crowd—a *public*. . . . The plays reproduce that opposition as a dramatic process, in which the two Englands—the one which descends from its hereditary rulers, and the one which ascends from the people as a whole—collide, transform one another, negotiate.[41]

With regular frequency, history intrudes upon itself in ways that are more whimsical than profound—Elizabethan taverns populate fourteenth-century London, rival actors of Burbage's company join in Cade's rebellion. But the incongruities of history and the multiple perspectives we gain from them extend far beyond such topical anachronisms or in-house, metatheatrical jokes.

"Constructed archaism" describes a performative as well as

an epistemological device. Enacted, performed, or produced by characters *and* spectators, it focuses on those aspects of performance that have always resisted theories of mimesis. Equally yearning, characters and spectators are equally necessary. Yet they never yearn for the same thing or from the same point of view or from the same historical space or time. The relationship between what takes place on stage and our experience and participation in it, between what the characters feel or dream and what the audience feels and dreams, is always double, dialogic, and never quite identical to itself. Constructed archaism is more ironic than mimetic, affective as well as cognitive, and inherently performative.

Theater in performance is an art of presence but it is also an art of absence, at one and the same time. The Prague structuralists realized this when they suggested that the theatrical sign could not be adequately comprehended by a Sausurean structure of signifier in relation to signified. They spoke instead of theatrical signification as a kind of a "derealized ostension," an idea they illustrated by describing what happens when a chair is placed on stage.[42] The chair is no longer a chair; in its derealization, it has instead become the sign of a chair. Peter Brook adopted this formulation in *The Empty Space* but others have found it wanting. For Herbert Blau, a chair placed on stage is no longer *merely* a chair.[43] It is *also* the sign of a chair: it is alternative to itself, in addition to itself, alien as well as identical to itself. It becomes a chair that resides "in the space of the story," as Jean Alter has suggested, and it also remains a chair that can be sat upon, picked up, or thrown into the audience.[44] At issue is not the prison house of language—the indeterminacy of what we mean by "chair"—but the generative capacity of certain modes of embodied performance. When we point to what we have in mind, whether it is a chair or a prop, an actor or a character, an embodied past or an experiential present, we discover that we cannot point to the one without pointing to the other. But neither can we point to both at once.

Gloucester's book of memory is itself a constructed archaism. He fears a profound historical amnesia, an epistemic break in continuity and legitimacy that will be retroactive as well as proleptic; he and the characters with whom he speaks, his on-stage audience, know that this is hyperbolic and hysterical; it will never happen. For the Elizabethan audience, however, or at least for some of its members, Gloucester remembers the future—the audience's present and recent past—in his fears. For the Elizabethan audience, the book of memory has indeed been blotted. Gloucester recalls all of the names stripped from village cemeteries during the reign of Edward VI, all of the parish statuary that sixteenth-century Protestant iconoclasts "de-faced" in their own acts of *damnatio memoriae*, and all of the bonds that had been weakened or shattered in the audience's own present time and place. All of the affective and cognitive relations, in brief, between the past and the present and what is yet to come, which are no longer securely anchored on the page or in collective memory. Gloucester does not directly allude to sixteenth-century efforts to undo, degrade, and disremember the past. Rather, he creates the space for an allusion. It is his offstage audience that constructs this memory of forgetting, this archaism.

The issue is one of legitimacy, legacy, memory; the questions are many. How do Elizabethans imagine historical continuity when the past is so discontinuous with the present? How can they remember, if not through forgetting? How, at last, do they (or we) forget? Theater is an art of presence, to be sure, but what is present is not "really" there at all. Henry V and Margaret of Anjou, the one dead but not yet buried when the tetralogy opens, the other dead but still occupying the English court as it draws to a close, are the specters that frame the first tetralogy, like metaphysical bookends. They represent very different ways in which the Elizabethan history play thinks through, by means of and beyond, its own absences.

"Brave Talbot," the terror of the French and the awe-inspiring nemesis and foil to Joan of Arc in *1 Henry 6*, provides another, more comprehensive example. It is not hard to fathom why Margaret was resurrected to haunt the reign of Richard III or why Shakespeare chose to bring her on stage as a living, ancient, posthumous but still-embodied voice. It is harder to understand why Talbot, who so fully occupies *1 Henry 6*, is so fully forgotten in the remainder of the tetralogy, and with a thoroughness that borders on the pathological.[45]

V

Talbot's legacy in Shakespeare's first history tetralogy would seem assured. Lucy assures all present—characters and spectators—that from Talbot's "ashes shall be reared / A phoenix that shall make all France afeard" (*1 Henry 6*, 4.7.93–94). In the remainder of the tetralogy, we would expect, at the least, the invocation of such an iconic figure. "Talbot" was clearly a name to conjure with; paying audiences were among the things that could be conjured with it. Talbot was apparently one of the most compelling attractions of the Elizabethan stage, a box-office draw for any company that managed to bring him back from the dead:

> How would it haue ioyed braue *Talbot* (the terror of the French) to thinke that after he had lyne two hundred yeares in his Tombe, hee should triumphe againe on the Stage, and haue his bones newe embalmed with the teares of ten thousand spectators at least, (at seuerall times) who in the Tragedian that represents his person, imagine they behold him fresh bleeding.[46]

Nashe captures something of Shakespeare's darker purpose in *1 Henry 6*, his "book" or play-script of historical consciousness. The point of resurrecting Talbot is not only to restore him to life but also to watch him die over and over again and to weep for him, to disanimate and "newe embalme" him as often as the audience desires. In the final analysis, Talbot is defined as much by his vanishing from the stage as by his heroic actions on it.[47]

Talbot is often viewed as the emblem of an idealized world no longer accessible, a reminder of a chivalric order that has no place in the emerging Tudor present. Cut adrift from medieval Christian history, he is also deprived of a place or *platea* in the uncertain structures of history and performance that will replace it.[48] He becomes, in this view, a kind of nostalgic archaism, a *figura* without a future. But nostalgia, in itself a powerful form of historical memory, only begins to work when a longed-for past is invoked or otherwise brought to mind. If we look for Talbot in the remainder of the tetralogy, he is not to be found at all: after his death in *1 Henry 6*, he is never invoked, referred to, remembered or recollected in any fashion—and this despite Lucy's prophetic promise that he will return "phoenix-like" to his men and his country, at least in name and reputation.

Why not rouse a cheer from Nashe's 10,000 spectators by invoking "the Talbot" in the subsequent plays of the first tetralogy? Shakespeare does precisely this in a scene written some years later, when Henry V makes a "household word" of Talbot's name on St. Crispin's day at Agincourt:

> Old men forget; yet all shall be forgot,
> But he'll remember, with advantages,
> What feats he did that day. Then shall our names,
> Familiar in his mouth as household words—
> Harry the King, Bedford and Exeter,
> Warwick and Talbot, Salisbury and Gloucester—
> Be in their flowing cups freshly remembered;
> And Crispin Crispian shall ne'er go by,
> From this day to the ending of the world
> But we in it shall be rememberèd.
> We few, we happy few, we band of brothers. (*Henry V*, 4.3.49–60)

This is historical memory in its official and hegemonic form, and it is worth noting that Talbot is given special significance in the roll call. With the exception of "Harry," the king himself, "Talbot" is the only lord who is personalized in a more familiar mode, invoked by proper name rather than the hereditary metonymies of office or title.[49]

Or so it seems, if we are not sensitive to the ironic structures of historical consciousness in Shakespeare's hands. Henry V promises an unchanging and heroic memory: until the "ending of the world," this band of brothers and this time and place will be remembered and commemorated on this holy day, St. Crispin's Day. An Elizabethan audience would have been confused, however. As Jonathan Baldo has noted, the battle of Agincourt was no longer celebrated on St. Crispin's Day by 1599, when *Henry V* was first performed at the newly erected Globe in Southwark. It had not, in fact, been officially remembered for most of Elizabeth's reign. "The mnemonic function of the speech in 1599," writes Baldo, "would most likely have been to remind audiences not of Agincourt . . . but of the absence of any national day of remembrance."[50] There is a stark contradiction between the historical consciousness Henry promises and the one the Elizabethan audience inhabited. Dramatic irony frames Tudor ideology. It extends beyond the stage and even the amphitheater to become another name for history.

No roll call "remembers" Talbot in *2 Henry 6*, *3 Henry 6*, or *Richard III*. Instead, his radical absence is highlighted, made starker and more paradoxical for the audience, when his death on the battlefield is also represented as the end of his line, the genealogical extinction of the name and heritage of "the Talbots." Which is, of course, inaccurate. The historical Talbot was succeeded as earl of Shrewsbury by one of his two surviving sons. On Shakespeare's stage, however, the case is altered. Talbot's eponymous son John is presented to the audience as his only heir. When both are killed, "the Talbot" will no longer be embodied in genealogy, which is the memory of the future as well as the past—a future that must be realized and incarnated in flesh and blood, as a corporeal memory composed in lineage and legacy and living, breathing descendants. Talbot's death forgets the future itself, producing an amnesia of infinite duration. Jean Howard and Phyllis Rackin have suggested that there is a paradoxical enhancement of the heroic Talbot, an inflation of Talbot's aura, in such misprision. The blotting out of Talbot's entire future line will earn for him an iconic afterlife, since it "means that only the name [Talbot] will survive—stripped of any living human referent but glorious in historical memory."[51] However, it is precisely the name that does *not* survive in dramaturgical memory. "In thee thy mother dies," as the father says to his dying and only son, "our household's *name*" (*1 Henry 6*, 4.6.38; emphasis added). He proves to be quite literally correct in the plays to come. His name, like his person and his descendants, vanishes from the remainder of the tetralogy.

But what does it matter? What if we don't know our Holinshed well enough to notice, don't remember when Margaret of Anjou died, or aren't startled by any of the other absences, disjunctions, inconsistencies, contradictions, or incongruities that characterize the early history plays? The issue, it seems to me, is not *whether* we take notice of such complicating aspects—the commentary on these plays testifies that we have long done so. Rather, do we view them as insignificant, signs of an apprentice playwright or the mark of poetic license taken for dramatic effect, or as something more substantial, significant, and clearly patterned? As alienation effects, in other words, capable of concentrating the minds of the audience? A default skepticism in such contexts—let us not make too much of it—is not, in and of itself, a more rigorous methodology. Hermeneutic skepticism is both necessary and problematic, not an end in itself but the beginning of further inquiry. Absence, disjunction, inconsistency, contradiction, incongruity—what do they matter? We might begin to answer that question by reminding ourselves that they are among the most important dramaturgical and epistemological devices available to the stage. They are among the tools that theater uses to think with, when it wants or needs to think about something else—and when it wants its audiences to do the same. Like any tools, they accomplish their work and perform their functions whether we notice them or not. We do not need to realize how thoroughly Talbot is forgotten by the remainder of the tetralogy in order to notice the effects of his absence. The remaining plays are made possible, in a sense, by that absence from the books of memory.

VI

There is one brief scene, long before his death, where Talbot vanishes right before our eyes. Talbot is captured by the Countess of

Auvergne in 2.3. She is proud to have apprehended "the Talbot" himself, but he denies that he is he. His name is Talbot but he's also merely a "shadow" of the real thing. "He will be here, and yet he is not here," the Countess of Auvergne complains. "How can these contrarieties agree?" (2.3.58–59).

The scene is brief, uncharacteristically comic, and entirely unrelated to the plot. It has consequently annoyed some and delighted others. E. M. W. Tillyard regarded it as a "startling but irrelevant anecdote."[52] And so it seems. In a rather prescient essay of 1967, however, Sigurd Burckhardt begged to disagree with his mentor on the purported irrelevance of the scene, finding in "this most episodic of episodes . . . the 'real' play, just as the Talbot in it is the 'real' Talbot."[53] "Reality" is properly put under question by Burckhardt and qualified with quotation marks: "reality" is an aporia rather than a given or embodied fact, something that the Countess (like Tillyard) seems unable to comprehend. She thinks that she has taken advantage of the earl's (outdated) chivalric courtesy with her invitation to supper; he will assume, as her guest, that he is protected by a host's traditional moral and ethical responsibilities. She traps him with her own, more devious, up-to-date, and proto-Machiavellian wiles. From her perspective, Talbot represents the outmoded legacies of a fading medieval and chivalric past, easy to regard as simple and naïve in the *Realpolitik* of the present.

Hitherto, the Countess could only possess Talbot in the form of his simulacrum, a painted portrait she describes as a mere shadow of the man himself. Now, at last, she has caught the substance, or so she thinks:

> Long time thy *shadow* hath been thrall to me,
> For in my gallery thy picture hangs;
> But now the *substance* shall endure the like,
> And I will chain these legs and arms of thine
> That hast by tyranny these many years
> Wasted our country, slain our citizens,
> And sent our sons and husbands captive.
> (*1 Henry 6*, 2.3.35–41; emphasis added)

Indulging in a display of metaphysical wit, the Countess announces her liberation from Plato's cave: even though the man named Talbot is a disappointment in and of himself—his demystified persona resembles a "weak and writhled shrimp" rather than a Hercules or Alexander—she no longer needs to be "captivated" by the mere shadows of mimetic art or heroic reputation. Her claim to possess Talbot's "substance," however, prompts the man himself to correct her Platonic understanding of the Real with a more Aristotelian one:

> No, no, I am but *shadow* of myself.
> You are deceiv'd; my *substance* is not here.
> For what you see is but the smallest part
> And least proportion of humanity.
> I tell you, madam, were the whole frame here,
> It is of such a spacious lofty pitch
> Your roof were not sufficient to contain't.
>   (2.3.50–56; emphasis added)

He understands "substance" and "shadow" differently, as a distinction between *substans* and *accidens*, the essence of a thing versus the "accidents" or incidentals of its phenomenological manifestation or sensible apprehension. Aristotle's distinction is not always analogous to Plato's ideal forms and their shadowy, inadequate, and misleading representations. Talbot's assertion that he's not "really" Talbot poses an epistemological and ontological riddle in the place of an anticipated certainty, which is what prompts the Countess to ask how these "contrarieties" can possibly agree.

It is not just that the physical, material, living and breathing Talbot looks a bit shrimpish. Talbot is not "really" there at all; he is not what or where he is. The "real" Talbot is not under the Countess's lock and key and so cannot be chained to her limited understanding of the essence of a thing. The full proportion of his humanity, what we might think of as the completion of himself as synecdoche, lies in a compound Talbot, a collective social entity that is partially embodied (but not entirely comprehended) in the English soldiers who burst into the room on cue:

> How say you, madam? Are you now persuaded
> That Talbot is but *shadow* of himself?
> These are his *substance*, sinews, arms, and strength,
> With which he yoketh your rebellious necks,
> Razeth your cities and subverts your towns,
> And in a moment makes them desolate.
>   (*1 Henry VI*, 2.3.61–66; emphasis added)

If the Countess's castle is insufficient to contain the "whole frame" of Talbot, this means that the soldiers who do fit under her roof are also material and embodied "shadows" of the collective thing itself. They too are always something else, here and yet not here at one and the same time: another meeting of contrarieties. "The Talbot" is always a virtual and collective self as well as an individual and embodied one—or rather, he is an individual self because he is a virtual and collective self, an *individuum* in the original but waning sense of the term in the sixteenth century. He is an indivisible, compound, or corporate entity. "The Talbot" cannot be captured because he is "really" something like an imagined community. And those are places none of us have been, that have to imagined to be seen.

Whether it takes the form of a nation or a public or another kind of social body, an imagined community is not the same as an imaginary one. The first is virtual but also entirely real; indeed, it is real only to the extent that it is virtual.[54] The other is the stuff of dreams or fantasies or delusions, not "real" in the same sense because something merely imaginary has not been grounded in the necessary virtuality of the real. Like Talbot's social body— "the Talbot"—imagined communities can never be fully embodied or manifested on a stage or in a castle, but this does not make them vague or ambiguous or obscure.

But is Talbot's social body an imagined or imaginary community? In terms of its immediate context—where the integrity imagined, the "tribe" that Talbot calls into being, is military— "The Talbot" could be said to be a limited but valid imagined community. The imagined whole would always be larger than any given or specific army. Insofar as he and his forces are them-

selves synecdoches for a more social, political, and representative
sovereignty, however, it is an imaginary or failed community, one
that is not yet capable of imagination. It cannot be called into
being if it cannot be *recalled* into being: remembered, embodied
as a legacy, an inheritance, a genealogy, or—in its most radical
political form—a form of participatory governance embodied
in a republic or democratic commonwealth. Like Henry IV's
crown or Shakespeare's coat of arms, it can only be legitimated
retroactively; it can only become imagined (rather than merely
imaginary) when it is successfully passed on to the future. Until
then, it is a constructed archaism, an unresolved dialectic of past
and present forms of community, cut adrift from any mode of
historical transmission or inheritance or systemic continuation.
"The Talbot" becomes a kind of social integrity that is alienated
from itself, which is another way of saying that it is alienated
from history itself.[55]

"History" is not merely one damned thing after the other,
in this context. Nor is it only an archaeology of the past. It is
a configuration of past, present, and future with a great many
variables included, including the time of configuration: a rela-
tivity of people and places and events, so to speak, rather than
a merely diachronic sequence. "The Talbot" has no lineal dimensions in the present or the future, severed so absolutely as
it is from genealogical or historical or theatrical consciousness;
neither its sociality nor its integrity exists once they cannot be
handed down by blood or political institutions or other mnemonic processes.[56] I would embrace Burckhardt's paradoxical
assertion that this scene—Talbot's capture by the Countess in
2.3—is "the 'real' play, and that the Talbot in it is the 'real' Talbot."[57] I would go a bit further: this scene is also the "real" tetralogy, albeit not in the way that Burckhardt meant. This Talbot is
not an avatar of the (Elizabethan) modern, as Burckhardt would
have it, or an icon of the medieval, as many others have regarded
him. He is instead an aporia, a *problématique* that brings the future and the anachronistic together. He is there (and not there)
in order to help us think about a present whose ties to the past

were at best under suspicion and at worst subject to dissolution, through various efforts to enforce a kind of affective amnesia in the Reformation. To cite Keith Thomas once again, to conceive a new generation that was "spiritually indifferent to the fate of its predecessors."[58]

Unlike the earl of Shrewsbury himself, however, the terms that are bandied about in this scene are not so easily forgotten or cut off from the future. "I am but *shadow* of myself . . . / my *substance* is not here." In and of themselves, "shadow" and "substance" make for an odd couple. The classical Latin distinction between *accidens* and *substans* is half-translated into Anglo-Saxon and this broken translation introduces a decided ambiguity. As a metaphysical term, "shadow" shuttles uncertainly between the Platonic and the Aristotelian: between an empty sign, an absence or a blocking of the light, and a double sign, one that is here and not here at the same time, substantial in both its physical and metaphysical dimensions. It is this shuttling that perplexes the Countess. She and her captive both speak in terms of "shadow" and "substance" but they seem to be speaking different languages when they do. The words on both of their tongues, keywords that should anchor a shared ontology and epistemology, register semiotic difference rather than community. The result is an uncertain semiotics of the Real whose dimensions will be charted and explored in the remaining plays, where "shadow" and "substance" are massively distributed and mediated. The terms recur together as a yoked singularity throughout the remainder of the tetralogy. Indeed, they are sounded in these four plays nearly as many times as they are in the rest of Shakespeare's dramatic corpus altogether. Coined to help us clarify the Real, they are instead scattered throughout history as a kind of sparagmatic *leitmotif.*[59] As in this brief scene, they are never identical to themselves in meaning; they are always shifting, consistently inconstant, becoming the source of ontological doubt rather than legitimacy as they migrate unpredictably among the material, the political, the psychological, the metaphysical, and the sacramental.

Or rather, as they migrate everywhere *except* the sacramental.

"Nor other satisfaction do I crave," says Talbot, as soon as the Countess has vowed to treat him with the "reverence" that is his due, "But only, with your patience, that we may / Taste of your wine and see what cates you have." This communion of wine and bread—one of the meanings of "cates"—is precisely not a sacramental one and not to be related to the Last Supper it nonetheless recalls. It remembers what is an ostensibly forgotten affective experience—Catholic, transubstantial communion—but at the same time strips that experience of any incorporative effects beyond the physiological body itself. It is affective but not effective and, like Talbot himself, this means it is remembered only in the forgetting of it. The repast to be enjoyed off stage is an ironic one, and the Countess, now Talbot's prisoner, will be able to serve her cates and wine only in the capacity of an ironic hostess, a literal captive. The one thing we would know for certain is that the wine and cates are precisely *not* a figure for the Eucharist. They might well constitute a substantial offering in a material sense of the term—we are to imagine the scene in question, it is capable of imagination—but they don't have a prayer, so to speak, of being substantial or transubstantial in the pre-Lutheran understanding of the word.

What sometimes hinders our efforts to understand the relation of the Elizabethan present to the Elizabethan past is an assumption that there is a pattern in the carpet waiting to be discovered. There must be a clue to unweave and follow in order to discover the correct answers to questions of Shakespeare's religion, artistic opportunism, powers of ideological deconstruction, or whatever else that might occupy us. What I want to suggest is that the pattern in this carpet—the first tetralogy of history plays—is instead an unraveling of pattern, in and of itself.[60] The plays pose a series of questions and undertake a wide range of experimental modes; they do not, however, pose answers or directions. The tetralogy is phenomenal in the experiential as well as the evaluative sense of that word: even more so than other instances of theater and performance, it constitutes an experience rather than an idea or argument—a use of theater, an art of absence as well as presence, to think about the social and its discontents.[61]

VII

As a constructed archaism, Talbot has a great deal of company in the first tetralogy. Late-medieval dramatic modes, figures, and scenes are scattered throughout these plays, cut loose from their theatrical, social, and epistemological moorings so that they wash ashore in unexpected places. Alienated from a once-defining matrix, one that had been structured by the performative and figural dynamics of late-medieval religious drama, such revenants can also be difficult to decipher. For example, Shakespeare's Duke of York opens *3 Henry 6* by reprising the role of Lucifer in the opening pageant of a Corpus Christi cycle. He usurps Henry's throne just as the soon-to-be-fallen angel tries to usurp the throne of God. However, unlike his damned predecessor, who occupies God's throne for the briefest instant if at all, York remains comfortably seated when the king, ostensibly God's anointed representative, enters to discover someone has been sitting in his chair. Lucifer fell on contact, as it were, the moment he sat down. The king's expressions of outrage have absolutely no effect on York, the rebellious overreacher.

Neither the infernal *figura* nor the parodic allegory is stable, however. At his death a short while later, York will play the part of Christ rather than the devil. In her martial and heroic mode—a part she has had to learn on the run, so to speak—Margaret wipes his face with a grisly reminder of Veronica's veil, a handkerchief stained with the blood of York's young son, Rutland. She then mocks him by placing a fake crown on his head—it might as well be a crown of thorns—before she removes that head and places it on the gates of York, "So York may overlook the town of York" (*3 Henry 6*, 1.4.180).

Which is the shadow here, and which the substance? Are we to imagine that York has changed so dramatically in a little over 300 lines? That he is meant to double as both Lucifer and Christ?

Or are we to imagine that medieval modes of theater are being parodied or exposed as obsolete, mere anachronisms, no longer capable of anchoring historical consciousness? Or do we explain such anomalies and contradictions by pointing out that Shakespeare was still a novice when he wrote these plays and hadn't yet developed the characterological brilliance he would later exhibit? Do we, in other words, explain them away as insignificant inconsistencies, signs of a talent that has not yet fully matured?

None of these solutions seems adequate, given the consistently inconsistent nature of character in these plays. York is made to stand on a molehill rather than a pageant wagon for his crowning moment in *3 Henry 6*. It is a place of such consequential insignificance that it need not have been rendered in any visible or physical sense on an Elizabethan stage. Even if a miniscule pile of dirt was used to present the role of Molehill, the prop would be occluded as soon as York stood on it. The tenor of its presence—something so small, so trivial and trivializing, that it might as well be nothing at all—could be conveyed even more fully if the hill itself was entirely absent, literally represented by its refusal of representation. Henry VI will also occupy a molehill a short while later in the same play, in a scene that also rehearses the architectonic powers of medieval drama but to quite different ends. When the king sits down on his molehill, he intends to moralize on the happy life of the homely swain he longs to be, but his abject narcissism is interrupted by a framing set of scenes: "*Enter at one door a soldier with a dead man in his arms. . . . Enter at another door another soldier with a dead man*" (*3 Henry 6*, 2.5.54–78). The first is a son who discovers, on stage, that the man he has killed is his own father; the second, a father who discovers he has killed his son. The two family dramas frame a king who has disinherited his own son, as if they were brought on stage to serve as allegorical psychomachias in Henry's own morality play. Henry becomes the center panel of a triptych representing the death of genealogy, the end of the line. Henry moralizes both tragedies as if they were instructive allegories, but for the audience they represent lived forms of meaning, not only embodied but also felt figures for the loss of history and the trauma of reform.[62] Generations in a single family, fathers and sons and daughters and mothers, rarely killed one another in a literal sense in Reformation England, but their divided faiths posited and imagined the death of one another's soul. In this mode of drama, in the play world on stage, these are "real" deaths; in this moment of the Protestant Reformation, in the unsettled world off stage, they are all the more "real," in an ontological and metaphysical and spiritual sense. Either way, these are real sons and fathers in the process of blotting one another from the book of memory. Henry's moralizing, however, has the effect of dehumanizing the figures before him in a way that medieval allegory never did. Abstract and far from specific in its individuations of "character," the morality play was nonetheless a complex and effective use of the two-eyed semiotics of the theatrical. It was designed to make the figural and the sacramental inseparable from (but never identical to) the human and the embodied. Henry treats medieval allegory as if it were imaginary rather than imagined: as if the formal qualities of its verse and the seemingly abstract or allegorical nature of its *mise en scène* were signs of its artificiality. He treats a "real" set of tragedies as if they were "only" allegories of the reductive kind, things to look past, signs to moralize, transcendent truths in personified allegorical disguise. It is a misprision of both tenor and vehicle, of two different modes of personation—early modern character and medieval exemplarity—and the effect is brutal. Sympathy for others, the sentiments felt in response to what Henry sees, should be a document of civilization. Here it becomes a layered document of barbarism.[63]

None of these—fathers or sons or the king himself—are "deep" characters in a verisimilar or psychological sense, of course. Henry's broodings on the molehill don't anticipate Hamlet or even Richard II, who will also sit on the ground to talk about the sad deaths of kings. Like community, character is scattered in fragments rather than developed over time in these plays, and the fragments often do not coalesce to become a symbolic or psychological integrity or any other kind of comprehensive whole. Characters in the first tetralogy are embodied in more affective than allegorical personae, but they are also, and often, self-contradictory and unpredictable in the extreme. They are not integrated identities in a psychological or thematic sense, and it is arguable whether they should be regarded as examples of Shakespeare's failed, early efforts to stage such identities. They resemble figures taken from a nonperspectival medieval painting, in which foreground and background could be imagined and represented from mutually exclusive points of view.

Is Joan the virgin saint that the French see and follow into battle, or is she the lascivious and demon-summoning witch that the English see from the beginning? The audience sees her as such only toward the end of the play (5.3), as the moment of her capture and immolation approach. Is she Pucelle or puzzel, a chaste farmer's daughter or a blasphemous whore? We tend to read the final moment in a dramaturgical sequence as revelatory, the place where the moral of the story is made plain. If every Jack marries his Jill at the end of the comedy, none of the gender hybridity and apparent patriarchal critique that came before such generic endings could have been serious rather than merely playful, for remembrance rather than oblivion when one left the theater. But such a teleological and diachronic epistemology, which looks to plot resolution for an ethical or moral *telos*, is regularly ironized and mocked in Shakespeare's plays. Puck's epilogue sweeps behind the door a great part of what has been most moving or disturbing in *A Midsummer Night's Dream*: the fruitful female bonds emblematized in a double-cherry or the mortal votaress of Titania's order; the humiliation of the Fairy Queen's love and desire in her heterosexual yet bestial (hence sodomitical, according to the laws of early modern England) union with Bottom. The point, of course, is that we leave the theater reminded that it's all still there, behind the door. A privileged and determinate sense of the ending seems foreign to the sparagmatic structure of these history plays as well. Is the final "truth" of Joan revealed or demystified in act 5, or is the audience meant to remember that she has always been a witch from the English point of view, which has always oscillated with the French perspective. To the victors goes historical consciousness, the record of what's remembered and what's forgotten.

It is even more difficult to bring Joan into a single focal plane if the same actor who plays Margaret doubles her. The two characters do not appear on stage at the same time; Joan exits to be burned at the stake, and Margaret makes her first entrance in quite rapid, and thus quite notable and dramatic, succession at the end of the play. In 2000 the Royal Shakespeare Company, under the direction of Michael Boyd, doubled the two women with the same Scottish actress and to significant effect. Margaret appears in all four plays, which means that, even without doubling, the stamina of the actor who plays her role adds to the epic dimensions of the history cycle in performance. On the page, it is all too easy to adopt singular viewpoints like York's—she is an "Amazonian trull" with a "tiger's heart wrapped in a woman's hide" (*3 Henry 6*, 1.4.115, 138)—or to allow isolated aspects of her behavior—she is an unchaste French bride, the savage killer of children like "young" Rutland—to overdetermine our own judgment. In *Engendering the Nation*, Jean Howard and Phyllis Rackin argued that Margaret's "spectacular rise" is "one of the many signs of gender disorder" in these plays: she is "represented as dangerous to men and to the good order of the kingdom."[64] When Phyllis Rackin saw the tetralogy on stage, however, she was surprised to discover that Margaret could become an exemplary and even heroic figure in performance. Our judgments of her character "might be different," Rackin surmised, "if we had more opportunities to see these plays performed":

> Reading a playscript from a printed text tends to privilege the represented action at the expense of its theatrical presentation. As a result, it tends to discount the charismatic theatrical appeal a character can have on stage. . . . Our negative estimation of women's place in the Elizabethan history play may be at least partly an artifact of our own construction.[65]

There is an epic scale to the first tetralogy, but Richmond, the crowning future of the Tudor line, is curiously marginal to its sweep. He is a late arrival, appearing for the first time in the decisive last scenes of *Richard III*. He does not occupy center stage as all the other Henrys (Bolingbroke and Hal, Henry IV and V, fathers and sons) will do in the later tetralogy. We think of the second history tetralogy as "the Henriad" in recognition of its epic scope. In Shakespeare's earlier venture, it is Margaret who provides the core energy for all of the plays in performance. These are her plays, her history cycle, her Margretiad.

Such consistent inconsistency extends beyond individual character. It characterizes the oddly complex shifts in dramatic mode and the perplexing multiplication of theatrical, affective, and ideological perspectives. The charisma that Rackin responded to in performance is a quality inseparable from the historical quandaries of legacy and memory that are at the heart of the tetralogy. Even if they flare up and vanish quickly from view, many of the scattered "representative" figures in these plays are also charismatic in their ability to be representative, brief though their moments of fame might be. "Charisma" literally means "a gift of grace."[66] In politics, as Max Weber suggested, charisma is the name we give to a kind of hierarchical power that isn't guaranteed by bloodline or inherited title or political structure.[67] It is an affective and ideological investment that the Many make in the One. In other words, it is something that the people give or grant to a leader, a character, or an actor, something bestowed by an audience or some other kind of group or community or public. We wrap such figures in a mantle of authority and immediately forget that we have done so; our investiture, once forgotten, serves to mystify the relation of agent to agency. Monarchy, aristocracy, class, gender and other hierarchies of power are also crowning mystifications of authority, of course.[68] But charisma is not a structural promise or assurance, as its kin tend to be. It cannot provide a vehicle for the passage from past to present to future. In terms of the *longue durée*, charisma is a relatively synchronic rather than a diachronic kind of legitimation. It is a barren form of authority: it produces no guarantee of continuance, no assured future, and no "natural" offspring.

Some of the charismatic figures in these plays are heroic in one scene and demonic in the next, like Joan of Arc or her reverse image, York. Some begin in disrepute like Margaret, who is French, female, and almost by definition unfaithful at the first; then, so heroic and moving in her losing struggle against the house of York that she can seem an early avatar of Henry V; and finally, in *Richard III*, a choral specter who, like Caliban, has learned how to curse. Jack Cade, who commands "actual" actors like Bevis and Holland as well as a grassroots ensemble of tanners and butchers and weavers who fill the stage "*with infinite numbers*" (*2 Henry 6*, 4.2.28 [SD]), makes tangible the leveling threat that underlies all of these charismatic, posthumous rehearsals of Talbot. Cade's reformation *qua* rebellion (4.2.59ff.) is nothing more or less than the "many-headed monster" of democracy—impossible to view as anything other than monstrous because it is historically premature, incapable of being actually reproduced in history due to the absence of a bureaucratic infrastructure in which democracy could be stabilized.[69] Cade's rebellion is another shadow of representative community rather than its substance. In this sense, he is another typical figure for the wreckage of history, a sign that the present—the Shakespearean or Elizabethan or Reformation present—has forgotten how to imagine continuity as well as community.

If we accept relatively recent speculations about the deep and everyday significance of eucharistic thought in late medieval society, this crisis of historical consciousness is precisely what we would expect to find in the early modern period, a time when such thought was intensely reformed, rejected, reinstituted, or disarticulated.[70] I am not suggesting that the first tetralogy is an allegory of such loss and reformation. An allegory would require some externalization of perspective, a capacity to view the relationship between substance and its various shadows or accidents, between the Real and the material, as a narrative: a historical transition from one mode of thought to another, from "Real Presence" to "real estate." For the early history plays, however, substance and shadow, theatrical sign and signified, are remarkably unstable in their various embodiments. When Suffolk speaks the opening lines of *2 Henry 6* and introduces the king to "his" French bride, the ontologies of sacred monarchy and sacramental matrimony are impossible to decipher:

> As by your high imperial Majesty
> I had in charge at my depart for France,
> As Procurator to your excellence,
> To marry Princess Margaret for your grace;
> So, in the famous ancient city of Tours,
> . . .
> I have performed my task and was espoused,
> And humbly now upon my bended knee,
> In sight of England and her lordly peers,
> Deliver up my title in the Queen
> To your most gracious hands, that are the substance
> Of that great shadow I did represent. (*2 Henry 6*, 1.1.1–5, 9–14)

We expect Suffolk to describe himself as the king's agent or representative—in other words, as his shadow, to be understood (like a literal shadow) as an immaterial sign of royal substance. Instead, it is the king's shadow that Suffolk has "represent[ed]," as though he could become the shadow of a shadow. As an agent without agency of his own, Suffolk should hold no title to the queen; he did not marry her in any "real" sense, even though he stood at the altar and enunciated the words. Yet he gives her to Henry as if she were something in his power to bestow: "The happiest gift that ever marquess gave, / The fairest queen that ever king receiv'd" (15–16). The merging of two bodies and souls into one, a union that should have been represented but not realized in the French ceremony, seems instead to have taken place. Suffolk, the representation of a shadow, acts as if he were quite substantial, in and of himself. And in terms of the union of body and heart (if not of soul), he not only seems to be but actually *is* possessed of full, free agency in relation to the queen's physical and affective love.

The tetralogy would seem to recover at the end, to find its historical grounding. The authorizing diachronic legitimacy of blood restores sacred majesty to the throne of England; Richmond ends the history cycle with the announcement of a genealogical as well as a martial triumph:

> And then—as we have ta'en the sacrament—
> We will unite the white rose and the red.
> Smile, heaven, upon this fair conjunction,
> That long have frowned upon their enmity.
> What traitor hears me, and says not 'Amen'?
> England hath long been mad, and scarred herself:
> The brother blindly shed the brother's blood;
> The father rashly slaughtered his own son,
> The son, compell'd, been butcher to the sire;
> All this divided York and Lancaster,
> United in their dire division. (*Richard III*, 5.6.18–28)

The god and the religion that Richmond invokes are Catholic, of course. Neither god nor religion will survive the next generation—Henry VIII's regime—intact. Decades before these plays were written or produced, the Eucharistic sacrament of communion announced by Richmond in this rousing conclusion had already been reclassified as the performance of a heresy rather a confirmation of the one true faith. Eucharistic communion had become a ritual passage into hell rather than an access to grace. The Elizabeth on the throne, the one who is descended from this union between another Elizabeth and another Henry Tudor, has herself renounced this god and this religion. By fiat of the church invoked above, she is a heretic; by the declaration of her father, she is a bastard and consequently an illegitimate queen. Any genealogical reference to her in the 1590s is also a reminder that she represents another end of the line, since she will die, like Shakespeare's Talbot before her, without an heir or any other means to secure the transmission of past into present and future.

VIII

"Be not afraid of shadows," counsels Ratcliffe at Bosworth Field (*Richard III*, 5.5.169). He has just discovered his unsettled king talking to himself, in voices more than one. Richard's startled waking soliloquy on the morning of his demise has long been celebrated for its anticipation of later introspective moments by later introspective characters. Some have taken the speech to task, at the same time, for its hyperbolic sentimentality. But most commentators agree that we are witnessing something like a fledgling Shakespearean interiority:

> Have mercy, Jesu!—Soft, I did but dream.
> O coward conscience, how dost thou afflict me?
> The lights burn blue. It is now dead midnight.
> Cold fearful drops stand on my trembling flesh.
> What do I fear? Myself? There's none else by.
> Richard loves Richard; that is, I am I.
> Is there a murtherer here? No. Yes, I am.
> Then fly. What, from myself? Great reason. Why?
> Lest I revenge. Myself upon myself?
> . . .
> My conscience has a thousand several tongues,
> And every tongue brings in a several tale,
> And every tongue condemns me for a villain.
> . . .
> Methought the souls of all that I had murther'd
> Came to my tent, and every one did threat
> To-morrow's vengeance on the head of Richard.
>   (*Richard III*, 5.5.134–160)

Richard has been descanting on shadows for much of his career. Ratcliffe's counsel is particularly well suited to this king, cast as it is in terms that are the king's own: a rhetoric of demystification that Richard has often used to empower himself and will employ again in this scene, when he reassures his troops that the king's fright in the night is no more yielding than a dream:

> By the apostle Paul, shadows tonight
> Have strook more terror to the soul of Richard

> Than can the substance of ten thousand soldiers
> (*Richard III*, V.v.216–19)

The fear he felt on awaking was the residue of sleep and has already been left behind and forgotten; it was all shadow and no substance, another shadow of a shadow.

The evocation of Paul seems out of character, however. It is as unexpected on the tongue of Richard Plantagenet as the revelation that a "conscience"—what conscience?—has discomfited his rest. Both the invocation of the apostle and the untoward suggestion of a moral or ethical self should give us pause. Richard's fear is expressed in terms that are quite familiar and that call to mind all the other times we've encountered the shadows and the substances of the Real, but Richard's evocation is different and differently overdetermined. The scene that precedes his awakening needs to be rescued from Richard's own misrecognition of it. Richard's uneasy sleep reverses the *mise en scène* we experienced when Henry VI was on his molehill, lamenting the loss of legacy. In *3 Henry 6*, the king was positioned in the center of the stage and was thus framed by the family tragedies he moralized upon. As I suggested earlier, the staging echoed or recalled the situation of a protagonist in a morality play who has reached a critical yet ambivalent point of decision. He is caught between antithetical desires, personified on stage by a good angel or spirit on the one side, talking into one ear, and a bad angel who glozes into the other ear, on the other side of the stage. Marlowe's *Faustus* has a number of "anachronistic" moments of this kind and in Marlowe, as in the medieval tradition, one is not always able to say whether the spirits on stage are to be understood as symbolic or actual beings. They might be psychological allegories of a divided conscience and (or) they might be genuine supernatural visitations by substantial yet spiritual beings from other realms.

In *Richard III*, however, the shadows of the dead would most likely occupy the center of the stage rather than its wings: the good Richmond would be sleeping on one side, the bad Richard on the other. The moral antinomies familiar to past theatrical modes of representation are displaced from the preternatural (good angel, bad angel) to the historical (good king, bad king).[71] In between the sleepers, the shadows alternatively curse and bless their royal auditors—but these shadows, embodied on stage, are neither angels nor allegories. They are the dead: quite substantial shadows, in other words. They are shades, in the sense that first emerges in the last decade of the sixteenth century, when shadows became shades, whether understood as ghosts or souls.[72] These are actual beings, the ghosts or souls of Richard's many victims. In terms of performance, what is being represented and what is doing the representing, the ghosts and the actors who embody them, are equally but antithetically substantial. Both are entirely "real" at this moment on stage. Richard calls them shadows but does not seem to realize that he is correct only in a sense he does not mean and could not mean, since it was not available to him or his fifteenth-century English. But it will be available to the ears of his sixteenth-century auditors. He intends to refer to something entirely insubstantial, the kind of shadow produced by an eclipse of the light or the dreams of a sleeping king. He refers, however, to shadows that are substantial and real even though they are not material—or rather, they are substantial and real insofar as they are not material. If "shade" or "shadow" refer to a ghost or spirit or soul, as I've suggested above, they refer to an immaterial but essential being and not a fantasy: to the substance of a person, the part that is immortal rather than the passing fancy of a dream. Richard means to say that the spirits of the dead were but a dream, his own deluded creation. He thinks he is speaking his own words and is able to say what he intends, but in this moment his language seems to speaking him instead.

What interests me is the fact that Richard's moment of guilty anagnorisis stems from a mistake, a fundamental error or misreading of the scene that the audience has watched and listened to. The dead have actually visited him in his sleep. He awakes thinking that he has dreamed about his dead victims and their curses, however; he knows, or thinks he knows, that their insubstantial voices came from within his own dreaming self. According to his own understanding, he has produced them and his fear is groundless. He is entirely mistaken, however—and his mistake is a substantial and profoundly consequential one.

In a Lacanian mirror stage, the infant realizes it is a self only when it misrecognizes its own image in the mirror. It mistakes that reflection for a better self, an other (self) who is more whole and complete than it can ever be. This is an error or misrecognition that is necessary if the self is to be born, in its early, rudimentary, always and already abject form. The mistake or error is a generative one, in other words. Richard mistakes one kind of shade for another and, in his error, assumes that he must be the kind of moral and ethical character who possesses something like a conscience. Richard's conscience is imaginary, just as the infant's self in the mirror is imaginary—and both are, as a consequence, entirely real.[73] Taking a substantial shade for a merely imaginary one, he mistakes the supernatural for the psychological, the actual for the imaginary, the real in a virtual sense for the figurative or merely fictional—as the shadow cast by a shadow, an insubstantial dream. Where the medieval stage left unresolved the ambiguity inherent in theatrical representation—are these allegories or angels?—Richard internalizes ambiguity as if it were the same thing as ambivalence. He knows that he is frightened by shadows but doesn't realize that the shadows are just as real as his fear. Born in error or misprision, his conscience is not the source of these several thousand tongues but it certainly feels as if it were—and his misapprehension, as it does for the Lacanian infant, has real consequences. Richard feels as if he has grown a new part of himself in the night, like an extra limb or a tumor. He calls it a conscience, and even though he will brand it, a moment later, as a fiction and disparage it as "but a word that cowards use, / Devised at first to keep the strong in awe" (5.6.339–40), this doesn't really change the new order of the self that he dies into. Richard's conscience depends upon its fictionality: the misrecognition of something actual and substantial as something merely imaginary is what brings the latter into existence. Internalizing the dead, psychologizing the sacred, Richard is fooled into inventing a soul.

In the larger disenchantment of the world, Protestantism attempted to demystify the old religion by "unmasking" the sacramental as the merely theatrical, the miraculous as simply a fake: *hoc est corpus meum*, the words of the priest that announce the "real presence" of Christ in the communion host—this is my body—was reduced to "hocus pocus," a charlatan's trick. When Richard unwittingly disenchants his own world, taking supernatural curses for the psychological stirrings of guilt, he mistakes the shades—the souls—of the dead for false imaginings, mere shadows. He internalizes the real and "substantial" souls that have visited him, mistakenly but effectively rendering them illusions projected by a conscience that neither he nor we imagined he could ever possess. Richmond may end the play with the hardly surprising, celebratory announcement of the remystified and sanctioned Tudor line. But the conclusion of the tetralogy, the end promised from the beginning by Margaret and Talbot and the rest, takes place here. Something like an Elizabethan understanding of modernity issues from the moment of Richard's awakening: an understanding of the modern as a radical form of misrecognition, a productive or generative *méconaissance* that is so fully woven into the structure of these plays that it sometimes seems as if it were the ironic signature of history itself.

IX

Shakespeare was a master at knowing what to leave out. The aura of psychological depth in Shakespearean characters often derives, as Stephen Greenblatt has noted, from what the playwright excised from his sources. In important instances, Shakespeare was especially keen to eliminate much of what explained *why* his characters acted as they did in the plot—he cut, in other words, key elements of rationale, motivation, or ethical principle that had been specified and spelled out by his sources:

> Shakespeare found that he could immeasurably deepen the effect of his plays, that he could provoke in the audience and in himself a peculiarly passionate intensity of response, if he took out a key

explanatory element, thereby occluding the rationale, motivation, or ethical principle that accounted for the action that was to unfold. The principle was not the making of a riddle to be solved, but the creation of a strategic opacity.[74]

This seems to me a brilliant observation. What isn't there can be or become more substantial than what is. T. S. Eliot came to a cognate realization in his discussion of the missing "objective correlative" in *Hamlet*, but he framed what was missing in terms of an aesthetic and psychological flaw rather than an integral dimension of an affective semiotics.[75]

We are drawn into a theatrical production as a participant; our participation is necessary, as it turns out, for the production of the play in a theatrical as well as an economic sense—as an aesthetic commodity. What is staged before us is not limited to that which is literally placed before our eyes or that which enters into our ears. What is not provided by the story or its characters must be filled in by us, the audience, and we are not one but many; we supplement the verbal and visual *mise en scène* in a heterogeneous and never entirely unanimous fashion. This is why affective character, one of the most recognizable signatures of Elizabethan drama, cannot be located on the page or on the stage alone. Affective character is a social relationship at heart, part of a complex yet everyday collaboration—a mode of production—between playwrights, actors, and audiences.[76]

If we limit this dynamic to character interiority or psychology, however, we have an incomplete picture. Nothing about Talbot or Margaret or even Richard III suggests or induces us to produce the kind of psychological interiority we project onto and into a Hamlet or a Macbeth. The affective intelligence of the early history plays is different—but it also takes place in the audience as much as it does in anything, however complex and brilliant, that is "represented" on the stage or articulated on the page. What is missing in the early histories—what Shakespeare has strategically occluded—tends to be more collective and social than individual or psychological—a missing history or genealogy, rather than an absent or removed motive. The audience is more likely to produce a "we" rather than an "I," more likely to be perplexed and compelled by a historical consciousness as opposed to an isolated or apparently individual consciousness. In either case, however, we are induced to think and feel *through* what is not there, to move not only beyond it but also by means of it. What is not supplied, represented, or otherwise manifested on stage does not constitute an emptiness or a lack. Instead, it functions as a necessary incompletion, a tool or a device that the audience can use to collaborate in the ostended extension of its own thought and feeling.

Theater is an art of absence as well as presence, and there are a great many theatrical forms of incompletion, amnesia, incongruity, and inconsistency: what the Countess labels "contrarieties"; what Burckhardt identifies as the "real" play in the case of *1 Henry 6*; what Womack terms the "constructed archaisms" of historical consciousness in the Shakespearean history play. Pierre Macherey went further in his *Theory of Literary Production* to suggest that a related economy of absence and presence is at the heart of what we call the literary. For Macherey, literature is always and necessarily structured around an internal displacement, caesura, or aporia. This is its strength, however, rather than its weakness: what is missing or absent is not a flaw or a register of indeterminacy or a reminder of the prison-house of language. Rather, it is the catalyst of a paradoxical production as well as a paradoxical induction of social meaning. This is what allows literature to "correspond[s] to a reality that is also incomplete, which it shows without reflecting":

> The literary work gives the measure of a difference, reveals a determinate absence, resorts to an eloquent silence. . . . What begs to be explained in the work is . . . the presence of a relation, or opposition, between elements of the exposition or levels of composition, those disparities which point to a conflict of meaning. This conflict is not the sign of an imperfection; it reveals the inscription of an *otherness* in the work, through which it maintains a relationship with that which it is not, that which happens at its margins. . . . The [work] is

not the extension of a meaning; it is generated from the incompatibility of several meanings, the strongest bond by which it is attached
to reality, in a tense and ever-renewed confrontation.[77]

It is important to note that the work does not imitate or merely
represent incompletion; the *otherness* is inscribed in the work and
"corresponds to a reality that is also incomplete." It is not the
sign of a poststructuralist variant on the pathetic fallacy. It is
closer to the "internal distantiation" that Althusser identified as
the literary work's capacity to apprehend the social as if outside
of ideology—something that only Theory, in Althusser's exalted
sense, was otherwise capable of doing.[78]

The relationship of art to society has always been difficult to
articulate in terms that can acknowledge relation without reflection, production without mimesis.[79] Or, to recall the question
framed at the beginning of this chapter, forms of forgetting that
are not simply opposed to forms of remembering. The oral history of the Gonja or the theatrical performance of historical
trauma are not examples of the failure of memory or the blindness of insight.[80] Theater and literature are not the same as theory. However, it is always good to remind ourselves that "theater"
and "theory" stem from the same Greek root: each designates a
powerful form of critical understanding, and at times, in certain
historical circumstances, both seem to be needed in equal ratio, each operating as the necessary supplement to the other. As
Kenneth Burke also and often reminded us,

> Theater can be especially useful in helping us think about the consti-
> tution and production of social reality. It is one of places where the
> critical understanding of theory (*theoria*) cannot always be separated
> from the poetic and world-making phenomenology of practice
> (*praxis*) or performance.[81]

The affective architectonics of theatrical performance engage an
audience in a kind of critical social thought that is more spatially
and collectively produced than many other modes of discursive
and nondiscursive art, but theater is hardly unique in its capacity
to help us think. Societies expand already existing forms of cul-

tural performance and develop new ones—oral, written, visual, and performed—for a variety of reasons. Sometimes they do so, as Tadeusz Kantor suggested, in response to a crisis or a shared and collective trauma. Sometimes, to quote Simpcox's wife in *2 Henry 6*, they do so "for pure need"—out of necessity, in order to think about themselves in ways they can't accomplish elsewhere or by other means or other media.

3

What's Hamlet to Habermas? Theatrical Publication and the Early Modern Stage

I

"*Preachers, Printers, & Players* . . . . be set vp of God, as a triple bulwarke agaynst the triple crown of the Pope, to bring him down" (1570: 1562). John Foxe's agents of reform were carefully selected. They occupy distinct media and overlapping social spheres, most often framed today in terms of oral, print, and performative cultures—when we include performative cultures at all. Foxe identifies three of the most significant and influential kinds of social media available to the early modern period, but he does not provide a complete list. Most prominently missing is "scribal publication," as Harold Love defined manuscripts that have achieved their final, public form as such: that intend, as it were, to remain manuscripts and should not be regarded as interim forms of writing that yearn to become print.[1] Love reminded us that manuscript production and circulation has a long and significant history as a form of publication in its own right, a history that extends well beyond and before the rise of the print-

ing press. It includes, for example, earlier forms of mass production like the medieval scriptorium. The printing press made the
process more efficient, of course, but it introduced neither mass
production nor the concept of publication. Gutenberg invented
the late medieval equivalent of an assembly line for textual reproduction. He was, if you will, the Henry Ford of his age.

None of which detracts from the staggering historical consequences of either Ford's or Gutenberg's inventions. Looking
backward, however, modern scholarship has sometimes granted
the printed book a nearly exclusive patent or copyright on the
concept of "publication." The emergence of digital media in
the past three decades has raised postmodern awareness of the
blindness this has produced; however, it is a lesson we could have
learned from late medieval and early modern culture just as readily. The hegemony of print has, until relatively recently, occluded
"scribal publication" from view—and continues to occlude another, quite different, and highly influential form of publication,
namely the performance or production of a play in a theater.
Foxe includes players as distinct agents of change because they
represented another medium altogether, another mode of production, and another form of publication—not in a figurative
sense but quite properly speaking.[2]

Francis Beaumont thought of theatrical performance in this
vein, as a mode of publication in and of itself. In the *first* printed
edition of *The Faithful Shepherdess* (c. 1609), Beaumont identified the material book as "this *second* publication [emphasis
added]" of the work.[3] The first publication of the play was the
one that took place on stage. Performance in these terms was an
act of *theatrical publication*, distinct from other modes of making something public and wielding entirely different capacities
to engage individual and collective identities.[4]

As Erica T. Lin has noted, the "initial physical form" of an
Elizabethan play was not the printed book. Bringing performance studies into dialogue with what she calls "material text
studies," she treats the performed play in concrete terms, as a
physical, material work in its own right, in performance.[5] There

is a "materiality of performance" found not only in the tangible accoutrements of theater (props, bodies, scaffold or stage, exits and entrances, and so forth) but also in its intangible dimensions. She encourages us to approach "the material" in less reified and fetishized ways, to resist separating the social from the material object, to think in terms of the materiality of history as well as the transactive and nonrepresentational dynamics of an affective technology like early modern theater. "Plays were first performed and only later published," she reminds us, "as numerous references on the title pages of playbooks attest" (12). Beaumont agrees that performance is the native mode of a play, but disagrees about what to call it. Plays were first *published* in performance, to amend Lin slightly, and only later published on the page.

Wresting the concept of "publication" back from the exclusive domain of print is not merely a quibble with words or terminology. The social and affective landscape of the early modern period looks and becomes quite different when we regard it less anachronistically and recognize "publication" in its various forms and modes as a multimedia concept. In terms of this study, such a corrective counterhistory will help to historicize the affective and cognitive technology I have explored directly—early modern amphitheater drama—as well as the many other affective and cognitive technologies I have passed by or merely gestured toward. It will help to clarify, or so I hope, the reason why I have been drawn to Michelle Rosaldo's concept of (social) emotions as forms of "embodied thought . . . steeped with the apprehension" of the social; as cultural performances, "social practices organized by the stories we both enact and tell";[6] and as ways of thinking as well as feeling, where the cognitive and the affective remain in full solution with one another. The early modern popular stage was one of the primary ways in which thoughts and feelings and beliefs could be *made public* in sixteenth-century England. This is what "publication" means, in the strong sense of the concept. Making something public is not only making it accessible or putting it into circulation. Publication is also, and more importantly, a key agent in the formation and reformation of collective and private identities.

Spoken or proclaimed, inscribed or imprinted on pages, performed at The Theatre or the Globe or the Rose: these were all modes of publication for early modern societies and each produced a different kind of literacy, as David Cressy has emphasized.[7] They were tools for the production of social knowledge. Early modern theater entered into the phenomenological dimensions of its audiences' private and public lives, including those places in the social imaginary where Elizabethans could think and feel and experience themselves and their worlds: where they could participate in their own lived and felt history—past, present, and what's to come—in dynamic, transactive, and often critical and internally distantiated ways. Players and their audiences were agents and actors in what we might call, with some necessary qualifications, an early modern public sphere.

II

The "bourgeois" public sphere, as imagined by Jürgen Habermas in *The Structural Transformation of the Public Sphere*, was fostered and strengthened by a number of social and cultural and economic developments. These included, for Habermas, the rise (at long last) of an actually existing bourgeoisie, the evolution of coffeehouses and lending libraries, and the emergence of new forms of print media that included gazettes, journals, newspapers, and, significantly, the early novel.[8] Theater did not participate in the resulting "bourgeois" public sphere, in Habermas's terms, until the drama of Congreve and Beaumarchais. Earlier instantiations of theater, including the amphitheater playhouses of Elizabethan London, were in fact—again, according to Habermas—most retrograde to the emergence of the public sphere. Early modern theater was entirely contained by the early modern *res publica* and served to maintain and promulgate what Habermas called the "representative publicity" of the early modern princely state. State and church together defined and largely controlled most forms of publicness in the period; it was their hegemony that had to be displaced or weakened before a classic Habermasian public sphere would be possible. The theater of Kyd and Marlowe and Shakespeare was one of the forms of the past that would have to be cleared away and replaced by new and radically reformed modes of theatrical performance if theater could hope to claim its membership in the new public sphere.

It is easy to dismiss such a view. Habermas's understanding of Elizabethan popular drama was limited, to say the least. In terms of theatrical and performance history, there can be little doubt that he simply had his facts wrong on some important points. For example, he assumed that leading figures of the aristocracy and even the monarch attended performances at the Globe and sat in prominent view of the rest of the audience. Asserting that the general populace "had been admitted" to theaters such as the Globe and the Comédie-Francaise "as far back as the seventeenth century," he argued that the lower-rank "public" were present only to authorize and legitimate the aristocracy: "They [the Globe and the Comédie] were all still part of a different type of publicity in which the "ranks" (preserved still as a dysfunctional architectural relic in our theater buildings) paraded themselves, and the people applauded."[9] Insofar as the Globe is concerned, this is of course pure fantasy. Neither the monarch nor the aristocracy was on display or applauded at the Globe. The Globe, like all of London's amphitheaters and most of its indoor playing spaces, was open to anyone with the price of admission. Habermas's reference to the aristocracy on display recalls certain aspects of French theater in the latter half of the seventeenth century, but those practices seem to have emigrated, in Habermas's imagination, across the Channel and back in time. It is a surprisingly anachronistic projection of an architecture of privilege that existed only at court, in so far as theatrical performance in early modern England is concerned.[10]

In addition, there is the matter of Habermas's conception of the "bourgeois public sphere" itself, which has been so thoroughly critiqued that any contemporary use of the phrase requires a disclaimer that one does *not* mean, for the most part, what Habermas meant. And yet, forgetting Habermas has been hard for history and theory to do. There is something important to be learned from Habermas about theater and publics. In an early and devastatingly thorough feminist critique, Nancy Fraser nonetheless concluded with a defense and recovery of the concept of a public sphere itself, asserting that "something like Habermas's idea of the public sphere is indispensable to critical social theory."[11] Recent and ongoing inquiries into the nature of historical civil societies have developed alternative and less teleological understandings of the ways in which "private people come together to form a public," long before the emergence of a *bourgeoisie* and in diverse cultural, social, and political contexts.[12] In its current working definition, a "public sphere" is an assortment (not quite an assemblage or ensemble) of publics and counterpublics that are themselves understood to be always partial and often conflictual forms of association.[13] For a growing body of early modern historians and literary scholars, speaking of an early modern public sphere or spheres no longer implies an anachronistic importation of an otherwise intact Habermasian model. "The public sphere," as Craig Calhoun has defined its post-Habermasian sense, "comprises an indefinite number of more or less overlapping publics, some ephemeral, some enduring, and some shaped by struggle against the dominant organization of others."[14] It is an uncentered congeries of publics and counterpublics rather than an organized or harmonious social body.

Habermas remains compelling in his understanding of the dynamic and inherently paradoxical relationships that can develop between the public and the private dimensions of the social.[15] But he understood theater as a cultural form more or less fixed in its publicness and even trapped by what he referred to as "representative publicity." For Habermas, theater was an inherently mimetic or representational mode whose purpose was to hold its mirror up to the nobility, with admiration. In so doing, early modern theater and most forms of theater before the late

eighteenth century helped to produce the "representative publicity" necessary to maintain a princely *res publica*. Left to its own
devices, theater was a conservative and regressive force in Habermas's terms. Indeed, it hindered the emergence of a public sphere
by enhancing and contributing to powers of church and state.

Such an understanding of the social life of theater marks
Habermas as one of the most influential antitheatricalists of the
twentieth century. And yet, as I hope to show, there is something
important to be learned from Habermas about theater and publics in the early modern period. In framing amphitheater drama
as a "public and performative" art, I have treated it as one of a
number of early modern forms of cultural performance. It is not
an exemplary or singular instance of the affective and cognitive
technologies that enabled early modern individuals to configure
or reform their collective selves. Each of these technologies offered its own distinct medium of enablement. If so, a number of
questions arise. What distinguishes early modern popular theater from other forms of cultural performance such as essays,
books, sermons, and so forth? Why is it necessary to emphasize
its experiential and affective dimensions as well as its cognitive
ones, the collective as well as the individual character of its en-
gagements with its audiences? Why enshrine "performance" in
this manner? Isn't a play on the page, printed in quarto or folio or
textbook or digital file, richer with possibility—alternative versions and interpretations—while performance on stage can at
best embody one concrete, limited version of "the play" itself?
What does it mean to argue, as I will do here, that theatrical
performance was a distinct and significant *mode of production* in
the early modern period? That theatrical performance, a form of
"publication" in its own right, engaged the embodied thoughts,
contradictions, and social traumas of its audiences—and thus
could serve as a catalyst for the making of various publics and
counterpublics, imagined communities and collective identities.
In what follows, I hope not to bury but to recover Habermas.
Despite his overt antitheatricalism, despite his fundamental

misunderstandings of English popular theater, Habermas in fact relied on the dynamics of theatrical performance in much of his thinking about the nature of the public sphere. Such dynamics played a significant role in Habermas's theoretical understanding of civil society—just as they played a significant role in the structures of feeling and social thought of many actual, historical civil societies, including the one that developed in early modern England.

III

Early in the pages of *The Structural Transformation of the Public Sphere*, Jürgen Habermas interrupts his own explication of the "representative publicity" of the sixteenth and early seventeenth centuries with a subsection entitled, "Excursus: The Demise of the Representative Publicness Illustrated by the Case of Wilhelm Meister." It is an odd moment for an unnecessary anecdote or digression, the customary meaning of "excursus," especially one like this, which transports us from the politics of the late-medieval and early modern *res publica* into the pages of a late eighteenth-century novel (1795) by Johan Wolfgang von Goethe.[16] Immediately after this brief *explication de texte romantique*, Habermas returns to the seventeenth century and continues his interrupted explanation of earlier forms of publicity, chronicling the economic, cultural, political, and other developments that would eventually give rise to the "bourgeois" public sphere.

But Goethe is not a digression, even if the literary turn seems odd or out of place at first. Like Freud finding a literary habitation and a name for the Oedipal complex in Sophocles, or Foucault using Cervantes and Velasquez to think his way into *The Order of Things*, Habermas looked to an aesthetic object for insight into his own sociological and historical hypotheses.[17] In Habermas's hands, Goethe's novel becomes a *bildungsroman* for an entire historical *episteme*. It is a parable, in fact, of the public sphere and its relation to varying forms of public and popular art. In the novel, young Wilhelm rejects the bourgeois world of business and politics for a career as an actor. He joins a company of traveling players, where he hopes to establish himself as a kind of "public person" (in Goethe's phrase) by representing on stage the one class of individuals for whom "seeming" and "being" had always been one and the same: the aristocracy. He eventually rises to the top of his acting troupe and as a reward is given the role of the prince of all princes, Hamlet the Dane.

For the aristocracy, as Habermas explains via Goethe, authenticity and authority were real "inasmuch as [they were] made present":

> The nobleman was what he represented; the bourgeois, what he produced: "If the nobleman [as Wilhelm writes in a letter to his brother-in-law], merely by his personal carriage, offers all that can be asked of him, the burgher by his personal carriage offers nothing; and can offer nothing. The former has a right to *seem*; the latter is compelled to *be*, and what he aims at seeming becomes ludicrous and tasteless."[18]

What the nobility made real by representing as such, in its own figure and presence and rites of display, was nothing less than the "representative publicness" of the princely state. It exercised a form of power produced (in part) by its own manifestations.[19] Goethe and Habermas seem to agree with such an appraisal of early modern power. What Wilhelm sought on stage was a surrogate for an already-archaic form of authority, a princely mode of publicity. And since he relied on the "secret equivocation"— Goethe's phrase—that theatrical performance shares with representative publicity, his enterprise seemed to be successful, at least for a short period of time.

What's Hamlet to Habermas? He's a sixteenth-century dramatic character played by a misguided late eighteenth-century novelistic character. He is also the emblematic representative of an anachronistic conjunction of theater and civil society: insofar as the public sphere is concerned, he is a mistake, a digression, a false lure. He is what keeps Wilhelm from assuming his proper place in the by then fully formed bourgeois public sphere:

> Wilhelm came before his public as Hamlet, successfully at first. The public, however, was already the carrier of a different public sphere, one that no longer had anything in common with that of representation. In this sense, Wilhelm Meister's theatrical mission had to fail. It was out of step, as it were, with the bourgeois public sphere whose platform the theatre had meanwhile become. Beaumarchais's Figaro had already entered the stage and along with him, according to Napoleon's famous words, the revolution.[20]

What is it that makes Figaro an agent in the formation of something we might call a theatrical public—or even, in this instance, a theatrical counterpublic (*Vive la Révolution!*)—while *Hamlet*, even when performed 200 years after its first performances at the Globe, cannot escape the representative publicity of the early modern *res publica*? Habermas's answer is a complex one, involving as it does an extensive account of significant historical transformations of both the theatrical apparatus of European popular drama and the reformed subjectivity of those private individuals who were its audiences. A key component can be economically identified, however. What separates these two modes of theatrical production—*Hamlet* from *Figaro*, Shakespeare from Beaumarchais—is the emergence of the novel.

Habermas's attention to the role played by literary and dramatic modes in the formation, transformation, and maintenance of different historical regimes of publicity is noteworthy, in and of itself. It should be of special interest to any post-Habermasian study of the relation of the individual to the social, the private to the public, and the historical reformation of such relations, especially those that include structures of feeling and social emotions. The turn to literary or dramatic and other performative forms, as in the seemingly out-of-place "Excursus" on *Wilhelm Meister*, is neither a whim nor a moment of mere illustration. Literature is not, in Habermas's hands, representing or merely reflecting social changes that are happening elsewhere. His emphasis is on the phenomenology of *reading* a novel, in the actual, ongoing, cognitive and affective experience of the reader:

> Especially Sterne, of course, refined the role of the narrator through the use of reflections by directly addressing the reader, almost by stage directions; he mounted the novel once more for a public that this time was included in it, not for the purpose of creating distance (*Verfremdung*) but to place a final veil over the difference between reality and illusion. The reality as illusion that the new genre created received its proper name in English, "fiction": it shed the character of the *merely* fictitious. The psychological novel fashioned for the first time the kind of realism that allowed anyone to enter into the literary action as a substitute for his own, to use the relationship between the figures, between the author, the characters, and the reader as substitute relationships for reality. The contemporary drama too became fiction ["*fiction*"] no differently than the novel through the introduction of the "fourth wall."[21]

Importing the English word and spelling, Habermas makes "fiction" do extra work as a critical concept: it is the name for a new "kind of realism," one that does not, surprisingly, have anything in common with representation. "Fiction" at first sounds as if entails a naturalistic verisimilitude, but its psychology is transactional and its bibliography includes Sterne as well as Defoe or Fielding. Habermas stresses the *metacritical* aspects of a novel like *Tristram Shandy*, in fact, and it is this metacritical inclusion of the reader that ultimately defines his phenomenology of reading "fiction."

When Habermas discusses the rise of the middle class, the increasing hegemony of print, the establishment of new discursive spaces in the civic topography such as coffeehouses, salons, public libraries, or the many other historical developments associated with the emergence of the "bourgeois" public sphere, it is often impossible to determine whether he is identifying a cause or an effect, an agent in or a symptom of, the social transformation he has in mind. Common to all of these developments, however, was a change that took place in the subjectivity of private individuals. A new kind of subjectivity began to develop:

first in the intimate sphere of the conjugal family, where the private yet social interactions of lived and everyday life took place, and afterwards in a host of other experiences which contributed to the production of this new or emergent subjectivity:

> The sphere of the public arose in the broader strata of the bourgeoisie as an expansion and at the same time a completion of the intimate sphere of the conjugal family. Living room and *salon* were under the same roof; and just as the privacy of the one was oriented toward the public nature of the other, and as the subjectivity of the privatized individual was related from the very start to publicity, so both were conjoined in literature that had become "fiction." On the one hand, the empathetic reader repeated within himself the private relationships displayed before him in literature; from his experience of real familiarity (*Intimität*), he gave life to the fictional one, and in the latter he prepared himself for the former. On the other hand, from the outset the familiarity (*Intimität*) whose vehicle was the written word, the subjectivity that had become fit to print, had in fact become the literature appealing to a wide public of readers. The privatized individuals coming together to form a public also reflected critically and in public on what they had read, thus contributing to the process of enlightenment which they together promoted.[22]

We have moved beyond "reading" in the everyday sense of the word. In the passage above, reading a novel is not a strictly private activity but rather a dynamic, social, yet imaginary transaction or dialectic of empathy. Reading "fiction" involves a great many literacies—social, emotional, ideological, and so on—beyond the linguistic or the aesthetic, and it does not take place only in the private aesthetic space between the reader and the text. It begins outside that literary relation, in the intimate sphere of family interactions, and it continues to circulate recursively between private and public realms, actual and virtual relations, feelings, and ideas. Fiction emerges within the lived self; lived relations "give life" to fictional ones. "Reading" is a name for a paradoxical reflexivity that can also be observed elsewhere.[23] A similar reflexivity organizes the proximate spaces of the reading room and the *salon*: "just as the privacy of the one was oriented toward the

public nature of the other, and as the subjectivity of the priva-
tized individual was related from the very start to publicity,"[24] so
were private and public, imagined and lived, virtual and actual
relations conjoined in the novel as a dialectical experience.

I will reserve judgment on the question of whether a historical
transformation of human subjectivity, unabashedly Hegelian in
Habermas's account, might in fact have taken place in the course
of the long eighteenth century. First, it is important to note that
his detailed and compelling account of the phenomenology of
reading imaginative "fiction" is presented as something less than
cause but more than mere example of the emergence of the public within the domestic or private sphere. Individual and collective subjectivities were also being transformed elsewhere, in the
social and spatial architecture of the salon as well as the study or
other sites of reading and writing: "The same Madame de Staël
who in her house cultivated to excess that social game in which
after dinner everyone withdrew to write letters to one another
became aware that the persons themselves became *sujets de fiction* for themselves and the others."[25] In his more extended consideration of reading fiction, Habermas clarifies the process by
which *sujets de fiction*, selves in the sense of subjects, are brought
into self-consciousness, to a stage where they become aware of
themselves as both subjects and objects of apprehension. As we
have seen, Habermas frames this process as a dynamic, intersubjective transaction between virtual and actual subjects. Wherever
it takes place, in the salon or the study or even, belatedly, in the
theater, this *sujets*-producing dialectic is a lived, experiential phenomenon. It happens in time and space, in everyday life: it is an
actual experience of a community (an "*audience*-oriented subjectivity") in the process of its own imagining. Reading novels took
place in, and helped to create, a new kind of social, psychological,
and experiential space, which then served as a kind of practice
field for the development of this "audience-oriented subjectivity."
Reading provided "a training ground," in Habermas's own terms,

> for a critical public reflection still preoccupied with itself—a process
> of self-clarification of private people focusing on the genuine expe-

rience of their novel privateness . . . [and] sparked by the products of culture that had become publicly accessible: in the reading room and the theater, in museums and at concerts. Inasmuch as culture became a commodity, and thus finally evolved into "culture" in the specific sense (as something that pretended to exist merely for its own sake), it was claimed as the ready topic of a discussion through which an audience-oriented (*publikumsbezogen*) subjectivity communicated with itself.[26]

An audience-oriented subjectivity, communicating with itself—but able to do so only late in the history of theater, where the actual audience had previously been authority-oriented rather than audience-oriented, in Habermas's curious physics of subjectivity.

Before the theatrical audience could become audience-oriented, complexly self-conscious of its private and public dimensions, theater had to be taken to school by the novel. It could free itself from representative publicity only when it acquired a new social and experiential architecture:

> The psychological novel fashioned for the first time the kind of realism that allowed anyone to enter into the literary action as a substitute for his own, to use the relationship between the figures, between the author, the characters, and the reader as substitute relationships for reality. The contemporary drama too became fiction ["*fiction*"] no differently than the novel through the introduction of the "fourth wall."[27]

Drama had to become a kind of enacted and embodied novel, establishing a new and quasi-readerly relationship with its now comfortably distanced audience. The public audience is recast as a collection of private but virtual readers. The fourth wall, according to Habermas, altered both the theatrical apparatus of live performance and the social consequences of seeing and hearing a play in this "novel" mode. It rescued theater from itself.

This is as unfair to the proscenium stage as it is to earlier modes of performance. However, it is a fairly accurate overview of the way Habermas thought about theater—or rather, of the way that he *thought* he thought about theater and its capacity to contribute to the bourgeois public sphere. There is more to his phenomenology of *fiction*, however, than fits within this explicitly antitheatrical philosophy. What interests me here is the degree to which Habermas seems incapable of describing novels and empathetic readers without recourse to the language of the stage, even though his express purpose was to differentiate the phenomenology of reading from the phenomenology of performance. Along with his readers, Richardson weeps over the "actors" in his novels and his plots "came to occupy center stage" despite the author's intentions. Sterne "refined the role of the narrator . . . by directly addressing the reader, *almost* by stage directions" (emphasis added).[28] It's the language—and a lot more. Habermas explicitly argues that theater could contribute to the public sphere only after it had denatured itself and become *less* theatrical, placing itself under the tutelage of prose fiction. What Sterne, Richardson, and other novelists produced, however, was "an audience-oriented subjectivity": a prosaic version of something derived, it would seem, from the spatialized dynamics of theatrical performance and production itself. The empathetic reader repeats within himself or herself[29] the private relationships "displayed before him" in a novel: the "subjectivity that was fit to print" emerges not from the page alone but from an intersubjective transaction between actual and virtual relations, feelings, and selves. Between reader and fictive character, scene of reading and story: a fully recursive dialectic restructures the relations of subject to object, private to public, active to passive, embodied to imagined. Each is constituted by the other: "from his experience of real familiarity (*Intimität*), he [the reader] gave life to the fictional one, and in the latter he prepared himself for the former."[30] It is a compelling and in many ways persuasive account of what happens when we read, a clarifying exposition of how reading imaginative fiction could be a process with public-making potential. It is also an inherently theatrical one. The same dynamic, the same complex dialectic between actual relations and their virtual or imagined counterparts, takes place between an audience member and a character or scene in a play, but in theatrical performance, unlike the act of reading, it takes place in a literal as well as a figurative sense.

At the phenomenological core of theatrical performance, according to Stanton Garner, is an "irreducible oscillation between represented and lived space."[31] It takes place not only on stage but also in the lived and imagined relations of the audience—in the dynamic interactions of audience and actor or character, spectator and scene, and even one member of the audience with his or her others. A play performed before an audience involves an intersubjective dynamic that is played out in all the virtual, empathetic dimensions that Habermas described so well in terms of reading fiction, but in a theater or other playing space, the audience-oriented subjectivity is a twice-behaved orientation, to adapt Richard Schechner's definition of performance.[32] It occupies and takes place in the actual, lived space inhabited by the audience, and it also takes place in the imagined and virtual space that theater shares with novelistic "fiction." Reading imaginative fiction is a complex, empathetic, and intersubjective process. It is also a performative and theatrical one, albeit in a more abstracted and figurative sense than we experience when seeing and hearing a play. Habermas's understanding of the social, spatial, and affective phenomenology of popular forms of art like the novel is quite persuasive, but not when its heritage is mistakenly and exclusively traced—mistakenly, because exclusively—to the wrong popular and public art. Theater operates as the ghost in Habermas's literary machine, despite his efforts to exorcise it. It is the Derridean supplement to his otherwise brilliant analysis of the reading process, a necessary imp of the Habermasian perverse.

IV

My point is not that Habermas contradicted himself. Indeed, his capacity to contradict himself, to think beyond and sometimes against his explicit historical and theoretical assumptions, is one of his strengths as a social theorist. Did an unprecedented or "novel" kind of human subjectivity evolve in the course of the eighteenth century, at least in certain European societies? Probably not. Were the dimensions and parameters of the social subject *recalibrated* or *reformed* during the same period? I'm sure they were, as they were also and quite massively reconfigured during the period of the Reformation. Our sense of self and other, the syntax and declension of our social emotions and thoughts, the cognitive and affective scaffolding we rely on in the everyday world—all of these aspects of the social habitus are subject to history and to culture, to regular and even constant reconfigurations and negotiations. Nor do I mean to suggest that Habermas's "audience-oriented subjectivity" was a product of the Reformation *rather* than the Enlightenment, or that the vehicle for such a shift or emergence was the Elizabethan play *rather* than the eighteenth-century novel. I do mean to suggest that Habermas's insistence on print as a primary agent of social change, capable of producing a new "familiarity [*Intimität*] whose vehicle was the written word, the subjectivity that had become fit to print" (51), should be met with skepticism rather than affirmation.[33] Print was a highly important if not quite new signifying medium in the sixteenth century. Its societal role in Europe and the world increased and expanded, for the most part, throughout the sixteenth, seventeenth, and eighteenth centuries.[34] In the period of the Reformation, it also was a significant force—but not the dominant medium that it would eventually become. Viewing the early modern period too narrowly from the perspective of print can obscure other modes of discursive production, especially those that combine the discursive and the nondiscursive, such as theatrical performance.[35]

What about the staged word, the subjectivity that had become fit to perform? It is a question that troubles modern theories of social media when it is raised at all. In *Oral and Literate Culture in England, 1500–1700*, for example, Adam Fox generally avoids the misleading binary opposition of his title and counsels us to think instead of different media in flux with one another, complex in their fluid boundaries and hybrid forms. Early modern England was a society "in which the *three* media of speech, script, and print infused and interacted with each other in . . . myriad ways."[36] Fox rightly shifts our terms of historical analysis from the linguistic equivalent of apples and oranges—"oral" is a medium of discourse, but "literate" describes a skill that is taught and learned[37]—to comparable yet distinct and different media. However, theater is notably absent from this complex inmixing and is scarcely mentioned elsewhere in Fox's study. Are we to assume that drama in performance, on the stage rather than the page, was not a significant factor as a signifying medium in the period? Or that performance is so much like speech that it need not be mentioned as such? That it goes without saying?

In *The Marketplace of Print*, Alexandra Halasz recognizes early modern theatrical performance as a separate and distinct medium of signification. She concludes, however, that early modern theater in performance was unable to contribute to the making of a public, counterpublic, or public sphere. Enacted on an actual stage, popular amphitheater drama in early modern England functioned, as she writes, "as a kind of lightning rod in the emergence of the public sphere": in other words, it *diverted* social and discursive energy from that emergence, just as a lightning rod diverts electrical energy from a house in a storm. Only when a play becomes less present and differently public—when it reappears on what Halasz calls the "paper stage," in the form of a printed book—can drama give us access to public events or issues from within the private sphere: "Disseminated from the stage, discourse remains in public. Embodied in the commodity-book, discourse enters into private spaces, indeed helps define them as private, as places where one might have privileged access to public events without having to enter into public space."[38] There is more than a whiff of magical thinking here. A book on a shelf, its pages uncut, defines a certain kind of private space—but not yet, I would argue, a discursive space. "Discourse" enters the study only when the physical object is read, something that might take place soon after the purchase of the commodity-book but might also take place, for the first time, decades or even centuries later—if ever. Discourse is the active agent here, not the book as a physical object that can be bought and sold. An argument on the street, a sermon in the square, a royal proclamation read out loud—these are not sold, are not marketed as "commodities," but they are discursive entities nonetheless, capable of functioning as both partial cause and telling effect of the public sphere.

According to Habermas, earlier forms of theater had to be weaned away from "representation" before theater could participate in the public sphere—but it did eventually do just that. According to Halasz, a play in performance, regardless of its period or the presence or absence of a "fourth wall," can never so participate. Halasz assumes that it is only through the "commodification of discourse" that discursive media can contribute to any kind of public. In her understanding, a performance cannot be a commodity even when it is bought and sold. Commodities, according to this school of thought, are "things" in a physical, material, tangible sense: "The marketplace commodification of discourse requires the conversion of social practices—storytelling, preaching, the dissemination of 'news' or knowledge—into things available for purchase."[39] Sixteenth-century popular drama, it seems to me, was quite inventive in the ways it converted other social practices into something available for purchase—biographical narratives, fictional and historical modes of storytelling, various forms of knowledge disseminated in new and sometimes original forms, and, most importantly, in the conversion of such sources from one regime of literacy to another, from the highly restricted world of reading into the much more broadly accessible experience of performance. But a play in performance lacks "thingness" in Halasz's sense—"things available for purchase"—even though it has a market and has been made available to any and all who can pay the price of admission. A play cannot become a commodity *qua* performance, in her terms, even when theater adopts the proscenium stage and the "fourth wall" that were so important to Habermas. Halasz's exclusion, in other words, is absolute. A play must shed its performative nature entirely and reappear in print, on the "paper stage," before it can give us access to the virtual dimensions of a public sphere.

According to Marx, however, commodities are *social* things as well as physical or material things. Indeed, in terms of their value-form, they are networks of association. They are "social relations between things," as Marx writes in the first volume of *Capital*, and "material relations between persons."[40] They are not contained in or by their physical or material properties.[41] They are never identical to themselves in their material guise, even when they are accessible to analysis in that form. Discourse does not need to be commodified in order to contribute to the making of a public or counterpublic, but even if it did, early modern theatrical performance constituted an intense and extensive commodification of the discourses of its own and other historical times.

Halasz clearly thinks otherwise; hers is a more radical anti-theatricality than Habermas's. "Disseminated from the stage, discourse remains in public." The assumptions underlying Halasz's thinking are not unusual ones. Performance is effervescent; theatrical productions do not last; they cease to exist once the performance is over. For Halasz, a play in performance is rooted in the immediate present and has no subsequent history or itinerary; it cannot travel in time or space after the epilogue is delivered and thus, from her point of view, it cannot enter into the private or intimate spheres of the social. Books last, on the other hand, and are not left behind in the bookstall after we have purchased them.[42] They accompany us home, where they can redefine our private spaces and private and public spheres. Words on the page are lasting forms of distributed memory as well as signification; they can be reread, transported elsewhere, conveyed to future generations, and so forth. By contrast, performance has limited duration and no lasting memorial existence. It is inaccessible once it has been experienced; even if we accept it as a commodity form, it is one with no shelf life. It is a signifying medium, but its poor memory and lack of retention mean that it cannot help us to imagine alternative communities or counterpublics or bring them into historical actuality. Publics always historicize; performance, like orality, suffers from a kind of structural amnesia.[43] It remains in public and in the present, which it can only hypostasize as the past.

V

Clearly, we are dealing with different kinds of blindness to performance, different strains of twentieth-century antitheatricality, and different misapprehensions of the stage as a potential catalyst for the formation of publics, counterpublics, public spheres, or other kinds of collective identities and selves. I can only assume, given his general silence on theater, that Adam Fox would regard a play in performance as a hybrid form of oral media, which would mean that its participation in the public sphere might be limited but not impossible. Habermas and Halasz would both privilege the book and its role in fashioning "the subjectivity that was fit to print." But Habermas has a more capacious understanding of the commodity form. He recognizes that theatrical performance did eventually contribute to the ongoing maintenance, if not to the initial formation, of the bourgeois public sphere. It is a denatured form of theater, unfortunately, stemming from Habermas's deep misunderstanding of the semiotics and phenomenology of performance and the specifics of theater history. Nonetheless—and it is a significant qualification—in his discussion of the novel he provides an insightful if unwitting phenomenology of the affective and cognitive dimensions of performance, even if only at the level of metaphor. In the oscillation of virtual and actual social relations that Habermas describes, reading becomes a *performative* process. Its virtual dimensions are less embodied, however, than those of theatrical performance. Reading is a more abstracted form of performance, less immediate in its sociality and its spatiality than performance on stage.

A public is different from an audience and other forms of "focused gathering," as Erving Goffman described a group of individuals who have gathered in one place for a shared purpose or agenda.[44] A public is a form of social and collective association that functions as a kind of imagined community. It is necessarily larger than any given set of individuals. Unlike an audience (in the strict sense of the term) or a crowd, its virtual or ideational dimensions are crucial. When Peter Womack described common players "addressing an unstructured and freely assembled crowd—a *public*," he confused one form of social collectivity for another.[45] A public is always larger than its embodiments or present members, like any other kind of imagined community. A crowd is indeed unstructured, but this is precisely what distinguishes crowds from publics or audiences. A crowd is an "unfocused" gathering; an audience, a focused one; a public, an evocation or interpellation of a social body rather than (or in addition to) any specific gathering of actual bodies in one place. To revise Goffman, it is what we might call a "focused virtuality," one that is crucial to the formation and reformation of collective identities.[46]

Habermas recognizes two distinct kinds of theatrical public in the late eighteenth century, when theater finally began to contribute to the bourgeois public sphere. The first, which he explicitly identifies and calls a "theater-going public," does not involve theatrical performance per se; the second, which bears no name but is exemplified by the theater of Beaumarchais, involves an etiolated form of performance—that is to say, theater only after it has been tutored and reformed by the novel. Provisionally, I'll call these the institutional and the ideological. The first, the theater-going public, would be made up of those private individuals whose self-interpellated identities, as members of a class that includes a great many other like-minded theatergoers, was the force that created a "cultural" kind of imagined community, in the sense of "high" or aesthetic culture.[47] Such a public would exceed any given audience by definition, since it would necessarily include an indefinable number of posited or virtual individuals who might not be attending any given theatrical performance but were nonetheless included in this culturally—or aesthetically—determined form of imagined community.[48]

The second kind of theatrical public, which we might call the ideological or perspectival, has outlines that are more amorphous. It would be composed of those private individuals who, in response to some aspect, large or small, of a particular performance, align themselves with a particular cognitive and affective position, a perspective or point of view extrapolated into a collective or public identity capable of supporting and authorizing such an individual alignment. In this kind of theatrical public, the play—in performance—is the thing. The public in question would be made up of those private individuals whose self-interpellated identity, as members of a class that included all those who might share a similar response to a specific moment or aspect of the performance, fostered an ideologically determined kind of imagined community. An ideological or perspectival public has the potential to transform or expand the architectonic space of performance into what Paul Yachnin has called a "critical social space."[49] Included within that space might be most or all of those present in the audience, but in an extreme case it could include only a single member of the actual audience, a private individual whose alignment with a like-thinking public would be entirely virtual. An example might be someone who doesn't laugh when Malvolio is taunted, even though all those around her do, or someone who responds with ambivalence or distress rather than relief or joy when the duke makes his queasy proposal to Isabella at the end of *Measure for Measure*. From this kind of theatrical public, new kinds of cognitive and affective alliance, powerful and real despite—or rather, because of—their imagined nature, can develop. New modes of social, ideological, or political thinking can even emerge.

Theatrical performance is always a form of symbolic *action*, as Kenneth Burke would say, with both discursive and nondiscursive attributes. Contemporaries of Kyd and Marlowe and Shakespeare hardly needed to be reminded that theatrical performance could be a potent social force. Even dedicated advocates of the Reformation, enemies of the visual and the spectacular, could at times regard early modern theater as instrumental to their cause, capable of bringing the Protestant revolution on stage. As a symbolic action, early modern theater had the potential to reconfigure and transform subjectivities and collective identities. Or rather, it created the critical social space in which some members of the audience, as full participants in the production of the play, could locate a critical perspective on such reformations of the heart and head. Theatrical performance offered a way to bring alternative forms of civil society to mind, to reimagine community and, as a consequence, to crystallize new powers of critical, embodied social thought into historical actuality.

VI

Media have two aspects. From one perspective, they operate as signifying or semiotic technologies: as signs inscribed on papyrus or parchment or vellum, or printed and bound in a book, or sounded by a harpsichord or a voice, or differently recorded images and words in a film, on a memory stick, and in "the cloud." From another perspective, however, they operate as forms of publication. "Publication," in this sense, refers to a social event rather than a material object or singular technology. It is a way of making something public, that is to say, for purposes of communication and the creation of social networks that are populated by actors, things, and knowledges. An undue or exclusive emphasis on the technology of media can easily distort the role those technologies play as agents of social change. We haven't fully digested the implications of Harold Love's work on "scribal publication," I would suggest, if we fail to realize its implications for other media, especially the oral and the performative.[50] Scribal publication, the circulation of a manuscript as the final, public, and perfected form of the work rather than a draft in search of a printing press, differs from print publication in significant ways. Works that are scribally published establish different audiences and encourage or make possible different forms of association; they contribute, in other words, to the imagining (and hence the production) of different kinds of community, different kinds of collective identities, and different kinds of publics or counterpublics. Love was not merely juggling terms when he described the circulation of a work in manuscript as an act of *publication*: he was shifting our focus from the mechanics of media to the public and social roles that different media can play. "Publication" is a symbolic action in a comprehensive sense that includes, at the least, oral, inscriptive, visual, and performative forms. Publication is the process of making something public; it produces public forms of signification and knowledge and feeling. These are social things, we might say, that can convey, interpellate, induce, challenge, analyze, or diagnose differing social and ideological perspectives, different social emotions, different imaginations of community.

The affective and cognitive media that were most significant for the early modern period included discursive, nondiscursive, and mixed forms. They included affective and cognitive technologies such as the oral, the inscribed, and the performative, and they also included ritual, visual, and other forms of publication. Each medium creates a critical and affective social space of its own: a sphere of publication that is rarely if ever isolated or autonomous but rather overlays, merges with, and bleeds into other spheres of publication. Amphitheater drama might be figured:

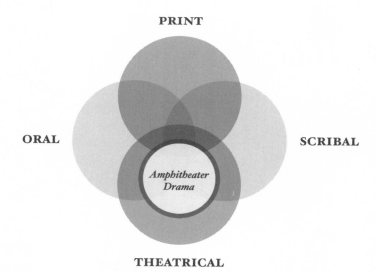

Spheres of early modern publication: the place of the amphitheater stage.

Any given genre of drama or any individual play will participate in a different ratio of these spheres of publication (my smaller figure quite approximately locates amphitheater drama). Likewise, other modes of public meaning—a sermon, a prose fiction, a lyric poem—will involve a hybrid conjuncture of different spheres of publication.[51] Each conjuncture locates itself in a different social and signifying space and thus requires a different combination of literacies.

Publication of the theatrical kind requires and develops in its audience a kind of literacy that is at once social and spatial, with a special affinity for the phenomenology of affective and cognitive space in its virtual as well as actual dimensions.[52] On stage, there are social relations and spaces that are represented, described, implied, or otherwise brought into virtual existence. In the playhouse, these represented or virtual relations and spaces are folded into the actual social relations and spaces inhabited by the audience. These are hybrid spaces, since they would include the actual, architectonic space of the theater as well as the social relations represented on stage: the relations actually and virtually established between character and audience and those between the actor and audience.[53]

What we see or hear in theater is precisely not what we get: an undue emphasis on what is presented, represented, or enacted would leave out the most important and heterogeneous components of the dramatic arts, namely ourselves. Theatrical performance vanishes in the instant of its flaring up before and within us, but this is also true of other modes of publication. The phenomenological experience of reading that Habermas describes so well is also a fleeting thing, unrepeatable and yet lasting and consequential, too. Like other forms of publication, theatrical publication shapes, induces, and disseminates knowledge as well as affect—and knowledge is not fully public if it is not remembered, circulated, and made capable of informing our private and public selves.

VII

Let us imagine, as a kind of corrective thought experiment—corrective to my own abstractions as well as our customary ways of thinking about theater as something strictly momentary or effervescent—let us imagine that the year is 1599 and we are in Elizabethan London. At a much-frequented bookstall, we buy a relatively new translation of Plutarch's *Lives*, realizing as we come across it that we know almost nothing about Roman history and would like to close that gap in our education. That same afternoon, we cross the Thames to Southwark to see the new play that has opened at the recently erected Globe. It is called *Julius Caesar* and is largely based on Plutarch, though we may or may not know this yet. The Globe is of course open to anyone who can pay the price of admission but the performance is fully accessible only to those who know how to give it attention and "prick up their ears," as Prospero says; the book, where the story of Caesar's assassination is also related, is available to anyone who has the price of purchase but not fully accessible to anyone who might buy it. We need different skills, different social, linguistic, spatial and other literacies, to get beyond the most significant threshold of either form of Roman history.

Press runs of books printed without patent were relatively small: 800 to 1,000 copies of a title would not be unusual.[54] Let's assume that every copy of the new Plutarch was sold and read immediately, in one and the same day. The scale of its synchronic dissemination would still pale in relation to what was regularly, even daily, achieved by early modern amphitheater drama. London amphitheaters seated from 2,500 to 3,000.[55] We have limited information about the number of performances that a relatively successful new play might enjoy, but we do know that the number of auditors and spectators at a single performance on a single afternoon could involve as many as three times the number of possible readers of the printed book. If we assume that an average performance played to an audience at half-capacity, as Erika T. Lin has suggested, "a single performance of a play in the theatre could [still] reach more people than the entire print run of that play as a book. . . . In terms of sheer exposure, the stage had far more influence than the page."[56]

In the actually existing world of print publication and commodity forms, it is more probable that none of the printed books were read, in whole or in part, on the same day as their purchase. There can be little doubt, however, that on any given afternoon a substantial percentage of the audience at the Globe heard and saw a significant portion, at least, of Shakespeare's play. They may have nodded off occasionally or let themselves be distracted by alluring glances or everyday worries, but they at least "skimmed" the performance. And a new audience, numbering in the thousands, did so the next day, and the next, for the duration of the run. Furthermore, there is no reason to suspect that leaving the theater after the performance caused some kind of collective amnesia. No one would remember the entire play, word for word, scene by scene—but in the case of a book, this is true as well. Only someone with a photographic memory could remember at such a comprehensive level. There would be gaps, seams, and inaccuracies in the memory of readers as well as theatergoers. And there would also be lots of new words, names, references, and so on, that had been consumed but not yet fully digested.

Early modern theater was not *merely* an enacted form of learning, of course, but it was also, in addition to its aesthetic and sociological roles, the occasion for a highly accessible and complex distribution of knowledge per se. The production of *Julius Caesar* would have injected a significant portion of Roman history, with its attendant republican debates—quite relevant to the late sixteenth century—into the hearts and minds of its audience, including all those who could not read and thus had no access to Plutarch's *Lives* in written or printed form. Furthermore, the play in performance was fully available to those individuals, since the literacies they did possess—social, spatial, oral, and so forth—were finely attuned to the public and performative culture they inhabited.[57] By the end of the performance, the individual and collective memories of our imagined audience would have grown deeper roots than before. That audience would have acquired a more complex and branching purchase on the historical past. And their affective and cognitive experiences would have accompanied them home or to the tavern, where they would continue to grow and develop, sometimes in face-to-face conversation or debate, sometimes in a virtual sense, as memories often do.

The printed or written word has a greater reach, of course, geographically as well as diachronically; its memory is distributed across the page as well as in the consciousness of the reader, which allows it to survive from one generation to the next and enjoy a multiplicity of readings and readers over time and space. However, we moderns and postmoderns, entranced by the powers of print and digital media, tend to regard theater as if it were strictly local in its effects as well as its conditions of possibility. We tend to underestimate how quickly and how far social things can pass from person to person, whether by word of mouth or breath or touch. When the audience of a video on YouTube expands at an exponential rate, we say that the video has "gone viral." No one can deny that modern media disseminate images and ideas efficiently and on a scale that is unprecedented. But "going viral" on YouTube is a metaphor, of course. It evokes other things that also spread at surprising rates and conquer great distances. The potency of the metaphor, in fact, lies in ancient as well as modern human catastrophes of biology. A virus that infects bodies has to travel by proximate means. Sometimes it is communicated by the passing of a breath from one person to another, sometimes by the touch of bodies or the intermixing of plasmas, but literal viruses and other virulent diseases can nonetheless travel quite efficiently in space and time, as we know from the history of medieval plagues, early modern syphilis, the Spanish flu of the early twentieth century, and the human immunodeficiency virus that is still killing large numbers of people in the twenty-first.

Theater is well woven into the fabric of a great many different societies. Many peoples have found it useful as a kind of social thought as well as an aesthetic pleasure, and even, as I have proposed here, as a much-needed if not necessary means to engage unsettling ruptures in the social imaginary and fundamental structures of feeling. It has served as one of the social tools available to Western cultures when they want to think about how they feel, or feel about what they think, and to do so in actual, experiential, and felt spaces as well as virtual or imagined worlds.[58] This seems to have been especially the case in a period like the early modern, when theater could still be part rival, part complement or ally, part alternative to other forms of publication like script and print and proclamation. All of these were important and consequential ways of making something public. All of them played significant roles in the structures of thought and feeling that made up the Elizabethan social imaginary, the publics and counterpublics that informed it, and were consequently, recursively, informed by it.

Epilogue

A relatively bare stage, a graveyard. A thing in hand but it too is doubled, at once a prop and an actual human skull, the one belonging to a dead man named Yorick and the other to a different man or woman, also dead but in a fashion that allows him or her to become the forgotten and unwitting donor of the skull used at the Globe c. 1600 in a play called *Hamlet*. The living body on stage, the actor personating Hamlet the Dane, occupies the same space, insofar as we can see, as the living body in the graveyard: two identities in one corporeality, two voices, two gestures, two grisly yet consoling and darkly comic moments of recognition and "earning."

"Alas, poor Yorick. I knew him, Horatio." It is an iconic moment in Elizabethan popular performance, of course—so familiar as to be a bit awkward to highlight or recall, so fully distributed and assimilated in so many cultures that it can seem, in its always and already inevitability, as if it has never truly been encountered for the first time.[1] It is a *memento mori*, of course, but so were all the anonymous bones strewn about the stage immediately before this moment in 5.1. Yorick's skull prompts a deeper, more resonant oscillation between the thing (or things) in the hand and the person (Yorick) who is trapped in the double-bind of Hamlet's heart and mind. He is reduced to a foul-smelling skull; he is nonetheless and also the childhood playmate and court jester who would give thrilling piggyback rides, until he died and went away. We learn that Hamlet was seven years old when Yorick left him, at the breeching age, as if the passage into the gendered world of men and women was also the point in time when his often-absent father could no longer be performed by a lively, jesting surrogate. His actual father left many times before his death, as fathers and kings often do. Hamlet the Elder couldn't even attend his own son's birth or play with the newborn infant prince: he was on the sledded ice killing Old Norway in battle while Gertrude was giving birth. Can we imagine Yorick supporting the head of the infant prince, kissing his lips we know not how oft, practicing the gibes and gambols that will soon make Hamlet laugh? Hamlet occupies Yorick's place and takes on his role in the scene, after all. He mocks the skull's own grinning, performing what it can no longer do. He exacerbates his own revulsion at it, this materiality of the dead, but then incorporates him, the living memory of Yorick, into his own body and feelings. This is a more dynamic moment of embodied thought than the shattered *mementi mori* scattered all around the stage. It is a brief, enacted, and successful act of mourning, an otherwise missing objective correlative to Hamlet's unresolved grief over his father's death.[2]

"[We] make the world smart," according to Andy Clark, "so that we can be dumb."[3] There is a truth in Clark's apothegm and there is also a lie, or rather, not so much a lie as a sleight of hand, a misdirection of attention worthy a magician. It isn't really "smart" and "dumb" he's concerned with, but "we." He is reminding us that our intelligence and feeling are not and never have been bound up in a skull, a heart, an ego or an id. We distribute ourselves in others: in other subjects as well as other objects, even in other subjects *as* objects in and of themselves, so that our limited and bounded individual selves don't have to do all the work of living, thinking, and feeling on their own.[4]

Clark gives colloquial and ironic expression to an issue that has bedeviled the philosophy of mind—thinking about how we think—at least since Plato. In the *Phaedrus*, Socrates puts forward a less ironic and more cautionary version of Clark's cognitive ecology when he retells the mythic invention of writing by Thoth, the Egyptian deity who presented written language as a gift to Thamus, the Egyptian king.[5] The point of the story is that writing, which promises to extend and enhance our memories, will in truth diminish our capacities for recollection. Writing will serve, not as the useful *aide-mémoire* it claims to be, but as its opposite, an *aide-amnésie*. It will be a poison for memory "rather than" a cure for forgetfulness—even though the remedy and the poison, in Plato's language, reside in the same thing, the same word, the *pharmakon*.[6]

Plato's cautionary tale makes the mistake of assuming that before writing, memory (and thought and feeling) took place more naturally, more natively and internally and entirely within "the boundaries of skull and flesh."[7] Cognitive ecologists would beg to disagree. And so, implicitly when not explicitly, would Elizabethan audiences attending a performance of *Hamlet* or any other Elizabethan play. Writing is only one the ways in which we use, and only one of the ways we have always used, the world around us—the world of things, persons, places, and experiences—in order to think and feel and remember. We think, feel, and remember *with* the world—by means of it, as a tool for living, and in tandem with it, alongside of it—as individual and collective selves, as part of a larger "*individual*" network of things, persons, places, and experiences.

In cognitive ecology, "mind" is understood as a kind of collaboration with the world; our cognitive and affective processes are recognized as social productions. In early modern studies, John Sutton and Evelyn Tribble have, individually and jointly, done much to establish the relevance of cognitive ecology to the literary and theatrical practices of sixteenth- and seventeenth-century England. "Cognitive ecology" combines the concept of "extended mind," which first developed in the philosophy of cognitive science, and the distinct but complementary concept of "distributed cognition," which first developed in cognitive anthropology. As Sutton and Tribble explain,

These models share an anti-individualist approach to cognition. In all these views, mental activities spread or smear across the boundaries of skull and skin to include parts of the social and material world. In remembering, decision making, and acting, whether individually or in small groups, our complex and structured activities involve many distinctive dimensions: neural, affective, kinesthetic, sensory, interpersonal, historical, political, cultural, technological; indeed, each dimension in this necessarily partial list is itself wildly heterogeneous. Many cognitive states and processes are hybrids, unevenly distributed across the physical, social, and cultural environments as well as bodies and brains, hooking up in both temporary and more enduring ways with other people and with certain things—artifacts, media, technologies, or institutions—each with its own history and tendencies. . . . Thought is distributed across insides (internal mechanisms constraining attention, perception, and memory); objects (artifacts and environments); and people (social systems). . . . The integrative label "cognitive ecology" particularly highlights the point that disparate but tightly interconnected elements within any such culturally specific setting operate in a complementary balance that shifts over time.[8]

Long before the invention of writing, material objects and specific places in the world served a similar function. They have enabled us to remember and lay to rest, in recoverable and returnable form, some of the most crucial aspects of our lived and felt history. Simonides could return the loved ones of the community to their families, but it was not because he had a photographic memory. Rather, he had the necessary literacy to be able to read a ruined banqueting hall: a spatial memory and the capacity to walk through the stones and the carnage of the dead to discover a topography of individual and collective mourning. He recovered the dead by consulting their distributed memories in the places they occupied. These places were the common places of felt knowledge: the *topoi* of grief that he alone could remember, decipher, and produce or perform.[9]

But we don't need Roman or Greek or Egyptian myth to illustrate the ways in which feeling and memory are regularly embodied, embedded, and distributed in the world around us.

As I have argued, the Protestant Reformation sought to sever, redefine, and reconfigure the affective ties that bound the living to the affective landscapes they inhabited. Structures of feeling were more resilient than radical reformers expected but they were nonetheless affected, sometimes profoundly, by the many radical efforts to sever historical, ideological, cognitive, and affective bonds. Evidence can be found in the language of selves and subjects as it changes in the course of the Reformation and Counter-Reformation. An *individuum* began to metamorphose into an individual, to cite once again one of the more startling and more substantive examples. The "modern individual" does not so much emerge into history as fall out of it, precipitated from a structure of feelings that had previously resolved the individual in the *individuum*. The "invention of the human" or the autonomous subject has always been a curious thing to celebrate as the mark of modernity within the early modern period, since the one can be found—invented in the less boastful meaning of the word—so readily in Homer, Plato, Sappho, Sophocles, Virgil, Augustine, Dante, and so on. The other, the notion of the "autonomous subject," is such an overt contradiction in terms that it records, as a phrase, another memory lapse. A subject is by definition *subjected* to the power or rule of another or—in a less hierarchical form—to a relation with another. The modern myth of the autonomy and unconstrained agency of the subject tells us more about modern and postmodern cultural performances— the stories we tell to ourselves, for ourselves—than it does about something that happened or hatched in the period of the Reformation in Europe.

Early modern theater was also way of thinking through things, one that didn't flinch at the dislocations or chop-fallen jowls of the past or present, any more than Hamlet does in the graveyard. It was a way of apprehending the disjunctions and abjections of its own climacteric present, sometimes by holding the mirror up to nature so that its audience might recognize and experience its own alienation effects: in the misrecognitions of Richard III, or the "surprising effects of sympathy" in moments of affective irony, or the oscillations between actual and virtual dimensions on stage, so resonant and dissonant with the audience off stage.[10] Whether we call it performance, production, or theatrical publication, the entire theatrical apparatus of early modern amphitheater drama was a dynamic and experimental form of distributed affect and cognition. It was more or less public, more or less private; more or less collective and more or less individual; more or less lodged in the architectonic structures of the amphitheater, and more or less lodged in the structures of feeling that comprised the broken ecologies of early modern hearts, heads, and worlds. Elizabethan amphitheater drama was a dissonant as well as a resonant form of cultural performance. In performance, it became a space for critical social thought as well as a space for sensual and aesthetic pleasures. Like the bones of the dead, it was a device that allowed counterhistories as well as histories to be experienced and embodied—a place to discover what it felt like, to be an Elizabethan.

Notes

PROLOGUE

1. John Stow, *A Survay of London* (1603), ed. C. L. Kingsford (Oxford: Clarendon Press, 1908), 330.

2. Henry Hart Milman, *Annals of S. Paul's Cathedral* (London: J. Murray, 1869), 156.

3. Natalie Zemon Davis, "Ghosts, Kin, and Progeny: Some Features of Family Life in Early Modern France," *Daedalus* 106, no. 2 (1977): 92.

4. Peter Marshall, *Beliefs and the Dead in Reformation England* (Oxford: Oxford University Press, 2002), 41.

5. Charnel practices varied a great deal throughout Europe, ranging from the in-mixing practices of the English to more discreet practices in countries like Spain and Italy, where separate shelves and compartments were reserved by and for specific families. See Vanessa Harding, *The Dead and the Living in Paris and London, 1500–1670* (Cambridge: Cambridge University Press, 2002) and Jeanine Curvers, "Burial Rituals and the Reformations in Early Modern Europe: A Comparative Study," MA Thesis, Utrecht University, 2010, http://igitur-archive.library.uu.nl/student-theses/2011-0221-200310/thesis.pdf (accessed November 3, 2012).

6. For Eamon Duffy's account of medieval burial practices, their cultural logic, and the logic of their disruption by reformers, see *The Stripping of the Altars: Traditional Religion in England, 1400–1580* (New Haven, CT: Yale University Press, 2005). For a recent and equally magisterial study of the affective landscapes of early modern communities,

see Alexandra Walsham, *The Reformation of the Landscape: Religion, Identity, and Memory in Early Modern Britain and Ireland* (Oxford: Oxford University Press, 2011). Philip Schwyzer combines the disciplines of literary studies and archaeology in an excellent book, *Archaeologies of Renaissance Literature* (Oxford: Oxford University Press, 2007). He discusses the evacuation of St. Paul's ossuary in chapter 4, "Charnel Knowledge."

7. The London population was around 40,000 for much of the late medieval period, with death and birth rates canceling one another out. Assuming a generation of twenty years, this means that 800,000 Londoners died in the city as a whole between 1100 and 1500. What percentage of these were buried at St. Paul's requires statistical-probability analysis that lies beyond this author's competence—and also lies beyond the general point being established here, namely that it was a considerable number.

8. Joseph Roach, *Cities of the Dead: Circum-Atlantic Performance* (New York: Columbia University Press, 1996).

9. Keith Thomas, *Religion and the Decline of Magic: Studies in Popular Beliefs in Sixteenth- and Seventeenth-Century England* (New York: Scribner's, 1971), 603.

10. Charnel clearances occurred in other parts of England, but these were scattered and form no pattern or progression.

11. D. J. Gordon, *The Renaissance Imagination: Essays and Lectures*, ed. Stephen Orgel (Berkeley: University of California Press, 1975), 18. The analogy of image and word to body and soul was a common but complex poetic figure in early modern theories of the emblem. See *Emblematica* 12 (2002) for a collection of essays devoted to it. For other work on such "reading," see Michael Bath, *Speaking Pictures: English Emblem Books and Renaissance Culture* (London: Longman, 1984); Daniel Russell, "The Emblem and Authority," *Word and Image: A Journal of Verbal/Visual Enquiry* 4 (1988): 81–87; Peter M. Daly, *The English Emblem and the Continental Tradition* (New York: AMS, 1988); Huston Diehl, "Graven Images: Protestant Emblem Books in England," *Renaissance Quarterly* 39 (1986): 49–66. For a discussion of the emblem as a form of Renaissance hypermedia, see Álvaro Llosa Sanz, "Shifting Our Vision: Reading Early Modern Emblems in the 21st Century" *eHumanista* 18 (2011): 385–91.

12. On the geopolitical significance of the extramural location of the playhouses, see Steven Mullaney, *The Place of the Stage: License, Play, and*

Power in Renaissance England (Chicago: University of Chicago Press, 1988; rpt. Ann Arbor: University of Michigan Press, 1995).

13. Jean-Pierre Vernant, "The Historical Moment of Tragedy in Greece: Some of the Social and Psychological Conditions," in *Myth and Tragedy in Ancient Greece*, ed. Jean-Pierre Vernant and Pierre Vidal-Naquet, trans. Janet Lloyd (New York: Zone, 1988), 27.

INTRODUCTION

1. Throughout *Emotions*, I will reserve the capitalized term for matters of the soul ("Reformation") and use lowercase for matters of the heart ("reformation"). The distinction is largely heuristic. Religious, social, and cultural aspects of the period form a matrix of changes rather than a set of separate or easily separable fields.

2. Raymond Williams, *Marxism and Literature* (Oxford: Oxford University Press, 1977), esp. 133–34. The concept and phrase appear frequently in his other writings and publications, including his extensive interviews with *New Left Review*. See Williams, *Politics and Letters: Interviews with New Left Review* (London: New Left Books, 1979). On "emotional communities," see Barbara Rosenwein, *Emotional Communities in the Early Middle Ages* (Ithaca, NY: Cornell University Press, 2007).

3. For the "rites of violence" in France in the 1560s, see Natalie Zemon Davis, *Society and Culture in Early Modern France: Eight Essays* (Stanford, CA: Stanford University Press, 1975), 152–88. I do not mean to suggest that England was free of popular or official forms of violence that were directed against persons as well as things (iconoclasm), but to note the well-recognized but difficult-to-explain differences in the scale of such violence from one region of Europe to another. Burning a Protestant at the stake as a heretic, arguably one of the most extreme types of deadly violence that occurred in England, was undoubtedly a traumatic event for family, community, and even those who read or heard about it. However, such events numbered in the hundreds rather than the tens of thousands, which is the number of Huguenot deaths estimated to have occurred in France in the 1560s.

Also important is the fact that the burning of a condemned heretic, however barbarous it might be to us—and to some of "them," sixteenth-century English men and women and children—was a legal and officially mandated act of violence, the enactment of a sentence that had been decided by both ecclesiastical and secular courts. This would not necessarily make it less traumatic, however, and could in fact heighten the trauma, since it would leave no recourse or appeal to a court of law. I owe this reflection to an insightful anonymous reader for The University of Chicago Press.

4. See A. G. Dickens, *The English Reformation* (London: B. T. Batsford, 1964). The evolution of opinion can be traced in works such as J. J. Scarisbrick, *The Reformation and the English People* (Oxford: Blackwell, 1984); Duffy, *Stripping of the Altars*; Christopher Haigh, *English Reformations: Religion, Politics, and Society under the Tudors* (Oxford: Clarendon Press, 1993); Patrick Collinson, *The Birthpangs of Protestant England: Religious and Cultural Change in the Sixteenth and Seventeenth Centuries* (Basingstoke: Macmillan, 1988) and also (among many of Collinson's relevant studies), *The Reformation: A History* (New York: The Modern Library, 2003). For a collection of essays that extend the period of the Reformation well beyond the sixteenth century, see Nicholas Tyacke, ed., *England's Long Reformation, 1500–1800* (London: University College of London Press, 1998). A number of literary studies have recovered the significant contributions of Elizabethan Catholics to the sixteenth-century flourishing of poetry and other imaginative forms over the past twenty years. See especially Ronald Corthell, Frances E. Dolan, Christopher Highley, and Arthur F. Marotti, eds., *Catholic Culture in Early Modern England* (Notre Dame, IN: University of Notre Dame Press, 2007).

5. In addition to Marshall, *Beliefs and the Dead in Reformation England*, see Peter Lake and Michael C. Questier, *The Anti-Christ's Lewd Hat: Protestants, Papists and Players in Post-Reformation England* (New Haven, CT: Yale University Press, 2002); Peter Lake and Steven C. A. Pincus, *The Politics of the Public Sphere in Early Modern England* (New York: Manchester University Press, 2007); Duffy, *Stripping of the Altars*; Collinson, *Birthpangs of Protestant England*.

For literary criticism, see Peter Cunich, "The Ex-Religious in Post-Dissolution Society: Symptoms of Post-Traumatic Stress Disorder?" in *The Religious Orders in Pre-Reformation England*, ed. James G. Clark (Woodbridge: Boydell, 2002), 227–38; Thomas Page Anderson, *Performing Early Modern Trauma from Shakespeare to Milton* (Aldershot: Ashgate, 2006); Scott Lucas, "Coping with Providentialism: Trauma, Identity, and the Failure of the English Reformation," in *Images of Matter: Essays on British Literature of the Middle Ages and Renaissance*, ed. Yvonne Bruce (Newark: University of Delaware Press, 2005), 255–73.

6. Marshall, *Beliefs and the Dead in Reformation England*, 4.

7. Alan Sinfield introduced the metaphor to contemporary discussions of Reformation England in *Faultlines: Cultural Materialism and the Politics of Dissident Reading* (Oxford: Clarendon Press, 1992). The emphasis in Sinfield's use of the term falls most strongly on ideological faultlines, which Marshall includes but is less centrally focused on. See below for a further discussion of Sinfield's use and the lasting influence of cultural materialism on early modern studies in general.

8. It is impossible to be specific about what does and doesn't constitute a state religion, given the fluctuations of official policy and practice during Henry VIII's reign—hence my circumlocution, "no fewer than." In my rough tally, I include Henrician Catholicism (after the break from Rome), Henrician Protestantism (with its many counter-reformations), Edwardian Protestantism, Marian Catholicism, and Elizabethan Protestantism. I do not count the preceding era of Roman Catholicism due to the fact that it was not a state religion.

9. Roger Williams, *Christenings Make Not Christians . . .* (London, 1645), 11–12.

10. On self as well as family divisions, conversions and counter-conversions, John Reynolds's conversion to Protestantism captures some of the sincere but topsy-turvy changes of faith that were experienced in the period. In a formal, face-to-face debate with his brother William on the respective merits their clashing faiths, John's defense of Catholicism was so persuasive that William, a Protestant when their debate started, converted on the spot. The family balance of faiths was preserved, however, since John was so impressed with his brother's presentation of Protestantism that he, too, converted—to his brother's now-abandoned faith. See Molly Murray, *The Poetics of Conversion in Early Modern Literature: Verse and Change from Donne to Dryden* (Cambridge: Cambridge University Press, 2009), 46–47, and Michael Questier, *Conversion, Politics, and Religion in England, 1580–1625* (Cambridge: Cambridge University Press, 1996), 95.

11. For a moving account of such an experience, see Peter Stallybrass, "Marx's Coat," in *Border Fetishisms: Material Objects in Unstable Spaces*, ed. Patricia Spyer (London: Routledge, 1998), 183–207. See also Ann Rosalind Jones and Peter Stallybrass, *Renaissance Clothing and the Materials of Memory* (Cambridge: Cambridge University Press, 2000), for an in-depth examination of clothing as a form of material and generational memory.

12. I have in mind a relation of place, space, and community that encompasses secular as well as devotional or magical relations, and that are as much a part of postmodern daily life as they were in ancient Greece or Elizabethan London. For a study of Reformation environments in particular, see Walsham, *Reformation of the Landscape*, and Kristen Poole, *Supernatural Environments: Spaces of Demonism, Divinity, and Drama* (Cambridge: Cambridge University Press, 2011). For a study of the symbolic and memorial topography of early modern London and its relationship to the emergence of amphitheater drama, see Mullaney, *Place of the Stage*.

13. J. Weever, *Ancient Funerall Monuments* (1631), 50–51, cited in Marshall, *Beliefs and the Dead in Reformation England*, 93.

14. Cicero recounts the story of Simonides in *De Oratore*; for its most notable and influential modern retelling, see Frances Yates, *The Art of Memory* (London: Routledge and Kegan Paul, 1966), 1–2. For Jacques Derrida's meditation on mourning, memory, and haunting—what he calls a "hauntology"—see *Specters of Marx: The State of the Debt, the Work of Mourning, and the New International* (New York: Routledge, 2006). Derrida examines *Hamlet* as well as Marx, and his ongoing remarks on the play reflect some of the issues of memory, forgetting, place, and historical consciousness that I explore in this book. For example, see page 9:

> First of all, mourning. We will be speaking of nothing else. It consists always in attempting to ontologize remains, to make them present, in the first place by *identifying* the bodily remains and by *localizing* the dead (all ontologization, all semanticization, philosophical, hermeneutical, or psychoanalytic—finds itself caught up in this work of mourning but, as such, it does not yet think it; we are posing the question of the specter, to the specter, whether it be Hamlet's or Marx's, on this near side of such thinking).

Also relevant would be Derrida's *Archive Fever: A Freudian Perspective* (Chicago: University of Chicago Press, 1996).

15. For an insightful study of the psychology of iconoclasm, see Margaret Aston, *England's Iconoclasts: Laws against Images* (Oxford: Clarendon Press, 2003). For nondoctrinal parallels, David Cressy has suggested the term "secular iconoclasms." See "Different Kinds of Speaking: Symbolic Violence and Secular Iconoclasm in Early Modern

England," in *Protestant Identities: Religion, Society, and Self-Fashioning in Post-Reformation England*, ed. Muriel McClendon, Joseph Ward, and Michael MacDonald (Stanford, CA: Stanford University Press, 2000), 19–42.

Elizabeth Williamson provides an excellent study of the relationship between structures of feeling, objects of devotion, and their migration to the stage as props in *The Materiality of Religion in Early Modern Drama* (Farnham, Surrey, England: Ashgate, 2009). Williamson's emphasis is on the "paradox of dematerialized devotion" (149ff.); for an illuminating counterargument, see Jennifer Waldron's recent study of the persistence of the material object and body in *Reformations of the Body: Idolatry, Sacrifice, and Early Modern Theater* (New York: Palgrave Macmillan, 2013).

16. See also Harding, *The Dead and the Living in Paris and London*, 64.

17. Michel Foucault, "Nietzsche, Genealogy, History," in *The Foucault Reader*, ed. Paul Rabinow (New York: Pantheon, 1984), 76–100; Marshall, *Beliefs and the Dead in Reformation England*, 100.

18. For relevant studies see David M. Loades, "Rites of Passage and the Prayer Books of 1549 and 1552," *Studies in Church History* 10 (1994): 205–15; Haigh, *Reformations*, 179; Matthew Milner, *The Senses and the English Reformation* (Farnham, Surrey, England: Ashgate, 2011); Duffy, *Stripping of the Altars*, 475.

19. Marshall, *Beliefs and the Dead in Reformation England*, 100, 123.

20. Patrick Collinson, *Elizabethans* (New York: Hambledon and London, 2003), 219.

21. William Binkes, quoted in F. G. Emmison, *Elizabethan Life: Disorder* (Chelmsford, England: Essex County Council, 1970), 46.

22. The plurality was first introduced by Haigh, *Reformations*.

23. For the contrast with Protestant Amsterdam, where religious tolerance was complex but also official and explicit, see Steven Mullaney, Angela Vanhaelen, and Joseph Ward, "Religion Inside Out: Dutch House Churches and the Making of Publics in the Dutch Republic," in *Making Publics in Early Modern Europe: People, Things, Forms of Knowledge*, ed. Bronwen Wilson and Paul Yachnin (New York: Routledge, 2010), 25–36. For intraprotestant divisions in early modern England at the parish level, see Christopher Haigh, *The Plain Man's Pathways to Heaven: Kinds of Christianity in Post-Reformation England, 1570–1640* (Oxford: Oxford University Press, 2007).

24. The instabilities of religious conversion in early modern England have received a great deal of attention in recent years. See especially Questier, *Conversion, Politics, and Religion in England*; Alexandra Walsham, *Church Papists: Catholicism, Conformity and Confessional Polemic in Early Modern England* (Woodbridge, UK: Boydell Press, 1999); Lake and Questier, *Anti-Christ's Lewd Hat*; Brian Cummings, *The Literary Culture of the Reformation: Grammar and Grace* (Oxford: Oxford University Press, 2002); Peter Marshall, *Religious Identities in Henry VIII's England* (London: Ashgate, 2006); Murray, *Poetics of Conversion in Early Modern Literature*.

25. What follows is my own formulation, but the idea of a "collective self" is not at all foreign to contemporary psychology. For an overview of scholarship on the social aspects of the self, see Constantine Sedikides and Marilynn B. Brewer, eds., *Individual Self, Relational Self, Collective Self* (Philadelphia: Psychology Press, 2001).

26. Sinfield, *Faultlines*.

27. Anthony Milton points out that moderate Calvinists like Joseph Hall and Thomas Morton, while "identifying the Pope as Antichrist and the Church of Rome as Babylon, allowed that the Church of Rome might still be a true church [and] . . . that her members might even owe her some obedience, and might yet attain salvation (according to certain carefully defined conditions) with her communion." See Anthony Milton, *Catholic and Reformed: The Roman and Protestant Churches in English Protestant Thought, 1600–1640* (Cambridge: Cambridge University Press, 2002), 106.

28. Cited in Norman Jones, *The English Reformation: Religion and Cultural Adaptation* (Oxford: Blackwell, 2002), 24–25.

29. Ibid., 25.

30. I borrow A. P. Rossiter's wonderful phrase for Shakespeare's capacity for mutually exclusive perspectives; see *Angel with Horns: Fifteen Lectures on Shakespeare*, ed. Graham Storey (London: Longman, 1989), xviii, 51.

31. For a reading of such strains in the play, see Stephen Greenblatt, *Hamlet in Purgatory* (Princeton, NJ: Princeton University Press, 2001).

32. *Hamlet* is not the only example of a play that takes advantage of theater's capacity, in violation of Newtonian physics, to allow two bodies to inhabit the same space at the same time. I discuss Kyd's *The Spanish Tragedy* in analogous terms in the following chapter.

33. Clifford Geertz, "The Growth of Culture and the Evolution of Mind," in *The Interpretation of Cultures* (New York: Basic Books, 1973), 81–82.

34. Edmund Leach, "Poetics of Power," *New Republic* 184, no. 4 (1981): 32.

35. John Leavitt, "Meaning and Feeling in the Anthropology of Emotions," *American Ethnologist* 23, no. 3 (1996): 517.

36. For the concept of the "betwixt and between," see Victor W. Turner, *The Forest of Symbols: Aspects of Ndembu Ritual* (Ithaca, NY: Cornell University Press 1967), 93–111.

37. Charles Darwin, *The Expression of the Emotions in Man and Animals*, intro. and commentary by Paul Ekman (Oxford: Oxford University Press, 1998), 212.

38. I owe this maxim to Peter Holland, who used it to marvelous effect in an SAA talk in 2010. Holland, however, attributed it to Stefan Collini, who used it without attribution in a 1989 article (rpt. in his *What Are Universities For?* [New York: Penguin, 2012], 20). Others have found earlier, mid-twentieth century examples, but no confirmed source or original use. Its Einsteinian origins are often mentioned but have never, to my knowledge, been verified. *Se non è vero, è ben trovato.*

39. The phrase psychological materialism comes from Gail Kern Paster, *Humoring the Body: Emotions and the Shakespearean Stage* (Chicago: University of Chicago Press, 2004), 12. See also Paster, Rowe, and Floyd-Wilson, eds., *Reading the Early Modern Passions*, and Paster, *The Body Embarrassed: Drama and the Disciplines of Shame in Early Modern England* (Ithaca, NY: Cornell University Press, 1993); Michael Schoenfeldt, *Bodies and Selves in Early Modern England: Physiology and Inwardness in Spenser, Shakespeare, Herbert, and Milton* (Cambridge: Cambridge University Press, 1999); Mary Floyd-Wilson, *English Ethnicity and Race in Early Modern Drama* (Cambridge: Cambridge University Press, 2003); and Douglas Trevor, *The Poetics of Melancholy in Early Modern England* (Cambridge: Cambridge University Press, 2004). Predating this work and a resource for much of it is Michael MacDonald, *Mystical Bedlam: Madness, Anxiety, and Healing in Seventeenth-Century England* (Cambridge: Cambridge University Press, 1981).

40. Of course, the etiology that humoral thought most directly explained was concerned with temperament rather than emotion. Humoral balance or imbalance is hard to change or correct, as early mod-

ern doctors recognized. Humors flowed and fluxed within the body, as contemporary humoral theorists emphasize, but their most pronounced clinical effects—temperament, various forms of illness—were relatively fixed and resistant to change. For a related critique of humoralism as a phenomenology of emotion, see Richard Strier's comments in Richard Strier and Carla Mazzio, "Two Responses to 'Shakespeare and Embodiment: An E-Conversation,'" *Literature Compass* 3 (2005): 15–31.

41. Under the pressure of what is sometimes called a "new materialism," there has been a marked tendency to pit the social and the material against one another, which often results in a strictly physiological understanding of the materiality of emotions. For example, earlier and groundbreaking work on literature, history, and emotions by scholars such as Adela Pinch and Julie Ellison is faulted in *Reading the Early Modern Passions: Essays in the Cultural History of Emotion*, ed. Gail Kern Paster, Katherine Rowe, and Mary Floyd-Wilson (Philadelphia: University of Pennsylvania Press, 2004) for being more social than material in its understanding of the passions or emotions. See p. 300 n. 81, where the relevance of such approaches to a "materialist psychology" is challenged due to their "transpersonal" and "transactional" use of terms, "in a social rather than material register." See Julie Ellison, *Cato's Tears and the Making of Anglo-American Emotion* (Chicago: University of Chicago Press, 1999), and Adela Pinch, *Strange Fits of Passion: Epistemologies of Emotion, Hume to Austen* (Stanford: Stanford University Press, 1999).

42. Michelle Z. Rosaldo, "Toward an Anthropology of Self and Feeling," in *Culture Theory: Essays on Mind, Self, and Emotion*, ed. Richard Shweder and Robert Levine (Cambridge: Cambridge University Press, 1984), 137–57. "Substances to be discovered in the blood" would include, I assume, the humors and spirits of Galenic medicine.

43. Modern scholarship on cardinal emotions extends at least as far back as Darwin's *Expression of Emotions* and continues through William James, *The Varieties of Religious Experience: A Study in Human Nature* (New York: Modern Library, 1902), and Paul Ekman.

44. Shlomo Hareli and Brian Parkinson, "What's Social about Social Emotions?" *Journal for the Theory of Social Behaviour* 38, no. 2 (2008): 190.

45. For a discussion of the social implications of "we" and an ethical defense of its use, see Stanley Cavell, "The Avoidance of Love," in *Must We Mean What We Say?* (Cambridge: Cambridge University Press, 2002), 167–353.

46. James Joyce, *Ulysses* (New York: Penguin, 1980), 31.

47. Milton Singer, "The Cultural Pattern of Indian Civilization: A Preliminary Report of a Methodological Field Study," *Far Eastern Quarterly* 15 (1953): 27. Clifford Geertz expands on the concept in *The Interpretation of Cultures* (New York: Basic Books, 1973), 113, and in "Blurred Genres: The Refiguration of Social Thought," *American Scholar* 49 (1980): 167. For an earlier formulation of this key concept, see Mullaney, *Place of the Stage*, passim. Huston Diehl provides an eloquent description in *Staging Reform, Reforming the Stage: Protestantism and Popular Theater in Early Modern England* (Ithaca, NY: Cornell University Press, 1997), 97–98.

48. See Steven Mullaney, "Affective Technologies: Toward an Emotional Logic of the Elizabethan Stage," in *Environment and Embodiment in Early Modern England*, ed. Mary Floyd-Wilson and Garrett Sullivan (Basingstoke: Palgrave Macmillan, 2007): 71–89.

49. Kenneth Burke, "Literature as Equipment for Living," in *The Philosophy of Literary Form*, 3rd ed. rev. (1941; Berkeley: University of California Press, 1971), 293–304.

50. Michael Macdonald, "The Fearefull Estate of Francis Spira: Narrative, Identity, and Emotion in Early Modern England," *Journal of British Studies* 31 (1992): 32–61. For another account, see John Stachniewski, *The Persecutory Imagination: English Puritanism and the Literature of Religious Despair* (New York: Oxford University Press, 1991), 37ff.

51. Macdonald, "The Fearefull Estate of Francis Spira."

52. John Foxe, *Acts and Monuments*, 4 vols. (1563, 1570, 1576, 1583), *The Unabridged Acts and Monuments Online* (Sheffield: HRI Online Publications, 2011). Available from http//www.johnfoxe.org; accessed April 30, 2014. For convenience, the URL for this citation is http://tinyurl.com/m8ccajf.

53. The episode was first brought to my attention by Carole Levin, "Women in *The Book of Martyrs* as Models of Behavior in Tudor England," *International Journal of Women's Studies* 4, no. 2 (1981): 196–207. Levin's article was one of the first to focus critical attention on the representation of women in Foxe, and I am indebted to it throughout. Since then, the account of the Massey family's death has received a great deal of attention. See (among others) Megan L. Hickerson, *Making Women Martyrs in Tudor England* (Basingstoke: Palgrave Macmillan, 2005); Susannah Brietz Monta, *Martyrdom and Literature in Early Modern England* (Cambridge: Cambridge University Press, 2005); David Lee

Miller, *Dreams of the Burning Child: Sacrificial Sons and the Father's Witness* (Ithaca, NY: Cornell University Press, 2003); Julie Crawford, *Marvelous Protestantism: Monstrous Births in Post-Reformation England* (Baltimore: Johns Hopkins University Press, 2005); D. M. Loades, *The Religious Culture of Marian England* (London: Pickering and Chatto, 2010).

54. For Foxe's rejoinder to Harding, see 1570:2169–73.

55. On the multivalence and reversibility of martyrological discourse, see Monta, *Martyrdom and Literature*.

56. Heywood, *An Apologie for Actors* (London, 1612): I: sig. B4r.

57. Many contemporary scholars have taken this and other passages in Heywood's *Apologie* as an instance of nationalism *avant le lettre*. See especially Jean Howard and Phyllis Rackin, *Engendering a Nation: A Feminist Account of Shakespeare's English Histories* (London: Routledge, 1997), and Crystal Bartolovich, "Shakespeare's Globe?" in *Marxist Shakespeares*, ed. Jean E. Howard and Scott Cutler Shershow (London: Routledge, 2001), 178–205.

58. Benedict Anderson, *Imagined Communities: Reflections on the Origins and Spread of Nationalism* (New York: Verso, 1983), 9–19, 144.

59. It is curious, then, that many discussions of ideology, from eighteenth-century *philosophes* to twentieth- and twenty-first-century Marxists, leave this necessary and problematic conjunction of thinking and feeling unsaid, unacknowledged, or at best mentioned only in passing or in parenthesis. As Jorge Lorrain writes, "ideology is more than a system of ideas; it has to do also with a capacity to inspire concrete attitudes and provide orientations for action." *A Dictionary of Marxist Thought*, ed. Tom Bottomore (Cambridge: Harvard University Press, 1983), 222.

60. Wierzbicka is persuasive for a number of reasons, some of them having to do with her professional qualifications and the esteem that her peers express for her work but most especially because her findings surprised her. She had set out to demonstrate the universality of human emotions—that even complex and culturally embedded emotions, whose terms do not translate well into other languages, can be accurately described and understood by using a neutral, nonevaluative set of descriptors. In its cultural specificity, *tęsknota* was one of her failures, a word for an emotion that couldn't be adequately paraphrased in her "Natural Semantic Metalanguage," which is a linguistically rigorous methodology she invented in order to study the affective dimensions

of what Leibniz called the "alphabet of human thought." She tried her best, in other words, to translate *tęsknota* into terms of affect that could be recognized by people in other cultures as something they also felt. She succeeded with many other words that had been regarded as untranslatable, in feeling as well as word, by one or another anthropologist, psychologist, linguist, or literary critic. *Tęsknota* resisted her efforts at a level that was significant. And like the best of researchers, she took such counterevidence seriously and with curiosity. She sought to understand her failure with *tęsknota*, even if such understanding might call into question the opening premise of her study.

Leibniz's alphabet was otherwise known as the *characteristica universalis*; see the *Concise Encyclopedia of Philosophy of Language*, ed. Peter V. Lamarque (Amsterdam: Pergamon, 1998), 486. For Anna Wierzbicka's account and her methodological explanation of her inquiries into the universality of emotions, see especially, "Human Emotions: Universal or Culture-Specific?" *American Anthropologist* 88, no. 3 (1986): 584–94; *Emotions across Languages and Cultures: Diversity and Universals* (Cambridge: Cambridge University Press, 1999).

61. My phrase "historical syntax" is meant as an accompaniment to Raymond Williams's "historical semantics"; see Raymond Williams, *Keywords: A Vocabulary of Culture and Society*, rev. ed. (New York: Oxford University Press, 1983), 23. I am indebted to Stephen Spiess for this reminder.

62. Unless otherwise noted, all quotations from Shakespeare's plays are from *The Norton Shakespeare*, ed. Greenblatt et al. (New York: W. W. Norton, 2008).

63. The title page of the 1594 quarto reads, *The Troublesome Reign and Lamentable Death of Edward the Second, King of England, with the Tragical Fall of Proud Mortimer*.

64. Christopher Marlowe, *Edward II*, ed. Martin Wiggins and Robert Lindsey (New York: W. W. Norton, 1997).

65. On derogated majesty, see David Scott Kastan, "Proud Majesty Made a Subject: Shakespeare and the Spectacle of Rule," *Shakespeare Quarterly* 37 (1986): 459–75.

66. Sigmund Freud, "The Antithetical Meaning of Primal Words," *The Standard Edition of the Complete Psychological Works of Sigmund Freud* 9 (1910); *Five Lectures on Psycho-Analysis, Leonardo da Vinci and Other Works*, 153–62. For the power and prevalence of antithetical or amphibolic terms in other early modern contexts, see Steven Mullaney,

"Lying Like Truth: Riddle, Representation and Treason in Renaissance England," *English Literary History* 47 (1980): 32–48.

67. "Theatrical apparatus" intentionally echoes Laura Mulvey's "filmic apparatus" (*Visual and Other Pleasures* [Houndmills: Palgrave MacMillan, 1989], but is also meant to register a significant difference in the structuring of the theatrical as opposed to the filmic gaze. A number of writers have transferred Mulvey's argument about the interpellative effects of film to the theater, but I would say the theatrical gaze is differently, and more heterogeneously, structured. At its most basic level, our point of view in film is highly determined: we cannot watch the film from a perspective that the camera is not showing us, so that our gaze or perspective is indeed conditioned and delimited by camera angle, movement, focus, and so on. The theatrical apparatus, by contrast, has no inherent point of view; it structures a more idiosyncratic and unpredictable gaze whose close-ups and tracking shots are entirely our own.

Using different zones on the stage to convey different kinds of signification—zones that included *platea* and *locus*—was not a new articulation of the playing space. It was an aspect of blocking that was significantly transformed in its amphitheater forms, however, as demonstrated by Robert Weimann, *Shakespeare and the Popular Tradition in the Theater: Studies in the Social Dimension of Dramatic Form and Function* (Baltimore: Johns Hopkins University Press, 1987). For an indispensable inquiry into the phenomenology of theatrical performance in general, including the relation of theatrical apparatus to the felt experience of performative space, see Bert O. States, *Great Reckonings in Little Rooms: A Phenomenology of Theater* (Berkeley: University of California Press, 1987). See also Bruce Smith, *The Acoustic World of Early Modern England: Attending to the O-Factor* (Chicago: University of Chicago Press, 1999). Erika T. Lin has recently challenged an overly spatial application of *locus* and *platea* in *Shakespeare and the Materiality of Performance* (New York: Palgrave Macmillan, 2012).

68. Craig Calhoun, "Imagining Solidarity: Cosmopolitanism, Constitutional Patriotism, and the Public Sphere," *Public Culture* 14, no. 1 (2002): 152.

69. See Anthony Giddens, *The Constitution of Society: Outline of the Theory of Structuration* (Berkeley: University of California Press, 1984), xxiii, xxx–xxxi, for the distinction between discursive and nondiscursive or practical consciousness. There is, as Giddens remarks, a "need to acknowledge the significance of practical consciousness. Where what

agents know about what they do is restricted to what they can say about it, in whatever discursive style, a very wide area of knowledgeability is simply occluded from view. The study of practical consciousness must be incorporated into research work. It would be an error to suppose that non-discursive components of consciousness are necessarily more difficult to study empirically than the discursive, even though the agents themselves cannot comment directly on them. The unconscious, on the other hand, poses altogether a different order of problem, certainly demanding techniques of interrogation distinct from those involved in descriptive social research." Note especially the distinction between nondiscursive or practical *consciousness* and the entirely different concept of the *unconscious*.

70. Catherine Gallagher and Stephen Greenblatt, *Practicing New Historicism* (Chicago: University of Chicago Press, 2000), 62.

71. For a persuasive account of the need to read literature less suspiciously, see Eve Sedgwick, "Paranoid Reading and Reparative Reading, or, You're So Paranoid You Probably Think This Essay Is about You," in *Touching, Feeling: Affect, Pedagogy, Performativity* (Durham, NC: Duke University Press, 2003), 67–92. I am indebted to Musa Gurnis for bringing this essay to my attention and for a number of other insightful suggestions.

72. See Gallagher and Greenblatt, 64: "The 'structures of feeling' that Williams analyzes are . . . invariably structures of repression."

73. Williams, *Marxism and Literature*, 133–34.

74. Fredric Jameson, *The Political Unconscious: Narrative as a Socially Symbolic Act* (Ithaca, NY: Cornell University Press, 1982).

75. For a formal explanation, see L. A. Zadeh, "Fuzzy Logic," *Computer* 21, no. 4 (1988): 83–93. Fuzzy logic is not the same as paradox, ambiguity, ambivalence, or other ways of holding two incompatible or opposite views simultaneously. Fuzzy logic is processural and variable rather than static or binary; it is not a form of duality, in other words, but an algorithm of possible views and depths of field that enables a fluid and "indiscrete" shift along a scale of differences. For an excellent explication of paradox and its crucial role in early modern popular theater, see Peter G. Platt, *Shakespeare and the Culture of Paradox* (Farnham, England: Ashgate, 2009).

76. Williams, *Marxism and Literature*, 132–33.

77. Berthold Brecht, *Brecht on Theatre: The Development of an Aesthetic*, ed. and trans. John Willett (New York: Hill and Wang, 1964), 161.

78. Louis Althusser, *Lenin and Philosophy and Other Essays* (New York: Monthly Review Press, 1978), 222–23.

79. Walter Benjamin, "Theses on the Philosophy of History," in *Illuminations*, ed. Hannah Arendt and trans. Harry Zohn (New York: Schocken Books, 1968), 255.

80. The quotations are from Michal Kobialka's summary of Kantor's views or statements, and may be his own articulation of Kantor's views; I have been unable to locate, at least, these specific assertions in Kantor's writings about theater. See Kobialka, "Forum on Tragedy," *Theatre Journal* 54, no. 1 (2002): 121.

81. Walter Benjamin, *The Origin of German Tragic Drama*, trans. John Osborne (London: Verso, 2003).

82. Henri Lefebvre, *The Production of Space* (Oxford: Blackwell, 1991).

83. For an evocative and influential exploration of such processes, see Michel de Certeau, *The Practice of Everyday Life* (Berkeley: University of California Press, 1984). Certeau's practices of everyday life contribute to the formation and are themselves the expression of the habitus as defined and elaborated by Pierre Bourdieu, beginning with *Outline of a Theory of Practice* (Cambridge: Cambridge University Press, 1977).

84. Burke, "Literature as Equipment for Living," 293–304.

85. Arjun Appadurai, "The Past Is a Scarce Resource," *Man* 16, no. 2 (1981): 201–19.

86. For the less technologically inclined, "What You See Is What You Get" (WYSWYG) was a common expression in the computer worlds of the 1980s. It emerged to highlight the transition from Emacs-based word processing, in which all formatting commands had to be inserted manually (with a series of special characters) and remained visible on the screen, to the present-day world of word processing, when what you see on the screen is what you get on the page when your words are printed.

87. For the original claim that it was, see Fredson Bowers, *Elizabethan Revenge Tragedy, 1587–1642* (Princeton, NJ: Princeton University Press, 1940).

88. E.g., David Bevington, *From Mankind to Marlowe; Growth of Structure in the Popular Drama of Tudor England* (Cambridge: Harvard University Press, 1962).

CHAPTER ONE

1. Thomas Wright, *The Passions of the Mind in General* (1604), intro. Thomas O. Sloan (Urbana: University of Illinois Press, 1971), 172. Wright's tears are a near-quote from Horace's *Ars Poetica*, line 102: "*Si vis me flere, dolendum est / primum ipsi tibi.*" (Horace, *Epistles, book II*, and *Epistle to the Pisones (Ars poetica)*, ed. and trans. Niall Rudd (Cambridge: Cambridge University Press, 1989). A literal translation would be, "If you wish me to weep, you yourself / Must first feel grief."

2. On the infectiousness of emotion from stage to audience, see Matthew Steggle, *Laughing and Weeping in Early Modern Theatres* (Burlington, VT: Ashgate, 2004).

3. For some well-formulated articulations of such approaches, see esp. Marshall, *Shattering of the Self*; Greenblatt, *Shakespearean Negotiations*; C. L. Barber, *Shakespeare's Festive Comedy: A Study of Dramatic Form and Its Relation to Social Custom* (Princeton: Princeton University Press, 1972); and Richard Schechner, *Between Theater and Ritual* (Philadelphia: University of Pennsylvania Press, 1985).

4. For influential examples of the "humoral turn," see Paster, Rowe, and Floyd-Wilson, eds., *Reading the Early Modern Passions*; Schoenfeldt, *Bodies and Selves in Early Modern England*; Trevor, *Poetics of Melancholy in Early Modern England*; Floyd-Wilson, *English Ethnicity and Race in Early Modern Drama*.

5. "Passions engender Humours, and humours breed Passions: how Passions cause Humors we have hitherto sufficiently declared; but how Humors stirre up Passions must now be delivered" (46). Gail Kern Paster understands this statement inversely from my own reading here, as if it were describing an inviolable causal relationship and not an occasional and somewhat mysterious one. See Paster, *Humoring the Body*, 85.

6. We do find such a strong relationship when we turn to the role that humors were thought to play in the formation of those deeply ingrained temperaments of character or personality—the choleric, the melancholic, and so forth—that Galenic theory has been most immediately associated with in the past.

7. I refer to the structure of the second edition (1604). The central books, on social emotions, received the most revision and expansion by Wright. As Thomas O. Sloan points out, the fifth book (the last on social emotion) was entirely new, "fashioned completely out of added

material" and not included in the earlier edition. See Sloan, introduction to Wright, *The Passions of the Mind in General*, xlviii.

8. Rosaldo, "Toward an Anthropology of Self and Feeling," 143.

9. Paster, *Humoring the Body*, 14.

10. For an insightful study of the inertial temperament and its role in geohumoral theory, see Floyd-Wilson, *English Ethnicity and Race in Early Modern Drama*.

11. See Macdonald, *Mystical Bedlam*, for an overview of Galenic medicine in practice.

12. Paster, *Humoring the Body*, 22.

13. Ibid., 4.

14. Ibid., 23.

15. I also have in mind the already cited work by scholars such as Michael Schoenfeldt and Douglas Trevor.

16. Paster, *Humoring the Body*, 34.

17. Ibid., 49.

18. As Marina Warner says, "His values are emotional: he wants to be moved to feel, to resemble the First Player in his ability to become involved, and not find himself on the side of the unmoved, like Pyrrhus in his momentary arrest, or the Gods and Fate who do not act, who are not moved but remain stuck, frozen, dried up, like Hamlet." Marina Warner, "Come to Hecuba," *Shakespeare International Yearbook* 11 (2011): 79.

19. Ellen MacKay argues that Elizabethan theatrical performance was, in a sense, designed to provide such nondiscursive evidence: it was "the promised end of a practice built on disappearance and erasure—a kind of fatal performance that left nothing behind but its self-effacing poetics." See *Persecution, Plague, and Fire: Fugitive Histories of the Stage in Early Modern England* (Chicago: University of Chicago Press, 2011), flyleaf.

20. "Consumption accomplishes the act of production only in completing the product as product by dissolving it, by consuming its independently material form, by raising the inclination developed in the first act of production, through the need for repetition, to its finished form; it is thus not only the concluding act in which the product becomes the product, but also that in which the producer becomes the producer." Karl Marx, *Grundrisse* (New York: Penguin, 2005), 93; cited by Herbert Blau, *The Audience* (Baltimore: Johns Hopkins University Press, 1990), 323.

21. All citations from *The Spanish Tragedy*, ed. J. R. Mulryne (New York: W. W. Norton, 1997).

22. The status of the Reformation in the play is complicated by uncertain dating (pre- or post-Armada?), the common and unanswerable questions of relevance of religion (nation) depicted on stage, and of course, the mutually exclusive cosmologies of the play, an apparently Catholic Spain that coincides with an entirely classical and pagan afterlife in Hades.

23. In addition to Peter Brook's "empty space," I have in mind the always-useful distinction between means of representation, what is being represented, and by whom, developed by Robert Weimann in a number of his essays and books, including "Bifold Authority in Shakespeare's Theatre," *Shakespeare Quarterly* 39, no. 4 (1988): 401–17. For an excellent overview of semiotic performance theory, see Keir Elam, *The Semiotics of Theatre and Drama*, 2nd ed. (New York: Routledge, 2002); for an influential and invaluable meditation on the phenomenology of performance, see States, *Great Reckonings. Critical Theory and Performance*, ed. Janelle G. Reinelt and Joseph Roach (Ann Arbor: University of Michigan Press, 2010), provides a wide-ranging collection of essays from influential performance theorists and practitioners who offer a variety of approaches and perspectives.

24. See Michael Hattaway, *Elizabethan Popular Theatre: Plays in Performance* (New York: Routledge, 1983), 101–28.

25. This production ended with a metatheatrical instance of doubling when Revenge removed his mask to reveal himself as Hieronimo, fully possessed, as it were, by the spirit of revenge.

26. William Shakespeare, *Titus Andronicus*, ed. Jonathan Bate (London: Arden Shakespeare/Thomson, 2002), 63.

27. Eugene Waith, "The Metamorphosis of Violence in *Titus Andronicus*," *Shakespeare Survey* 10 (1957): 39–49.

28. Rough recordings of both the Stratford and the London productions can be viewed at the Shakespeare Institute Library in Stratford-Upon-Avon.

29. Alan C. Dessen, *Shakespeare in Performance: "Titus Andronicus"* (Manchester: Manchester University Press, 1989), 60.

30. In this violation of the audience's generic expectations, she occupies the Proppian place customarily held by a ghost or a displayed corpse (*The Spanish Tragedy*) or skull (*The Revengers Tragedy*); she is also a reminder of how many Elizabethan plays, especially tragedies, are

haunted by the dead in one way or another, including literal hauntings by ghosts.

A rich strand of contemporary thinking about theater and performance has emphasized the strong relation between "haunting" and the affective semiotics of theater. See Marvin Carlson, *The Haunted Stage: The Theatre as Memory Machine* (Ann Arbor: University of Michigan Press, 2003); Greenblatt, *Hamlet in Purgatory*; Herbert Blau, *Take Up the Bodies: Theater at the Vanishing Point* (Urbana: University of Illinois Press, 1982); Peter Marshall, "Deceptive Appearances: Ghosts and Reformers in Elizabethan and Jacobean England," in *Religion and Superstition in Reformation Europe*, ed. Helen Parish and William G. Naphy (Manchester: Manchester University Press, 2002), 182–208; Richard Dutton, Alison Gail Findlay, and Richard Wilson, eds., *Theatre and Religion: Lancastrian Shakespeare* (Manchester: Manchester University Press, 2003). In *Take Up the Bodies*, Blau introduced "ghosting" as a term that captures the metacritical dynamics of many instances of "haunting." The concept is theorized by Jacques Derrida in *Specters of Marx*. For a recent, insightful expansion of the concept, see Andrew Sofer, *Dark Matter: Invisibility in Drama, Theater, and Performance* (Ann Arbor: University of Michigan Press, 2013).

31. Shakespeare, *Titus Andronicus*, ed. Bate, 63.

32. Equally essential is Heather James, *The Light in Troy: Drama, Politics, and the Translation of Empire* (Cambridge: Cambridge University Press, 1997), 42–84.

33. Alexander Leggatt, *Shakespeare's Tragedies: Violation and Identity* (Cambridge: Cambridge University Press, 2005), 18. Howell's film captures this quite well; for example, in the scene where Lavinia must scratch out her story with Marcus's staff, she puts it (following Marcus's instruction) in her mouth, and it comes out bloody. Her uncle's counsel has reopened her wounds and made them bleed anew. Curiously, given the tenor of her film, Taymor ignored this internal stage direction and allowed Lavinia to place the staff on her shoulder rather than in her mouth.

34. Cited by Paul Woodruff, *The Necessity of Theatre: The Art of Watching and Being Watched* (Oxford: Oxford University Press, 2008), 168.

35. Pascale Aebischer, *Shakespeare's Violated Bodies: Stage and Screen Performance*, (Cambridge: Cambridge University Press: 2004), 26. Musa Gurnis provides an equally insightful and related study in her unpublished essay, "Lavinia's Speaking Body: Physical Indecorum and Stagings of Rape in *Titus Andronicus*."

36. Kenneth Burke, *Permanence and Change: Anatomy of a Purpose* (Berkeley: University of California Press, 1954).

37. For detailed and comprehensive information on performance history, see Charles Edelman, ed., *The Merchant of Venice: Shakespeare in Production* (Cambridge: Cambridge University Press, 2002) and James C. Bulman, *Shakespeare in Performance: The Merchant of Venice* (Manchester: Manchester University Press, 1991).

38. See John Gross, *Shylock: Four Hundred Years in the Life of a Legend* (New York: Touchstone, 1992), 121–22.

39. Maria Edgeworth, *Harrington*, ed. Susan Manly (Peterborough, Ontario: Broadview Press, 2004), 135.

40. Ibid., 137.

41. Hole does not clarify what might cause this shift in point of view, other than the innate virtue of sympathy. His essay is nonetheless remarkable in the ways in which it anticipates audience-response as well as performance theory of twentieth-century criticism. See Richard Hole, "An Apology for the Character and Conduct of Shylock,'" cited in *The Merchant of Venice*, ed. W. Moelwyn Merchant (Harmondsworth: Penguin Books, 1967), 47; for "prepossessions," 53.

42. Barber, *Shakespeare's Festive Comedy*, 218.

43. The same is true of Marlowe's *Jew of Malta*; there, the contradictions of genre are posed more directly, since we are asked to accept the play as a "tragedy" despite the fact that this is the one thing, or at least one of the things, it refuses to be.

44. As Linda Gregerson pointed out to me, the fact that he includes laughter is extraordinary: who imagined that the Jew that Shakespeare drew might be ticklish? All citations of the play are from *The Merchant of Venice*, ed. John Drakakis (London: Arden/Methuen, 2011).

45. Harold Bloom, introduction to *William Shakespeare: Comedies and Romances*, ed. Bloom (New York: Chelsea House, 1986), 11.

46. Henry Turner, "The Problem of the More-than-One: Friendship, Calculation, and Political Association in *The Merchant of Venice*," *Shakespeare Quarterly* 57, no. 4 (2006): 413–42. On theories of genre and its complexity, see John Frow, *Genre* (New York: Taylor and Francis, 2006), and Jacques Derrida, "The Law of Genre," in *Modern Genre Theory*, ed. and intro. by David Duff (Harlow: Longman, 2000), 219–31.

47. "Thoroughly conventional" is James E. Siemon's phrase for Shylock's role as a "villain" in his essay, "The Canker Within: Some Observations on the Role of the Villain in Three Shakespearean Comedies," *Shakespeare Quarterly* 23 (1972): 435–43. Bulman, in *Shakespeare in Per-*

formance (17), regards Shylock's contractual and legal bond to be no less barbarous and, like many critics, labels his proposed act of legally sanctioned manslaughter a "murder"—which by definition is precisely what it is not.

48. Francis Bacon, "Of Revenge," in *Francis Bacon: The Major Works*, ed. Brian Vickers (Oxford: Oxford University Press, 2002), 147.

49. The edition used is *Thomas Middleton: The Collected Works*, ed. Gary Taylor and John Lavagnino (Oxford: Clarendon Press, 2007).

50. For less rationalized, more historically accurate views on the status of revenge in Elizabethan society, see Michael Neill, "English Revenge Tragedy," in *A Companion to Tragedy*, ed. Rebecca Bushnell (Malden: Blackwell, 2005), 328–50; Katharine Eisaman Maus, "The Spanish Tragedy; Or, the Machiavel's Revenge," in *Revenge Tragedy*, ed. Stevie Simkin (Basingstoke: Palgrave, 2001), 88–106. Linda Woodbridge, *English Revenge Drama: Money, Resistance, Equality* (Cambridge: Cambridge University Press, 2010); Kiernan Ryan, *Shakespeare* (Basingstoke: Palgrave, 2002), esp. 16–37.

51. In his claim that Elizabethan England was still a revenge culture, Bowers cites pastoral remonstrations against "revenge" that are largely about bearing grudges and Jacobean sermons or treatises against dueling, an emerging rather than residual social practice with a practical and ethical code quite distinct from revenge. He also posits an archival loss, itself unrecorded, which must have eliminated all the juridical evidence one would expect to find in and of such a culture. See Bowers, *Elizabethan Revenge Tragedy*, esp. chaps. 1–3.

52. Maus, "The Spanish Tragedy," xi.

53. Woodbridge remarks, "To the Halletts' pigeon-holing rhetorical question, 'What is to be gained by defining revenge tragedy so broadly that it cuts across well-established genre borders to herd together a mass of plays having very little in common?' . . . I reply that much is to be gained by transgressing such boundaries. I will be generously inclusive because my quarry is not genre definition but the cultural work that literary revenge performs. Why did revenge permeate this drama? England was not a feud culture like Scotland, or Friuli in Italy. Why did a Christian nation relish vengeful and (often) religiously skeptical plays? (While I give different answers from those of Prosser and other religiously oriented writers, the question they raise is crucial: what is a substantial body of revenge drama doing in a Christian society?) Why, in a monarchy, did stage avengers assassinate kings? Why did a hierar-

chical nation relish scenes of commoners killing dukes? What cultural work did revenge perform?" Woodbridge, *English Revenge Drama*, 5.

On revenge comedy, see Ann Rosalind Jones, "Revenge Comedy: Writing, Law, and the Punishing Heroine in *Twelfth Night, The Merry Wives of Windsor*, and *Swetnam the Woman Hater*," in *Shakespearean Power and Punishment: A Volume of Essays*, ed. Gillian Murray Kendal (Madison, NJ: Fairleigh Dickinson University Press, 1998), 23–38.

54. Diehl, *Staging Reform, Reforming the Stage*, 3.

55. Neill, "Accommodating the Dead," 244, 252.

56. Davis, "Ghosts, Kin, and Progeny," 95–96; cited by Neill, "Accommodating the Dead," 244.

57. Cynthia Marshall, *The Shattering of the Self: Violence, Subjectivity, and Early Modern Texts* (Baltimore: Johns Hopkins University Press, 2002), 4, 7 (emphasis added).

58. Bertolt Brecht, *Brecht on Theatre*, trans. John Willett (New York: Hill and Wang, 1964), 203.

59. Howard Eiland, "Reception in Distraction," *boundary 2*, 30, no. 1 (2003): 51–66.

60. In Walter Benjamin, *Illuminations*, ed. Hannah Arendt and trans. Harry Zohn (New York: Schocken Books, 1968).

61. Eiland, "Reception in Distraction."

62. Russ McDonald, "Telling Stories," in *Shakespeare Up Close: Reading Early Modern Texts*, ed. Russ McDonald, Nicholas D. Nace, and Travis D. Williams (London: Arden Shakespeare, 2012), 222.

63. Portia's prejudice is uglier on the surface but, like the caskets, what's inside is sometimes surprising. She equates Morocco's skin color with the devil, but she doesn't call him one (as Antonio calls Shylock) and she doesn't justify her prejudice as truth or essentialize Morocco's nature to legitimize her dislike. "If he have the condition of a saint and the complexion of a devil, I had rather he should shrive me than wive me" (1.2.124): if the inner man is such, she would entrust her everlasting soul to him and allow for the possibility that he is graced by God, which is no small thing, but she still wouldn't want to marry him due to his differences from her own kind and a skin color she doesn't like.

64. The contrast between Leah's ring, notable for her husband's continued and express fidelity to the bond it represents, and Portia and Nerissa's rings, notable for the Christian husbands' violation of the vows and bonds they embody, is at once striking and repeatedly emphasized in the last two acts. Other rings, such as the one that Roderigo

Lopez acquired and offered to the queen—the ring that was the one thing Elizabeth kept for herself when she returned his estate to his family after his death—may be echoed in these as well.

65. Stephen Orgel, *Imagining Shakespeare* (Basingstoke: Palgrave Macmillan, 2003): 151. Orgel's rediscovery stems from a close rereading of the Furness Variorum of 1898, where the heritage of the name was first clarified. "Jessica" is also British but proves to be of Scottish rather than Saxon origin. Emma Smith explores the pseudo-facts we have long accepted about "the Jew that Shakespeare drew" and, siding with Orgel, presents a compelling case for an extensive reconfiguration of critical views on the play; see "Was Shylock Jewish?" *Shakespeare Quarterly* 64, no. 2 (2013): 188–219.

66. Ryan, *Shakespeare*, 36.

67. For "studious abandonment," see Eiland, "Reception in Distraction," 63. For the concept of rehearsal I have in mind here, see Steven Mullaney, "Strange Things, Gross Terms, Curious Customs: The Rehearsal of Cultures in the Late Renaissance." *Representations* 1, no. 3 (1983): 40–67.

68. Martha Nussbaum points out that "empathy does not suffice for compassion" and can even be antithetical to it. A torturer, she notes, may be "acutely aware of the suffering of the victim, and able to enjoy the imagining of it, all without the slightest compassion." Empathy, one might say, is one of the fundamental job qualifications for someone who wants to be an effective torturer. See Nussbaum, *Upheavals of Thought: The Intelligence of Emotions* (Cambridge: Cambridge University Press, 2001), 329.

69. The agency of audience, the degree to which the entire auditorium defines the playing space we sometimes reduce to the stage itself, is neither comprehensive nor unlimited. Any and all responses from individuals in the audience are not equally legitimate, however. Some are unexpected and undesired—laughter in a serious scene, a void of silence at a joke—and might be prevented in future performances by adjustments to blocking or acting or script. I tend to agree with Alan Dessen: we stand to learn a great deal about the dynamics and dimensions of theater and its place in historical cultures when we try our best to "trust" the play-text enough to make room for the affective and cognitive contributions of its varied audiences. For a critique of Dessen's emphasis, see Cary M. Mazur, "Historicizing Alan Dessen: Scholarship, Stagecraft, and the 'Shakespearean Revolution,'" in *Shakespeare,*

Theory, and Performance, ed. James C. Bulman (New York: Routledge, 1996), 149–67.

CHAPTER TWO

1. Ernst Renan, "What Is a Nation?" in *Nation and Narration*, ed. Homi K. Bhabha (London: Routledge, 1990), 11. For the concept of "creative misremembering," see Colin Burrow, "Shakespeare and the Humanities," in *Shakespeare and the Classics*, ed. Charles Martindale and A. B. Taylor (Cambridge: Cambridge University Press, 2013), 13.

2. I've adapted from the lyrics of "Walk On" by U2: "a place / None of us has been / A place that has to be believed / To be seen."

3. The one exception would be habitual memory, a term that refers to highly somatic forms of memory. One can best accomplish certain physical actions, like complex movements in sports or driving a car, if one has learned them well enough to forget them with the mind so that the body can more fluidly remember them. See Edward S. Casey, "Keeping the Past in Mind," *Review of Metaphysics* 37, no. 1 (1983): 77–95, esp. 85.

4. Of course, she is also not "really" there in terms of her theatricality, since "she" was actually a boy actor playing Margaret at either the Theatre or the Rose. However, her cross-dressed dimensionality—the doubling of her gender in terms of actual and virtual identities—is nowhere foregrounded in this play; since it was English custom with all female roles on popular stages, the layered gender is largely unmarked. Her historical impossibility, by contrast, is a singular attribute of this play; her posthumous incongruity is marked and always on stage for the audience.

5. Blau, *Take Up the Bodies*.

6. The literature on social and/or collective memory in the social sciences is extensive; for an insightful overview, see Jeffrey K. Olick, "Collective Memory: The Two Cultures," *Sociological Theory* 17, no. 3 (1999): 333–48. On distributed cognition and memory, see John Sutton, *Philosophy and Memory Traces: Descartes to Connectionism* (Cambridge: Cambridge University Press, 1998). For approaches to Shakespeare's history plays, see Dermot Cavanagh, Stuart Hampton-Reeves, and Stephen Longstaffe, eds., *Shakespeare's Histories and Counter-Histories* (Manchester: Manchester University Press, 2007).

7. See J. A. Barnes, "The Collection of Genealogies," *Rhodes-Livingstone Journal* 5 (1947): 52–53. For a critique of our customary distinction between "oral and literate" cultures, see chapter 3.

8. Jack Goody and Ian Watt, "The Consequences of Literacy," *Comparative Studies in Society and History* 5. no. 3 (1963): 304–45.

9. For a succinct critique of the myth of a purely oral culture, see Brian V. Street, *Literacy in Theory and Practice* (Cambridge: Cambridge University Press, 1984), 45–47.

10. Ian Watt, who served as Goody's assistant during this stage of the anthropologist's fieldwork in Ghana, would later become famous in his own right for his seminal contribution to literary history, *The Rise of the Novel: Studies in Defoe, Richardson and Fielding* (London: Chatto and Windus, 1957).

11. As Street notes, Goody acknowledged in a later essay that he knew of no cultures in the past 2,000 years that were not mixed. See Street, *Literacy in Theory and Practice*, 45. In the case of the Gonja, Goody later wrote about the premodern influence of Islamic scribes in the region; see "The Impact of Islamic Writing on the Oral Cultures of West Africa," *Cahiers d'Etudes Africanes* 11, no. 43 (1971): 455–66. My thanks to Stephen Spiess for this citation.

12. See especially Cathy Caruth, *Unclaimed Experiences: Trauma, Narrative, and History* (Baltimore: Johns Hopkins University Press, 1996) and the essays collected in *Trauma: Explorations in Memory*, ed. Cathy Caruth (Baltimore: Johns Hopkins University Press, 1995). For a useful overview of trauma theory across the humanities and sciences, see Ruth Leys, *Trauma: A Genealogy* (Chicago: University of Chicago Press, 2000). On individual trauma, narrative, and recovery, see Susan J. Brison, *Aftermath: Trauma and the Remaking of a Self* (Princeton, NJ: Princeton University Press, 2002). An excellent set of explorations in modern cultural traumas can be found in Jeffrey C. Alexander, Ron Eyerman, Bernhard Giesen, Neil J. Smelser, and Piotr Sztompka, eds., *Cultural Trauma and Collective Identity* (Berkeley: University of California Press, 2004).

13. To be sure that my articulation here is not mistaken for a trivialization, I might add that the stakes of the game are often high and costly. Memory matters, as Walter Benjamin would often remind us, and the lesson is one that Reformation England would immediately recognize. I have in mind Thesis VI from Benjamin's "Theses on the Philosophy of History": "Only that historian will have the gift of fanning the spark of hope in the past who is firmly convinced that even the dead will not be safe from the enemy if he wins." For the full thesis, see

Illuminations, ed. Hannah Arendt and trans. Harry Zohn (New York: Schocken Books, 1968), 255. For Freud, of course, fort/da was the game his grandson would tirelessly repeat with his favorite objects, losing and finding, forgetting and remembering them with pleasure at the loss as well as the gain. For Lacan, fort/da marked the entry into the Symbolic.

14. Casey, "Keeping the Past in Mind," 77. Such complex relations of forgetting and remembering (or disremembering) are also related to the twinned and inseparable processes of introjection and incorporation that Nicholas Abraham and Maria Torok analyze as a melancholic relation of present to past. See Nicolas Abraham and Maria Torok, "Introjection—Incorporation: Mourning or Melancholia," in *Psychoanalysis in France*, ed. Serge Lebovici and Daniel Widlöcher (New York: International Universities Press, 1980), 3–16, esp. 13–14; and *The Wolf Man's Magic Word: A Cryptonomy*, trans. Nicholas Rand (Minneapolis: University of Minnesota Press, 1986), passim.

15. "Paradox" may be inadequate here, as Jacques Derrida suggests in "Fors," his foreword to Abraham and Torok, *Magic Word*, trans. Barbara Johnson, xi–xlviii.

16. V. S. Ramachandran and D. Rogers-Ramachandran, "Synaesthesia in Phantom Limbs Induced with Mirrors," *Proceedings of the Royal Society of London* 263 (1996): 377–86.

17. See V. S. Ramachandran's remarkable account in *The Tell-Tale Brain: A Neuroscientist's Quest for What Makes Us Human* (New York: Norton, 2011), 24–40.

18. As discussed in the introduction to *Reformation of Emotions*, historians have never been able to agree on some quite basic historical issues, including why or whether or when the English Reformation succeeded, the relative health or decrepitude of pre-Reformation English Catholicism, or what explains the apparent ease with which the English negotiated such a massive yet relatively peaceful tectonic shift in politics, culture, and religion. Eamon Duffy's vibrant Catholic England and Diarmaid MacCulloch's vibrant Protestant one are equally well drawn, compelling, and convincing, yet the two views of successive historical moments are hard to reconcile. David Cressy's study of suppression, persistence, and polysemy in English festivity offers one cogent account. See Duffy, *Stripping of the Altars*, 475; Diarmaid MacCullough, *The Later Reformation in England 1547–1603* (Houndmills: Palgrave MacMillan, 1990); David Cressy, *Bonfires and Bells: National*

Memory and the Protestant Calendar in Elizabethan and Stuart England
(Berkeley: University of California Press, 1989).

19. Miri Rubin, *Corpus Christi: The Eucharist in Late Medieval Culture* (Cambridge: Cambridge University Press, 1991), 361.

20. Christopher Elwood, *The Body Broken: The Calvinist Doctrine of the Eucharist and the Symbolization of Power in Sixteenth-Century France* (New York: Oxford University Press, 1999), 4, 5.

21. Some aspects of eucharistic thought were absorbed into the political, social, religious, and dramaturgical worlds of Elizabethan England, but what this means is far from clear. Was it a sign of residual Catholicism? Or rather, a sign of a canny cooptation and appropriation, secularizing all but the affective aspects of eucharistic thought? For cogent voices in the debate, see Richard C. McCoy, *Alterations of State: Sacred Kingship in the English Reformation* (New York: Columbia University Press, 2002); Lee Palmer Wandel, *The Eucharist in the Reformation: Incarnation and Liturgy* (Cambridge: Cambridge University Press, 2011); Antony Dawson and Paul Yachnin, *The Culture of Playgoing in Shakespeare's England: A Collaborative Debate* (Cambridge: Cambridge University Press, 2005); Susannah Brietz Monta, "It Is Required You Awake Your Faith: Belief in Shakespeare's Theater," in Degenhardt and Williamson, *Religion and Drama*, 115–38; and Jean-Christophe Mayer, *Shakespeare's Hybrid Faith: History, Religion and the Stage* (New York: Palgrave-Macmillan, 2006).

22. My reference is to the ancient Roman ritual known as *damnatio memoriae*, in its original, pre-Christian sense, which referred to the "condemnation" or erasure of an individual from social memory, an act accomplished by eliminating any mention of that individual from the historical record: from all inscriptions, coins, statues, papyri, and so forth. When "damnation" later took on the Christian sense of "consignment to hell," *damnatio memoriae* became associated with the Christian ritual of excommunication, casting the most severe punishment that could be visited on a member of the church as the ultimate act of enforced and collective amnesia, a banishment of the individual from God's memory itself—a total and complete annihilation.

23. Thomas, *Religion and the Decline of Magic*, 603.

24. See my prologue.

25. See Christopher Haigh, *English Reformations: Religion, Politics, and Society under the Tudors* (Oxford: Oxford University Press, 1993).

26. Williams, *Keywords*, 257.

27. Evelyn B. Tribble, "The Partial Sign: Spenser and the Sixteenth-Century Crisis of Semiotics," in *Ceremony and Text in the Renaissance*, ed. Douglas F. Rutledge (Newark: University of Delaware Press, 1996), 23–34.

28. On *figura*, see Erich Auerbach, "La cour et la ville," in *Scenes from the Drama of European Literature*, trans. Ralph Mannheim (Manchester: Manchester University Press, 1984), 133–82. I am indebted to Sarah Beckwith's argument about the York cycles in *Signifying God: Social Relation and Symbolic Act in the York Corpus Christi Plays* (Chicago: University of Chicago Press, 2003), but also have a different understanding of the relationship between sacramental and theatrical signs. She sometimes seems to collapse the theatrical into the sacramental when dealing with medieval drama, and to overlook the degree to which theater is inherently an art of "epistemological doubt," an epithet that Beckwith correctly applies to Elizabethan drama but fails to recognize in its medieval theatrical manifestations. Epistemological doubt or aporia is a state of being I would associate with the ambivalence of the theatrical sign itself, in and of itself; "sacramental" is the one thing that "sacramental" theater could never be. In my understanding of religious medieval drama, it was not understood to be so.

29. Peter Womack, "Imagining Communities: Theatres and the English Nation in the Sixteenth Century," in *Culture and History 1350–1600: Essays on English Communities, Identities, and Writing*, ed. David Aers (Detroit, MI: Wayne State University Press, 1992), 99.

30. Diehl, *Staging Reform, Reforming the Stage*, 3.

31. Michael Neill, *Putting History to the Question; Interrogation, Torture, Truth* (New York: Columbia University Press, 2000).

32. There is considerable debate about the sequence of composition for the three plays devoted to the reign of Henry VI. The first to appear in print (in a quarto of 1594) was the play that would later, in the Folio, be identified as *The Second Part of Henry VI* but was titled *The First Part of the Contention of the Two Famous Houses of York and Lancaster*. Most modern editors regard *1 Henry 6* as a prequel written after the other two plays; for my purposes, the question of sequence is largely moot.

33. Womack, "Imagining Communities," 136.

34. Ibid.

35. For a fine exploration of the Pauline roots of citizenship in the early modern period, see Julia Reinhardt Lupton, *Citizen-Saints: Shakespeare and Political Theology* (Chicago: University of Chicago Press, 2005).

36. For key literary explorations, see Richard Helgerson, *Forms of Nationhood: The Elizabethan Writing of England* (Chicago: University of Chicago Press, 1992) and Howard and Rackin, *Engendering a Nation.*

37. I am paraphrasing his opening statement in *The Eighteenth Brumaire of Louis Bonaparte* (New York: International Publishers, 1994), 1.

38. *Mustapha*, Chorus 207–8, cited in J. W. Lever, *The Tragedy of State: A Study in Jacobean Drama* (London: Methuen, 1971), 8.

39. Womack, "Imagining Communities," 145. Womack's phrase derives from S. L. Collins, *From Divine Cosmos to Sovereign State* (Oxford: Oxford University Press, 1989). Collins's study is one example of the many interpretations of the cycle which argue the position—teleological and ideological—that Womack explicitly rejects.

40. Womack, "Imagining Communities," 137. Endings do not always have the final word: this is especially the case when the drama before us is so clearly dialectical rather than didactic in its engagement with its audience. Endings are sometimes the point, the promised end, or the image of it; but they are always the attribute of form and genre, the frame rather than the work itself. What outlasts the fleeting interim of performance, what has the capacity to surprise us, to change the way we think and sometimes even the way we live, are not the endings—a series of marriages that threatens to include everyone on stage, the final demise of a Richard or a Macbeth—but what are often extremely brief moments, punctuations rather than plots. It is the inquisitive, probing, and defamiliarizing energy of early modern drama, not the embrace of the familiar or normal, that so many different minds—from Bradbrook and Rossiter to Lever or Brecht, Rabkin, Berger, Greenblatt, and countless others—have found so remarkable. For a particularly insightful and probative analysis of closure and deferral in performance, focused especially upon the English history plays, see Barbara Hodgdon, *The End Crowns All: Contradiction and Closure in Shakespeare's History* (Princeton, NJ: Princeton University Press, 1991).

41. Womack, "Imagining Communities," 137–38.

42. See Elam, *Semiotics of Theatre and Drama*, 5–28.

43. For Herbert Blau's brief overview of the chair on stage as a performance theory trope, see Blau, *Audience.*

44. Jean Alter, *A Sociosemiotic Theory of Theatre* (Philadelphia: University of Pennsylvania Press, 1990), 23. See also Andrew Sofer's excellent discussion in *The Stage Life of Props* (Ann Arbor: University of Michigan Library, 2003), 6–11; Stanton Garner, *Bodied Spaces: Phenomenology*

and Performance in Contemporary Drama (Ithaca, NY: Cornell University Press, 1994); and Blau, *Take Up the Bodies*, 249 passim.

45. On the pain of memorial reformation, see Elizabeth Mazzola, *The Pathology of the English Renaissance: Sacred Remains and Holy Ghosts* (Leiden: Brill, 1998), in which she suggests that "the habits and projects of the Renaissance are some of the most self-consciously sophisticated methodologies for the burial and retrieval of cultural knowledge," and notes that "the disowning of cognitive stances or epistemological frameworks can cause tremendous psychic pain" (2).

46. Nashe, *Works of Thomas Nashe*, 1:212.

47. For a subtle exploration of asymptotic aspects of the early history plays, see Christopher Pye, *The Vanishing: Shakespeare, the Subject, and Early Modern Culture* (Durham, NC: Duke University Press, 2000).

48. In the figural structure of history that had informed some forms of medieval biblical theater, past and present and future were implied, contained, and completed in one another, in what might be called a sacramental dialectic. I would note that the sacramental is not the theatrical and should not be confused with the figural history that unfolds on a stage or pageant wagon. On *figura* and the shape of Christian history, see Auerbach, "La cour et la ville." For an influential counterargument about sacramental theater, see Beckwith, *Signifying God*.

49. His title at this time would have been Baron of Blakemere; he was not created Earl of Shrewsbury until 1442; Shakespeare awards him this title prematurely in *1 Henry 6*.

50. See Baldo, "Wars of Memory in Henry V," *Shakespeare Quarterly* 47, no. 2 (1996): 132–59, esp. 138. I owe this reference to Jean-Christophe Mayer and his SAA seminar paper, "Shakespeare's Memorial Drama."

51. For Howard and Rackin's approach to Talbot, see *Engendering a Nation*, 54–61.

52. E.M.W. Tillyard, *Shakespeare's History Plays* (New York: Collier Books, 1962), 183.

53. Sigurd Burckhardt, "'I Am But Shadow of Myself': Ceremony and Design in 1 Henry VI," *Modern Language Quarterly* 28, no. 2 (June 1967): 139–58.

54. For "virtual," "actual," and their relation to the real, see Gilles Deleuze, "The Actual and the Virtual," in *Dialogues II*, trans. Eliot Ross Albert (New York: Columbia University Press, 2002), 148–52. I define my use more fully in chapter 3, "What's Hamlet to Habermas?"

55. The integrity of "the Talbot" is heroic, martial, masculine, and so forth, but it is neither medieval nor early modern, neither a figure for

an anachronistic feudal community nor an early modern anticipation or reflection of an emerging Reformation kind of popular sovereignty. We could think of it as a highly mystified medievalism (with the emphasis on "highly") or as a distorted image of a kind of representative authority that could eventually be thought of as a "nation" in the modern sense, but when we do so, we translate an early modern dilemma into a more familiar nostalgia, whether we assign that nostalgia to Shakespeare (yearning for a past that never was) or to ourselves (yearning for a less forgetful genealogical understanding of ourselves).

56. For a medieval, eucharistic analogy, see Caroline Walker Bynum's discussion of the "problem of the cannibal," in *The Resurrection of the Body in Western Christianity, 200–1336* (New York: Columbia University Press, 1995). Hypothetical cannibalism provided a limit-case, a theological thought experiment, used to clarify the paradoxical relation of body to soul, material to spiritual substance. What body will be resurrected at the end of history? Will the norm be the body as it died or at its prime? What happens to the nails and hair cut off during a lifetime? What happens to the food, plant and animal, ingested during that lifetime and converted into the substance of the eater's body? What if an infant were fed only human flesh, whose substance will be returned to its original owner for the resurrection—and thus would be subtracted from the resurrected body of the cannibal? He or she would only have the substance passed on from the father and the mother. However, if the cannibal in question fostered a child who was only fed with human flesh, there would be no material body to resurrect—and no spiritual body to reunite with it.

57. Burckhardt, "I Am But Shadow of Myself," 155.

58. Thomas, *Religion and the Decline of Magic*, 603. The dramatic method exemplified in this instance is also manifested in the experiments with dramatic character throughout the tetralogy, most notable in the radical inconsistency of any given character as she or he moves from one scene to the next; in the scattered, fragmentary, yet incongruously effective way in which bits and pieces of medieval theater, cut adrift from the figural associations that once bound past and present together, are strewn throughout the fifteenth century as rehearsed here and now, on the late Elizabethan stage; and in a host of other absences, disjunctions, inconsistencies, contradictions, and incongruities that are too persistent to be consigned to the null category of the immature, the apprentice, or the dramaturgically inept author. Taken one by one, such

characteristics are not hard to explain away in this fashion. But taken all together, as they are more likely to be taken in performance than on the page, they are something strange and admirable: an experiment in historical thinking that is sparagmatic rather than linear or teleological.

59. The culmination of the substance-shadow pairing is in the last scene of *Richard III*; see the final section of this chapter.

60. "No figure in the carpet is the carpet. There is in the pointing out of patterns something that is opposed to life and art, an ungraciousness which artists in particular feel and resent." Barber, *Shakespeare's Festive Comedy*, 4.

61. For the importance of the unknown in knowledge formation, see also Valerie Traub, *Making Sexual Knowledge: Thinking Sex with the Early Moderns* (forthcoming, 2015).

62. For similar reflections on York's death and Henry's scene, see Wikander, "Something Is Rotten: English Renaissance Tragedies of State," in *A Companion to Tragedy*, ed. Bushnell, 311.

63. In Michael Boyd's production of the first tetralogy (Ann Arbor, MI, 2000), he evoked a haunted allegory of the past, present, and future by having the "dead" Talbot and son, with all their wounds of battle, play the roles of father and son, son and father.

64. Howard and Rackin, *Engendering a Nation*, 72, 73.

65. Rackin, "Staging Women in Shakespeare," 4–5; my citations are from a written version of the talk that Rackin delivered in Ann Arbor, Michigan, in the year 2000. My thanks to the author for sharing this manuscript with me.

66. Cf. OED (a): "A free gift or favour specially vouchsafed by God; a grace, a talent."

67. See Max Weber, *The Theory of Social and Economic Organization*, trans. A. M. Henderson and T. Parsons (Oxford: Oxford University Press, 1947).

68. It might be mystified so that it looks like a kind of representative authority—the title page of Hobbe's *Leviathan*, where the prince is composed of and by the people, comes to mind—but it still wears a crown or a title. It incorporates authority rather than serves or represents it in a more republican or democratic semiotics of power.

69. For a recent study of this topic, see Kai Wiegandt, *Crowd and Rumor in Shakespeare* (Burlington, VT: Ashgate, 2012).

70. As Evelyn Tribble has argued, these radical changes are signs that bear witness to an epistemological and social crisis as well as a

semiotic one, pointing "not only toward shifts in signifying practices, but also toward shifts in the entire way of conceiving human society." Tribble, "The Partial Sign," 23–24.

71. See Patricia A. Cahill, *Unto the Breach: Martial Formations, Historical Trauma, and the Early Modern Stage* (Oxford: Oxford University Press, 2008), for a similar reading of this scene.

72. OED (II.6.b): "a spectre, a phantom." This OED locates the earliest usage in 1598, in *The Merry Wives of Windsor*. For the status of ghosts in early modern France, see Timothy Chesters, *Ghost Stories in Late Renaissance France: Walking by Night* (Oxford: Oxford University Press, 2011).

73. I am using Lacan's terminology here; elsewhere, I have discriminated between the imaginary (a phantasy) and the imagined (a component of the real).

74. Stephen Greenblatt, *Will in the World: How Shakespeare Became Shakespeare* (New York: Norton, 2004), 323–24.

75. Hamlet is such a mystery (the play and its protagonist) because it lacks an objective correlative, understood as "a set of objects, a situation, a chain of events which shall be the formula of [a] particular emotion; such that when the external facts, which must terminate in sensory experience, are given, the emotion is immediately evoked" (58). See T. S. Eliot, "Hamlet and His Problems," in *The Sacred Wood and Major Early Essays* (Mineola, NY: Dover, 1998), 55–59.

76. See esp. Elam, *Semiotics of Theatre and Drama*.

77. Pierre Macherey, *A Theory of Literary Production*, trans. Geoffrey Wall (London: Routledge and Kegan Paul, 1978), 79–80. I have modified Wall's translation from "book" to "work," to the discursive rather than the physical or material object, to clarify what I take to be Macherey's meaning. Macherey uses "livre" for "work" as well as "book."

78. Althusser's thinking about the literary was critically influenced, indeed, by Macherey's work. See Louis Althusser, "A Letter on Art in Reply to André Daspre," in *Lenin and Philosophy and Other Essays* (New York: Monthly Review Press, 2001), 151–56.

79. Macherey's theory of the literary is hampered in part, however, by its lingering debt to a repressive model of literary signification. The literary text is "haunted by the absence of certain repressed words which make their return [emphasis added]." If the text represses, however, the critic must adopt a suspicious and corrective stance toward literature in order to set it right and replace it with an act of read-

ing that is sometimes called ideological demystification. From such a critical perspective, literature inevitably becomes the stooge of a dominant ideology rather than a form of critical and affective thinking in and of itself. From the latter point of view, literature becomes instead an experiential tool for living, a means by which we apprehend more than we can otherwise comprehend. I say that Macherey is hampered only in part, however, because he also seems to credit the literary with something like a tacit theoretical insight or—to unmix my metaphor a bit—a tacit sounding out of its corresponding reality. It is a reality that is also incomplete, something it can show to us only because it does not or cannot reflect or represent it.

80. Paul de Man's paradoxical paradigm for the relationship between blindness and insight involves an altogether different dynamic of production. De Man described a zero-sum relationship between memory and forgetting; a certain blindness or occlusion toward one thing is the price we pay for insight into another. In the performance of historical trauma, blindness and insight are simultaneous, inseparable, and mutually deconstructive. See *Blindness and Insight: Essays in the Rhetoric of Contemporary Criticism* (London: Routledge, 1983).

81. The arts and other forms of cultural performance (including myth) are described and regarded as tools for living throughout Burke's work and career; I have in mind the address he gave to the American Writers' Congress in 1935: "A hammer is a carpenter's tool; a wrench is a mechanic's tool; and a 'myth' is the social tool for welding the sense of interrelationship by which the carpenter and the mechanic, though differently, can work together for common social ends. In this sense a myth that works well is as real as food, tools, and shelter are." For this talk, see "Revolutionary Symbolism in America. Speech by Kenneth Burke to American Writers' Congress, April 26, 1935," reprinted in *The Legacy of Kenneth Burke*, ed. Herbert W. Simons and Trevor Melia (Madison: University of Wisconsin Press, 1989), 267.

CHAPTER THREE

1. Harold Love, *The Culture and Commerce of Texts: Scribal Publication in Seventeenth-Century England* (Amherst: University of Massachusetts Press, 1998).

2. For an opposing view, see Lucas Erne, *Shakespeare as Literary Dramatist* (Cambridge: Cambridge University Press, 2003).

3. "To my friend Maister *John Fletcher* upon his Faithfull Shepheard-

esse," in *The Faithful Shepherdess*, in *The Dramatic Works in the Beaumont and Fletcher Canon*, vol. 3, ed. Fredson Bowers (Cambridge: Cambridge University Press, 1976).

4. See Julie Stone Peters, *Theatre of the Book 1480–1880: Print, Text, and Performance in Europe* (Oxford: Oxford University Press, 2000), 238, for other examples.

5. Lin, *Shakespeare and the Materiality of Performance*, 11–12.

6. Rosaldo, "Toward an Anthropology of Self and Feeling," 143.

7. See especially David Cressy, "Literacy in Context: Meaning and Measurement in Early Modern England," in *Consumption and the World of Goods*, ed. John Brewer and Roy Porter (London: Routledge, 1993), 305–19. For those uneasy with such an expansion of "literacy" to describe social knowledges and skills that extend far beyond the root meaning of the term as the ability to read and/or produce writing, it might help to remember that being able to read and/or write was not the referent for "literacy" in this period. Reading and/or writing in Latin were the proof of literacy. Those who could read Foxe's first edition of *Actes and Monuments* were literate: it was published in Latin. Those who could not do so were not strictly literate. Access to and production of writing in English or any other vernacular became the threshold for literacy only after the Reformation.

8. Jürgen Habermas, *The Structural Transformation of the Public Sphere: An Inquiry into a Category of Bourgeois Society*, translated by Thomas Burger (Cambridge, MA: MIT Press, 1989).

9. Ibid., 38.

10. Habermas seems to imagine a "box" reserved for nobility whose "coin" was calculated in bloodlines rather than species. The display was of rank in this sense and not of wealth, which could be displayed in some Elizabethan and Jacobean theaters with the purchase of a place on stage or in the balcony.

11. Nancy Fraser, "Rethinking the Public Sphere: A Contribution to the Critique of Actually Existing Democracy," in *Habermas and the Public Sphere*, ed. Craig Calhoun (Cambridge, MA: MIT Press, 1989), 110.

12. Habermas, *Structural Transformation of the Public Sphere*, 25.

13. For a recent example, see Wilson and Yachnin, eds., *Making Publics in Early Modern Europe*, esp. 1–21.

14. Calhoun, "Imagining Solidarity," 162.

15. Most important and sometimes overlooked is his emphasis that

the public sphere can only develop within the private or domestic sphere rather than in the open or in open public spaces where it might afterward manifest itself. "The public's understanding of the public use of reason was guided specifically by such private experiences as grew out of the audience-oriented (*publikumsbezogen*) subjectivity of the conjugal family's intimate domain (*Intimsphäre*). . . . Included in the private realm was the authentic 'public sphere,' for it was a public sphere constituted by private people" (28, 30).

16. Habermas, *Structural Transformation of the Public Sphere*, 12–14. *Excurs* in the German, which has, to the best of my knowledge, quite similar connotations. For the German text, see *Strukturwandel der Öffenlichkeit: Untersuchungen zu einer Kategorie der bürgerlichen Gesellschaft* (Neuwied a. Rh. & Berlin: H. Luchterhand Vlg., 1965), 22.

17. If the Frankfurt school is sometimes remembered for its suspicion of the aesthetic object and a form of critique devoted to the demystification and correction of art and its ideological complicities, this is a reminder that there was always another side to that distrust. Art also mattered a great deal to the Frankfurt school, and the cultural sphere (in the aesthetic sense of the term) was for Habermas a kind of laboratory for new collective and individual subjectivities to develop—and a place where the social theorist can sometimes discover new algorithms for the historical relation of public to private, social to individual.

18. Habermas, *Structural Transformation of the Public Sphere*, 13.

19. A cognate understanding of early modern power was embraced by a host of twentieth-century theorists, especially new historicists who laid special emphasis on the kinship between such state or princely power and the theater. I would include Michel Foucault, Roy Strong, Stephen Orgel, Ed Muir, Stephen Greenblatt, Louis Montrose, Leonard Tennenhouse, Steven Mullaney, and a host of others.

20. Habermas, *Structural Transformation of the Public Sphere*, 14.

21. Ibid., 50.

22. Ibid., 50–51.

23. One example would be Dutch *huiskerken* or "house churches" in early modern Amsterdam: Catholic churches that thrived in a Calvinist city-state because they were both hidden (they looked exactly like the Dutch homes on either side of them) and yet they were also known to all, public secrets to Protestant and Catholic alike. Steven Mullaney, Angela Vanhaelen, and Joseph Ward describe the paradoxical expansion of the public within the private in this fashion: "If 'house church'

is a conundrum or portmanteau word, the sociological entity it refers to is a conundrum or portmanteau creature as well. It is as if a single room in a home were discovered to house, in a Mobius strip sort of way, another room within it, and that this second, interior space also violated the normal laws of physics by being larger than the space in which it was contained. In the *huiskerk*, private space opens up into, opens up as, public space in this fashion." See Mullaney, Vanhaelen, and Ward, "Religion Inside Out," 33–34.

24. Habermas, *Structural Transformation of the Public Sphere*, 50.

25. Ibid., 50.

26. Ibid., 29.

27. Ibid., 50.

28. Ibid., 49, 50.

29. The gendered dimension of such empathy is even more complex. Since the affective point of view in most fiction was (and still is) structured as male rather than female, there is another stage to the dialectic for the female reader and a more complex subjectivity would be one of the results.

30. Ibid., 50.

31. Garner, *Bodied Spaces*, 42. See also Peter Brook, *The Empty Space* (London: Penguin, 2008), and Blau, *Audience*.

32. See Richard Schechner, *Between Theater and Anthropology* (Philadelphia: University of Pennsylvania Press, 1985).

33. Habermas, *Structural Transformation of the Public Sphere*, 51.

34. See David Cressy, "Levels of Illiteracy in England, 1530–1730," *Historical Journal* 20 (1977): 1–23.

35. We can observe this in a wide range of studies of the printing press or printed book as an agent of social transformation; see, among many examples, Elizabeth L. Eisenstein, *The Printing Press as an Agent of Change: Communications and Cultural Transformations in Early Modern Europe* (Cambridge: Cambridge University Press, 1979), and David Zaret, *Origins of Democratic Culture: Printing, Petitions, and the Public Sphere in Early Modern England* (Princeton, NJ: Princeton University Press, 2000).

36. Adam Fox, *Oral and Literate Culture in England, 1500–1700* (Oxford, Oxford University Press), 2000), 5.

37. The lasting hold of such an ill-sorted and misleading dichotomy suggests that it has strong ideological roots, which in this case seem to be the residue of an embarrassed ethnography. The dichotomy makes

sense only if we sufficiently deconstruct it to realize that "oral" is a cover term for its repressed original in literacy studies of the past: for the illiterate conceived as the "primitive." It is a mystified distinction that continues to impede even the best studies of public and private forms of meaning in the early modern era.

38. Alexandra Halasz, *The Marketplace of Print: Pamphlets and the Public Sphere in Early Modern England* (Cambridge: Cambridge University Press, 1997), 182, 185.

39. Ibid., 29.

40. Karl Marx, *Capital: A Critique of Political Economy*, vol. 1, trans. Ben Fowkes (New York: Vintage Books, 1977), 165, 166.

41. Marx uses a wide range of metaphors to convey what he calls the transubstantial or mysterious aspects of commodities. Commodities are described as pupae metamorphosing into other commodities or into money, sometimes as sirens who cast "wooing glances" at money, and sometimes they are even cast as dramatis personae. They are animated social entities, intersubjective as well as interobjective.

42. In so far as this is true, it should be true of books written, marketed, circulated, and read long before the invention of the printing press. Halasz is not alone in her fetishization of print, by which I mean the attribution of new powers that have always been characteristic of written language, whatever the mode of its inscription.

43. For the concept of structural amnesia, see Barnes, "Collection of Genealogies," 52–53.

44. For "focused gathering," see Erving Goffman, *Behavior in Public Places* (New York: Free Press, 1966), 91.

45. Womack, "Imagining Communities," 138. It is possible that he meant to emphasize the transformative, illocutionary speech-act—addressing of a group, whether a crowd or an audience, in a manner that brings a public into existence.

46. Some of these distinctions are my own, but they grow from the many rich discussions and forums that took place during in the multidisciplinary research project called "Making Publics: Media, Markets and Association in Early Modern Europe, 1500–1700" (MaPs), which spanned the years 2005–2010 and in which I was fortunate to participate as a co-investigator. For more specific and detailed articulations of publics, counter-publics, and non-Habermasian public spheres, see the two anthologies: Wilson and Yachnin, eds., *Making Publics in Early Modern Europe*, and Angela Vanhaelen and Joseph P. Ward, eds., *Mak-*

ing Space Public in Early Modern Europe: Performance, Geography, Privacy (New York: Routledge, 2013).

47. See Habermas, *Structural Transformation of the Public Sphere*, 29: "the products of culture . . . had become publicly accessible: in the reading room and the theater, in museums and at concerts. Inasmuch as culture became a commodity, and thus finally evolved into "culture" in the specific sense (as something that pretended to exist merely for its own sake), it was claimed as the ready topic of a discussion through which an audience-oriented (*publikumsbezogen*) subjectivity communicated with itself."

48. Most of us would agree, contra Habermas, that this kind of theatrical public was a significant social phenomenon at least as early as the rise of Elizabethan professional theaters, which precipitated new forms of critical and aesthetic thinking about drama as well as new debates about the relation between theater and commonwealth, theater and morality, theater and religion.

49. Paul Yachnin, "The Reformation of Space in Shakespeare's Playhouse," in *Making Publics in Early Modern Europe*, ed. Wilson and Yachnin, 212–13.

50. Love, *Culture and Commerce of Texts*.

51. My diagram omits, of course, the visual arts, music, ritual, and a number of other distinct media and modes of production.

52. By actual, I do not mean "real," nor do I merely mean physical or sensible. The Real is rather understood here as a complex algorithm of the actual and the virtual, neither one of which functions separately as literal or figurative, extant or imagined, present or absent. See Deleuze, "The Actual and the Virtual." For a different conception of the Real, developed in dialogue and disagreement with Deleuze, see Slavoj Žižek, *Organs without Bodies: On Deleuze and Consequences* (London: Routledge, 2004).

53. This is what Stanton Garner calls "the irreducible oscillation between represented and lived space" in *Bodied Spaces*, 42. Stanton's irreducibility includes bodies on stage (who occupy two spaces at the same time, as actors and characters), props, and other examples. It is this simultaneity of the actual and virtual that accounts for differences between performed, written or printed, filmed, and other phenomenological forms.

54. Greg Walker estimates that drama would be even lower, from 500–600 copies. See Greg Walker, *The Politics of Performance in Early*

Renaissance Drama (Cambridge: Cambridge University Press, 1998), 13. For an overview of the size of print runs, see Peter Blayney, "The Publication of Playbooks," in *A New History of Early English Drama*, ed. John D. Cox and David Scott Kastan (New York: Columbia University Press, 1997), 383–422.

55. For estimates of audience sizes, see Andrew Gurr, *Playgoing in Shakespeare's London*, 3rd ed. (Cambridge: Cambridge University Press, 2004).

56. Lin, *Shakespeare and the Materiality of Performance*, 13. Lin's own thought-experiment, which came to my attention only after the publication of an early version of this chapter, focused on the printed play rather than a related text like Plutarch. Our point is largely the same, and I'm grateful to Lin's more detailed statistics for the printed play.

57. See especially Cressy, "Literacy in Context," 305–19.

58. The literature on the social construction of space is too extensive to chronicle here. In terms of "virtual" space, my own thinking began long ago when reading Suzanne Langer's insightful inquiry into the role of space in various arts; see *Feeling and Form: A Theory of Art Developed from Philosophy in a New Key* (New York: Macmillan, 1977). Langer fundamentally misunderstands theatrical space, however; like Habermas, she objects to performance that does not hew to the architecture of the fourth wall.

EPILOGUE

1. For two studies of *Hamlet* and the "drama—and the trauma—of reform," see Diehl, *Staging Reform, Reforming the Stage*, and Greenblatt, *Hamlet in Purgatory* (esp. 244). For my own previous analysis of this scene, see Steven Mullaney, "Mourning and Misogyny: *Hamlet, The Revenger's Tragedy*, and the Final Progress of Elizabeth I, 1600–1607," *Shakespeare Quarterly* 45, no. 2 (1994): 1–23.

2. For a more extended reading of the process of surrogate mourning in the scene, see Mullaney, "Mourning and Misogyny." For a classic study of memorial surrogacy, see Roach, *Cities of the Dead*.

In her rethinking of romance as a popular and compelling genre in the period, Gail Kern Paster has persuasively suggested that wet-nursing cultures like Elizabethan England developed different and differently alienated affective bonds with the nonmaternal breast, the wet-nurse's family, and a wide range of other parental surrogates: "From wet-nursing right through apprenticeship, the culture so widely employed surrogacy as the institutional model for parenthood. Thus, the loss and magical return of children structuring the Jacobean romance plots may really mask a suppressed anxiety originating not from the subject position of grieving parent but from that of grieving child." Paster, *The Body Embarrassed*, 219.

3. Andy Clark, *Being There: Putting Brain, Body, and World Together Again* (Cambridge, MA: MIT Press, 1997), 180.

4. In contemporary theory, complementary paths have been charted for the study of such distribution in terms of relations (network-actor theory) and in terms of materiality (thing theory). Theories of extended mind and distributed affect-cognition have drawn from and enabled both perspectives. At their best, such paths and perspectives can be immensely productive for critical social thought in a wide range of fields and disciplines and interests. *The Reformation of Emotions* is not a book about them per se but I do regularly draw upon such ways of thinking as the resources I understand them to be: tools for historical and social and literary and performative analysis. For more on thing theory and actor-network theory, see Bill Brown, "Thing Theory," *Critical Inquiry* 28, no. 1 (2001): 1–22; and Bruno Latour, *Reassembling the Social: An Introduction to Actor-Network-Theory* (New York: Oxford University Press, 2007).

5. *Phaedrus*, 274C–D. The phrase "cognitive ecology" was introduced by Edward Hutchins, *Cognition in the Wild* (Cambridge, MA: MIT Press, 1985), xiv passim.

6. For Derrida's masterful reading of *Phaedrus*, see "Plato's Pharmacy," in *Dissemination*, trans. Barbara Johnson (Chicago: University of Chicago Press, 1981).

7. Evelyn Tribble and John Sutton, "Cognitive Ecology as a Framework for Shakespearean Studies," *Shakespeare Studies* 11 (2011): 94.

8. Ibid., 94–95. On the related concept of "distributed cognition," see John Sutton, "Distributed Cognition: Domains and Dimensions," in *Cognition Distributed: How Cognitive Technology Extends our Minds*, ed. Itiel E. Dror and Stevan Harnad (Amsterdam: John Benjamins, 2008), 45–56, as well as his earlier book on "extended mind," *Philosophy and Memory Traces*; Evelyn Tribble and John Sutton, "Interdisciplinarity and Cognitive Approaches to Theatre," in *Affective Performance and Cognitive Science: Body, Brain, and Being*, ed. Nicola Shaughnessy (London: Bloomsbury, 2013); Evelyn B. Tribble, *Cognition in the Globe: Attention and Memory in Shakespeare's Theatre* (New York: Palgrave Macmillan,

2011); and Laurie Johnson, John Sutton, and Evelyn Tribble, eds., *Embodied Cognition and Shakespeare's Theatre: The Early Modern Body-Mind* (New York: Routledge, 2014). The work of Bruce McConachie came to my attention late in the completion of *Reformations*; however, his use of cognitive theory to understand the affective experience of an audience watching a play resonates with my own efforts here. See Bruce A. Mc-Conachie, *Engaging Audiences: A Cognitive Approach to Spectating in the Theatre* (New York: Palgrave Macmillan, 2008).

9. For Cicero's tale and its application to later memory theaters, see Frances Yates, *The Art of Memory* (London: Routledge and Kegan Paul, 1966), 17–18.

10. The phrase "surprising effects of sympathy" comes from the title of Marivaux's first novel; for an excellent exploration of this and other structures of feeling in the eighteenth and early nineteenth centuries, see David Marshall, *The Surprising Effects of Sympathy: Marivaux, Diderot, Rousseau, and Mary Shelley* (Chicago: University of Chicago Press, 1988).

Index

Abraham, Nicolas, 209n14
Aebischer, Pascale, 75, 200n35
affective irony, 48–51, 69, 74–75, 89, 92, 101–81; defined, 48–51
affective technologies, 23, 26, 50, 87, 146, 150, 168, 191n48; as embodied in print and other media, 4, 23, 26–31, 46, 50, 87; as embodied in theatrical production, 23, 46, 87, 94, 146, 150, 167–68; and thinking through things, 17, 50–51, 103–6, 163, 167–79
Alexander, Jeffrey C., 206n12
Alter, Jean, 114, 210n44
Althusser, Louis, 44, 142, 196n78, 214n78
Anderson, Benedict, 30, 111, 192n5
Anderson, Thomas Page, 184n5
Arendt, Hannah, 196n79, 203n60, 207n13
Aston, Margaret, 86n15
Auerbach, Erich, 107, 211n48

Bacon, Francis, 83, 202n48
Baldo, Jonathan, 118, 211n50
Barber, C. L., 79, 82, 89, 91, 197n3, 201n42, 213n60

Barnes, J. A., 96, 205n7, 219n43
Bate, Jonathan, 68–73, 199n26, 200n31
Bath, Michael, 182n11
Beckwith, Sarah, 209n28, 211n48
Benjamin, Walter, 44–45, 89, 92, 196n79, 196n81, 203n60, 206n13
Bevington, David, 196n88
Blau, Herbert, 198n20, 200n30, 205n5, 210n43, n44, 218n31
Bloom, Harold, 81, 201n45
Bourdieu, Pierre, 41, 196n83
Bowers, Fredson, 48, 83–84, 196n87, 202n51, 216n3
Boyd, Michael, 65, 130, 213n63
Brecht, Berthold, 44, 74, 88, 89, 195n77, 203n58, 210n40
Brewer, John, 216n7
Brewer, Marilynn B., 185n25
Brook, Peter, 69, 70, 114, 199n23, 218n31
Brown, Bill, 222n4
Bulmàn, James C., 201n37, n47, 205n69
Burckhardt, Sigurd, 120, 123, 141, 211n53, 212n57
Burke, Kenneth, 23, 47, 76, 142, 166, 201n36, 215n81

Burrow, Colin, 205n1
Bynum, Caroline Walker, 212n56

Cahill, Patricia, 214n71
Calhoun, Craig, 40, 149, 194n68, 216n11, n14
Carlson, Marvin, 200n30
Caruth, Cathy, 49, 59, 206n12
Casey, Edward S., 49, 101, 205n3, 207n14
Cavell, Stanley, 190n45
Certeau, Michel de, 196n83
charnel house (ossuary), 1–10, 46
Chesters, Timothy, 214n72
Clark, Andy, 176–77, 222n3, n7
cognitive ecology, 50, 177–78, 222n5
collective self, 14–15, 20, 29, 32, 47, 87, 104, 122, 150, 164, 177, 188n25, 217n17
Collinson, Patrick, 13, 16, 86, 184n3, 174n5, 187n20
Conflict of Conscience, The, 25
constructed archaism, 112–14, 123, 126, 141. *See also* Womack, Peter
conversion, viii, 9, 78, 105; of social practices, 162, 185n10, 188n24
Corthell, Ronald, 184n4
Crawford, Julie, 192n53
Cressy, David, 147, 186n15, 207n18, 216n7, 218n34, 221n57
cultural performance, 23, 26, 34, 42, 45–47, 62, 107, 146, 150, 179, 180, 215n81
Cunich, Peter, 184n5

Daly, Peter M., 182n11
damnatio memoriae, 105, 109, 115, 208n22
Darwin, Charles, 189n37, 190n43
Davis, Natalie Zemon, 2, 86, 181n3, 183n3, 203n56
dead, the: and charnel houses, 2–4, 8–11, 50, 72, 85–86, 137, 180, 186n14;

as embodied memory, 11–12, 178; Protestant alienation from, 3, 13, 86, 105, 124; Protestant rage against, 11–12
Deleuze, Gilles, 211n54, 220n52, 200n30, 201n46, 207n15, 222n6
de Man, Paul, 215n80
Derrida, Jacques, 186n14
Dessen, Alan C., 72, 73, 199n29, 204n69
Dickens, A. G., 184n4
Diehl, Huston, 85, 105, 182n11, 191n47, 203n54, 209n30, 221n1
distraction, 79, 12, 88; as alienation effect, 88–90; Berthold Brecht and, 88–89; Walter Benjamin and, 89–92, 203n59, n61, 204n67
Dolan, Frances E., 184n4
Drakakis, John, 201n44
Duffy, Eamon, 181n6, 207n18
Dutton, Richard, 200n30

early modern drama: as affective technology, 26, 40, 46, 62, 92, 146, 180; amphitheater productions of, 23–26, 40–49, 62–64, 76–77, 84, 91–93, 146–50, 161, 168–70, 180; architectonics of, 49, 180; and defamiliarization, 201n40; mimetic and antimimetic aspects of, 48–49, 53, 61, 114, 121, 149. *See also* Kyd, Thomas; Marlowe, Christopher; Shakespeare, William
Edelman, Charles, 201
Edgeworth, Maria, 79–80, 201n39; *Harrington*, 78–92, 201n39
Eiland, Howard, 89, 203n59, n61, 204n67
Einstein, Albert, 21, 189n38
Eisenstein, Elizabeth L., 218n35
Ekman, Paul, 18–20, 189n37, 190n43
Elam, Keir, 199n23, 210n42, 214n76

Ellison, Julie, 190n41
Elwood, Christopher, 104, 208n20
Emmison, F. G., 187n21
emotions: as embodied thought,
    19, 22, 49, 55, 93, 146; emotional
    communities, 5, 23, 24, 69, 82;
    etiologies of, 21, 54; and Galenic
    theory, 21, 54, 56–61; and histori-
    cal trauma, 8–34, 46, 85–87, 93, 99,
    106, 108; histories of, 17, 21, 32–34,
    61; intersection with ideologies,
    29–31; and language, 19, 21, 24, 32–
    34; phenomenology of, 21, 24, 28,
    33, 38–41, 48, 61; as points of view,
    76; reformation of, 8, 22, 62, 93;
    representation of, 51; social, 17, 18,
    22, 29, 32–34, 48, 53, 160; in social
    landscape, 8, 33, 87–102; as stories,
    22, 24, 25; theatrical, 45, 52, 60, 64,
    74–76; universal versus cultural,
    17, 20, 32, 55. *See also* structures of
    feeling
Erne, Lucas, 215n2
Eucharist, 125, 134, 104; and eu-
    charistic thought, 49, 104, 132,
    208nn19–21; and materiality, 106,
    120–22, 138; substance of, 107,
    212n56
Eyerman, Ron, 206n12

Findlay, Alison Gail, 200n30
Floyd-Wilson, Mary, 13, 21, 58, 189n39,
    190n41, 191n48, 197n4, 198n10
Foucalt, Michel, 12, 42–43, 187n17,
    217n19
Fox, Adam, 160–64, 218n36
Foxe, John: account of Perotine
    Massey's death, 27–29; *Actes and
    Monuments* (*The Book of Martyrs*),
    87, 108, 144–45, 191n52, 192n54,
    216n7; and representation of
    women, 191n53

Fraser, Nancy, 149, 216n11
Frow, John, 201n46

Gallagher, Catherine, 42, 195n70
Garner, Stanton, 159, 210n44, 218n31,
    220n53
Geertz, Clifford, 17–18, 189n33, 191n47
Giddens, Anthony, 41, 194n69
Giesen, Bernhard, 206n12
Goethe, Johan Wolfgang von, 151–52
Goffman, Erving, 164, 219n44
Goody, Jack, 97–102, 206n8, n10, n11
Gordon, D. J., 4,, 182n11
Greenblatt, Stephen, 52, 139, 188n31,
    193n62, 195n70, n72, 197n3, 200n30,
    210n40, 214n74, 217n19, 221n1
Gross, John, 201n38
Gurr, Andrew, 221n55

Habermas, Jürgen, 49–50, 147–60,
    163–66, 211n54, 216n8, n10, n11,
    12, 217n16, n17, 18, 20, 218n24, n33,
    220n47, n48, 231n58
Haigh, Christopher, 106, 184n4,
    187n18, n22, n23, 208n25
Halasz, Alexandra, 161–64, 219n35, n42
Harding, Thomas, 27, 28, 192n54
Harding, Vanessa, 181n5, 187n16
Hareli, Schlomo, 190n44
Hattaway, Michael, 64, 191n24
Helgerson, Richard, 209n30
Henry VIII, 10, 134, 185n8
Heywood, Thomas, 30, 192n56, n57
Hickerson, Megan L., 191n53
Highley, Christopher, 184n5
Hodgdon, Barbara, 210n40
Hole, Richard, 78–80, 201n41
Holland, Peter, 189n38
Howard, Jean, 118, 130, 192n57, 210n36,
    211n51, 213n64
Howell, Jane, 70–72, 200n33
Hutchins, Edward, 222n5

imagined communities, 31, 40, 94,
    101, 111–12, 122, 150, 164–66; and
    publics, 150, 164–66
individual, 20–22, 28–29, 32, 78, 87,
    150, 135–38; and collective self, 17,
    20–22, 29, 33, 46, 86–87, 96, 101,
    122. 140, 145, 150, 153, 171, 176–79;
    and medieval individuum, 46,
    106, 122, 179; in relation to private
    and public selves, 165–66, 177,
    154n55, n56
inverted sympathy, 77–78

James, Heather, 200n32
Jameson, Fredrick, 43, 195n74
Jones, Anne Rosalind, 185n11, 203n53
Jones, Norman, 86, 188n28
Joyce, James, 191n46

Kantor, Tadeusz, 43, 143, 196n80
Kobialka, Michal, 196n80
Kyd, Thomas, 16, 49, 64–69; *Spanish
    Tragedy*, 62–68

Lake, Peter, 184n5, 188n24
Langer, Suzanne, 221n58
Latour, Bruno, 222n4
Leach, Sir Edmund, 18–19, 34,
    189n34
Leavitt, John, 18–19, 34, 189n35
Lefebvre, Henri, 45, 196n82
Leggatt, Alexander, 73, 200n33
Levin, Carole, 191n53
Levine, Robert, 190n42
Leys, Ruth, 206n12
Lin, Erika T., 170, 194n67
Loades, David M., 87n18, 192n53
Lorrain, Jorge, 192n59
Love, Harold, 144–45, 167–68, 215n1,
    220n50
Lucas, Scott, 184n5
Lupton, Julia Reinhardt, 209n35

MacCullough, Diarmaid, 207n18
Macdonald, Michael, 23–25, 61,
    187n15, 189n40, 191n50, n51,
    198n11
Macherey, Pierre, 141, 214n77, n78, n79
Macklin, Charles, 76–79
Marlowe, Christopher, 36–45, 49,
    73, 136, 148, 166, 193n64, 201n43;
    Edward II, 36–45, 193n64; *Jew of
    Malta*, 86, 201n43
Marotti, Arthur F., 184n4
Marshall, Cynthia, 86–87, 203n57
Marshall, David, 223n10
Marshall, Peter, 8, 12, 86, 181n4,
    188n24, 200n30
Marx, Karl, 43, 112, 163, 186n14,
    198n20, 219n40, n41
Maus, Katharine Eisaman, 85,
    202n50, n51, n52
Mazur, Cary, 204n67
Mazzio, Carla, 190n41
Mazzola, Elizabeth, 211n45
McClendon, Muriel, 187n15
McConachie, Bruce A., 223n8
medieval drama: morality plays, 25–
    26, 48, 108; pageant and Corpus
    Christi cycles, 107, 108, 126–27;
    as sacramental drama, 211n48; in
    Shakespearean drama, 127–28, 136
Miller, David Lee, 192n53
Milman, Henry Hart, 181n1
Milner, Matthew, 187n18
Milton, Anthony, 188n27
Monta, Susannah Brietz,
    191n53,192n55, 208n21
mourning. *See* trauma
Mullaney, Steven, 182n12, 186n12,
    187n23, 191n47, n48, 193n66,
    204n67, 217n19, n23, 218n24,
    221n1, n2
Mulvey, Laura, 194n67
Murray, Molly, 185n10, 188n24

Nashe, Thomas, 116–17, 211n46
Neill, Michael, 85–86, 108, 202n50, 203n55, n56, 209n31
Nussbaum, Martha, 204n68

Olick, Jeffrey K., 205n6
Orgel, Stephen, 90. 204n65, 217n19

Parkinson, Brain, 190n44
Paster, Gail Kern, 18, 21, 56–59, 189n39, 190n41, 197n4, n5, 198n9, n12, n16; 221n2
performance, phenomology of, 38–61; and audience-oriented subjectivity, 156–60; dimensionality of, 48–50, 61, 64–65, 70, 89, 147, 150, 164–65, 169, 180, 205n4; and "ghosting," 95, 200n30. *See also* cultural performance; early modern drama; medieval drama
Peters, Julie Stone, 216n4
Pinch, Adela, 190n41
Pincus, Steven C. A., 184n5
Pollock, Linda, 15
Poole, Kristen, 186n12
publication: oral, scribal, printed, and performed kinds of, 50, 144–47; spheres of, 168–69; as theatrical performance, 50, 145, 150
public sphere, 147; post-Habermasian, 149, 153, 220. *See* Habermas, Jürgen; publication
Pye, Christopher, 211n47

Questier, Michael, 184n5, 185n10, 188n24

Rackin, Phillis, 118, 130–31, 192n57, 210n36, 211n51, 213n64, n65
Ramachandran, V. S., 102–3, 207n16
Reformation, English: Book of Common Prayer, 12; and dis-

solution of monasteries and chanceries, 10–11, 110; Elizabethan compromise as "don't ask, don't tell" society, 14; and historical consciousness, 12, 49, 86, 103, 108–9. *See also* individual: and collective self
Renan, Ernst, 94, 205n1
revenge drama, Elizabethan, 48, 81–88; the dead in, 72; ghosts in, 62
Roach, Joseph, 3, 182n8, 199n23, 221n2
Rogers-Ramachadran, D., 207n16
Rosaldo, Michelle, 22. 34, 55, 61, 146, 190n42, 198n8, 216n6
Rosenwien, Barbara, 183n2
Rossiter, A. P., 188n30, 210n40
Rowe, Kathrine, 21, 189n39, 190n41, 197n4
Royal Shakespeare Company productions: *The Spanish Tragedy* (1997), 65–66; *Titus Andronicus* (1987), 70–72
Ruben, Miri, 104, 208n19
Russell, Daniel, 182n11

Sanz, Álvaro Llosa, 182n11
Scarisbrick, J. J., 184n4
Schechner, Richard, 159, 197n3, 210n32
Schoenfeldt, Michael, 21, 189n39, 197n4, 198n15
Schwyzer, Philip, 182n6
Sedgwick, Eve, 195n71
Sedikides, Constantine, 188n25
Shakespeare, William: *Hamlet*, 16, 49–50, 58–61, 67, 81–86, 95, 128, 140, 152–53, 175–77, 179, 186n14; *2 Henry 4*, 39, 112; *1 Henry 6*, 109–12, 115–18, 129–30; *2 Henry 6*, 109, 118, 132, 133, 146; *3 Henry 6*, 118, 126–27,

Shakespeare, William (*continued*)
130, 136; *Henry 5*, 112; *The Merchant of Venice*, 35, 49, 76–93; *Richard II*, 128; *Richard III* 94–95, 115, 122, 128, 131–32, 134–43; *Titus Andronicus*, 49, 51, 68–93
Siemon, James E., 201n47
Sinfield, Alan, 15, 185n7
Singer, Milton, 23, 191n47
Sloan, Thomas O., 197n1, n2, n7
Smelser, Neil J., 206n12
Smith, Bruce, 194n67
social imaginary, 5, 14–15, 43, 92–93, 101–5, 107, 147
Sofer, Andrew, 200n31, 210n44
Spiera, Francisco, 24–26, 61
Stallybrass, Peter, 185n11
States, Bert O., 194n67, 200n30
Steggle, Matthew, 197n2
Stow, John, 1, 181.1
Street, Brian V., 206n9, n11
Strier, Richard, 190n40
structural amnesia, 96–101, 108–9, 114, 164, 208.22, 219n43
structures of feeling, 8, 24–26, 32–34, 195n72, 223n10. *See also* emotions; Williams, Raymond
Sutton, John, 177–78, 205n6, 222n7, n8
Sztompka, Piotr, 206n12

Taymor, Julie: *Titus* (1999), 69–70, 73, 200n33
Thomas, Keith, 3, 105, 124, 182n9
Tillyard, E. M. W., 120, 211n52
Torok, Maria, 207n14, n15
trauma: early modern popular drama as response to, 45, 87, 184n5, 206n12, 214n71; and historical consciousness, 49, 108; kinds of, 49, 99–109; and the Reformation,

8–11, 85–87, 222; remembering and forgetting, 100–106, 142, 216n43
Trevor, Douglas, 21, 189n32, 197n4, 198n15
Tribble, Evelyn, 107, 177–78, 214n70, 222n7, n8, 209n24
Turner, Henry, 201n46
Turner, Victor, 111, 189n36
Tyacke, Nicholas, 184n4

Vanhaelen, Angela, 13, 187n23, 219n46, 217n23
Vernant, Jean-Pierre, 5, 183n13

Waith, Eugene, 69, 199n27
Waldron, Jennifer, 187n15
Walker, Greg, 220n54
Walsham, Alexandra, 182n6, 186b12, 188n24
Ward, Joseph, 13, 187n15, n23, 219n46, 217n23
Warner, Deborah, 70–73
Warner, Marina, 198n18
Watt, Ian, 97–102, 206n8, n10
Weever, J., 11, 186n13
Weimann, Robert, 194n67, 199n23
Wiegandt, Kai, 213n69
Wierzbika, Anna, 32–35, 192–93n6; and the historicity of emotions (e.g. Polish *tęsknota*), 32–35
Williams, Raymond, 8, 41–44, 106, 183n2, 193n61, 195n72, n73, 208n26. *See also* structures of feeling
Williams, Roger, 9, 185n9
Williamson, Elizabeth, 187n16, 208n21
Wilson, Bronwen, 187n23
Wilson, Richard, 200n30
Womack, Peter, 108, 111–13, 141, 165, 209n29, n31, 210n39, n40, n41, 219n45

Woodbridge, Linda, 85, 202n50, n53
Woodes, Nathaniel, 25–26
Woodruff, Paul, 200n34
Wright, Thomas, 48, 51–55; and humors, 54–56; *Passions of the Minde in Generall*, 48–56; and semiotics of tears, 51–52, 60; and social emotions, 55–56, 60

Yachnin, Paul, 208n21, 216n13, 219n46, 220n49
Yates, Frances, 186n14, 223n9

Zadeh, L. A., 195n75
Zaret, David, 218n35
Žižek, Slavoj, 220n52
Zohn, Harry, 196n79, 203n60, 207n13